JANE AUSTEN: *Emma* (Revised) David Lodge
JANE AUSTEN: *'Northanger Abbey'* & *'Persuasion'* B. C. Southam
JANE AUSTEN: *'Sense and Sensibility'*, *'Pride and Prejudice'* & *'Mansfield Park'*
B. C. Southam
BECKETT: *Waiting for Godot* Ruby Cohn
WILLIAM BLAKE: *Songs of Innocence and Experience* Margaret Bottrall
CHARLOTTE BRONTE: *'Jane Eyre'* & *'Villette'* Miriam Allott
EMILY BRONTE: *Wuthering Heights* (Revised) Miriam Allott
BROWNING: *'Men and Women'* & *Other Poems* J. R. Watson
CHAUCER: *The Canterbury Tales* J. J. Anderson
COLERIDGE: *'The Ancient Mariner'* & *Other Poems*. Alun R. Jones & W. Tydeman
CONRAD: *'Heart of Darkness'*, *'Nostromo'* & *'Under Western Eyes'* C. B. Cox
CONRAD: *The Secret Agent* Ian Watt
DICKENS: *Bleak House* A. E. Dyson
DICKENS: *'Hard Times'*, *'Great Expectations'* & *'Our Mutual Friend'* Norman Page
DICKENS: *'Dombey and Son'* & *'Little Dorrit'* Alan Shelston
DONNE: *Songs and Sonnets* Julian Lovelock
GEORGE ELIOT: *Middlemarch* Patrick Swinden
GEORGE ELIOT: *'The Mill on the Floss'* & *'Silas Marner'* R. P. Draper
T. S. ELIOT: *'Prufrock'*, *'Gerontion'* & *'Ash Wednesday'* B. C. Southam
T. S. ELIOT: *The Waste Land* C. B. Cox & Arnold P. Hinchliffe
T. S. ELIOT: *Plays* Arnold P. Hinchliffe
HENRY FIELDING: *Tom Jones* Neil Compton
E.M. FORSTER: *A Passage to India* Malcolm Bradbury
WILLIAM GOLDING: *Novels 1954–64* Norman Page
HARDY: *The Tragic Novels* (Revised) R. P. Draper
HARDY: *Poems* James Gibson & Trevor Johnson
HARDY: *Three Pastoral Novels* R. P. Draper
GERARD MANLEY HOPKINS: *Poems* Margaret Bottrall
HENRY JAMES: *'Washington Square'* & *'The Portrait of a Lady'* Alan Shelton
JONSON: *Volpone* Jonas A. Barish
JONSON: *'Every Man in his Humour'* & *'The Alchemist'* R. V. Holdsworth
JAMES JOYCE: *'Dubliners'* & *'A Portrait of the Artist as a Young Man'* Morris Beja
KEATS: *Odes* G.S. Fraser
KEATS: *Narrative Poems* John Spencer Hill
D.H. LAWRENCE: *Sons and Lovers* Gamini Salgado
D.H. LAWRENCE: *'The Rainbow'* & *'Women in Love'* Colin Clarke
LOWRY: *Under the Volcano* Gordon Bowker
MARLOWE: *Doctor Faustus* John Jump
MARLOWE: *'Tamburlaine the Great'*, *'Edward II'* & *'The Jew of Malta'* J. R. Brown
MARLOWE: *Poems* Arthur Pollard
MAUPASSANT: *In the Hall of Mirrors* T. Harris
MILTON: *Paradise Lost* A. E. Dyson & Julian Lovelock
O'CASEY: *'Juno and the Paycock'*, *'The Plough and the Stars'* & *'The Shadow of a
Gunman'* Ronald Ayling
EUGENE O'NEILL: *Three Plays* Normand Berlin
JOHN OSBORNE: *Look Back in Anger* John Russell Taylor
PINTER: *'The Birthday Party'* & *Other Plays* Michael Scott
POPE: *The Rape of the Lock* John Dixon Hunt
SHAKESPEARE: *A Midsummer Night's Dream* Antony Price
SHAKESPEARE: *Antony and Cleopatra* (Revised) John Russell Brown
SHAKESPEARE: *Coriolanus* B. A. Brockman

SHAKESPEARE: *Early Tragedies* Neil Taylor & Bryan Loughrey
SHAKESPEARE: *Hamlet* John Jump
SHAKESPEARE: *Henry IV Parts I and II* G.K. Hunter
SHAKESPEARE: *Henry V* Michael Quinn
SHAKESPEARE: *Julius Caesar* Peter Ure
SHAKESPEARE: *King Lear* (Revised) Frank Kermode
SHAKESPEARE: *Macbeth* (Revised) John Wain
SHAKESPEARE: *Measure for Measure* C. K. Stead
SHAKESPEARE: *The Merchant of Venice* John Wilders
SHAKESPEARE: *'Much Ado About Nothing'* & *'As You Like It'* John Russell Brown
SHAKESPEARE: *Othello* (Revised) John Wain
SHAKESPEARE: *Richard II* Nicholas Brooke
SHAKESPEARE: *The Sonnets* Peter Jones
SHAKESPEARE: *The Tempest* (Revised) D. J. Palmer
SHAKESPEARE: *Troilus and Cressida* Priscilla Martin
SHAKESPEARE: *Twelfth Night* D. J. Palmer
SHAKESPEARE: *The Winter's Tale* Kenneth Muir
SPENSER: *The Faerie Queene* Peter Bayley
SHERIDAN: *Comedies* Peter Davison
STOPPARD: *'Rosencrantz and Guildenstern are Dead'*, *'Jumpers'* & *'Travesties'*
T. Bareham
SWIFT: *Gulliver's Travels* Richard Gravil
SYNGE: *Four Plays* Ronald Ayling
TENNYSON: *In Memoriam* John Dixon Hunt
THACKERAY: *Vanity Fair* Arthur Pollard
TROLLOPE: *The Barsetshire Novels* T. Bareham
WEBSTER: *'The White Devil'* & *'The Duchess of Malfi'* R. V. Holdsworth
WILDE: *Comedies* William Tydeman
VIRGINIA WOOLF: *To the Lighthouse* Morris Beja
WORDSWORTH: *Lyrical Ballads* Alun R. Jones & William Tydeman
WORDSWORTH: *The 1807 Poems* Alun R. Jones
WORDSWORTH: *The Prelude* W. J. Harvey & Richard Gravil
YEATS: *Poems 1919–35* Elizabeth Cullingford
YEATS: *Last Poems* Jon Stallworthy

Issues in Contemporary Critical Theory Peter Barry
Thirties Poets: 'The Auden Group' Ronald Carter
Tragedy: Developments in Criticism R.P. Draper
The Epic Ronald Draper
Poetry Criticism and Practice: Developments since the Symbolists A.E. Dyson
Three Contemporary Poets: Gunn, Hughes, Thomas A.E. Dyson
Elizabethan Poetry: Lyrical & Narrative Gerald Hammond
The Metaphysical Poets Gerald Hammond
Medieval English Drama Peter Happé
The English Novel: Developments in Criticism since Henry James Stephen Hazell
Poetry of the First World War Dominic Hibberd
The Romantic Imagination John Spencer Hill
Drama Criticism: Developments since Ibsen Arnold P. Hinchliffe
Three Jacobean Revenge Tragedies R.V. Holdsworth
The Pastoral Mode Bryan Loughrey
The Language of Literature Norman Page
Comedy: Developments in Criticism D.J. Palmer
Studying Shakespeare John Russell Brown
The Gothic Novel Victor Sage
Pre-Romantic Poetry J.R. Watson

Keats

The Narrative Poems

A CASEBOOK

EDITED BY

JOHN SPENCER HILL

MACMILLAN

First published 1983 by
MACMILLAN PRESS LTD
Houndmills, Basingstoke, Hampshire RG21 6XS
and London
Companies and representatives
throughout the world

ISBN 0–333–27677–9

A catalogue record for this book is available
from the British Library.

14   13   12   11   10   9   8
03   02   01   00

Printed in China

CONTENTS

Part Three: *Twentieth-Century Studies*

ACKNOWLEDGEMENTS

The editor and publishers wish to thank the following who have given permission for the use of copyright material:

Mario L. Avanzo, extract from 'La Belle Dame Sans Merci' in *Keats' Metaphors for the Poetic Imagination* (1967), by permission of Duke University Press, copyright © 1967 by Duke University Press; Newell F. Ford, extract from 'Endymion' in *The Prefigurative Imagination of John Keats* (1951), by permission of Stanford University Press, copyright 1951 by the Board of Trustees of the Leland Stanford Junior University, renewed 1979; Walter E. Houghton, essay 'The Meaning of Keats' *Eve of St Mark*' in *English Literary History*, XIII (1946), by permission of The Johns Hopkins University Press; Kenneth Muir, essay 'The Meaning of Hyperion' from *John Keats: Reassessment* (1969), by permission of the author; David Perkins, extract from *The Quest for Permanence: The Symbolism of Wordsworth, Shelley and Keats* (1959), by permission of Harvard University Press, copyright © 1959 by the President and Fellows of Harvard College; Paul D. Sheats, essay 'Stylistic Discipline in *The Fall of Hyperion*' from *Keats–Shelley Journal*, XVII (1968), by permission of the editor; Louise Z. Smith, article 'The Material Sublime: Keats and Isabella' from *Studies in Romanticism*, 13 (1974), by permission of the Trustees of Boston University; Stuart M. Sperry, extract from 'The Allegory of Endymion' in *Keats the Poet* (1973), reprinted by permission of Princeton University Press, copyright © by Princeton University Press; Jack Stillinger, extract from *The Hoodwinking of Madeline* (1971), by permission of the author and University of Illinois Press; Earl R. Wasserman, extracts from 'The Eve of St Agnes' in *The Finer Tone: Keats' Major Poems* (1955), by permission of The Johns Hopkins University Press.

GENERAL EDITOR'S PREFACE

The Casebook series, launched in 1968, has become a well-regarded library of critical studies. The central concern of the series remains the 'single-author' volume, but suggestions from the academic community have led to an extension of the original plan, to include occasional volumes on such general themes as literary 'schools' and genres.

Each volume in the central category deals either with one well-known and influential work by an individual author, or with closely related works by one writer. The main section consists of critical readings, mostly modern, collected from books and journals. A selection of reviews and comments by the author's contemporaries is also included, and sometimes comment from the author himself. The Editor's introduction charts the reputation of the work or works from the first appearance to the present time.

Volumes in the 'general themes' category are variable in structure but follow the basic purpose of the series in presenting an integrated selection of readings, with an Introduction which explores the theme and discusses the literary and critical issues involved.

A single volume can represent no more than a small selection of critical opinions. Some critics are excluded for reasons of space, and it is hoped that readers will pursue the suggestions for further reading in the Select Bibliography. Other contributions are severed from their original context, to which some readers may wish to turn. Indeed, if they take a hint from the critics represented here, they certainly will.

A. E. DYSON

INTRODUCTION

When John Keats made up his mind in the winter of 1816–17 to devote his life to poetry, he had just passed his twenty-first birthday. Longer in choosing a literary career than most aspiring young poets of his day, he was still further handicapped at the beginning because he lacked the formal education and broad experience of Classical and English literature enjoyed by the majority of his most creative contemporaries. Unlike Wordsworth and Coleridge, or Shelley and Byron, he had not studied at one of the universities, with leisure to contemplate an appropriate career. Since 1811, when he had been apprenticed to Dr Thomas Hammond, surgeon and apothecary of Edmonton, Keats had been preparing himself for a practical career in medicine; and poetry-writing (which he began, apparently, only in 1814) was no more than a pleasing diversion, a temporary escape from the harsh realities witnessed daily in Hammond's surgery and, later, in the wards of Guy's Hospital in London. But 1816 changed all that. It was, for Keats, a year of growing commitment to poetry, a year leading to the major turning-point of his short life – his decision to abandon medicine for poetry.

Through the autumn and early winter of 1816, following an inspirational stay at Leigh Hunt's Hampstead cottage in early October, Keats laboured over *Sleep and Poetry*, by far the longest (404 lines) and most serious poem he had thus far attempted. On the verge of a momentous commitment he tried to set down his conception of the end and aim of poetical endeavour and to map out, as best he could at so early a stage, an outline of his own hopes and ambitions. Part assertion and part aspiration, part discovery and part continuing quest, *Sleep and Poetry* is a personal manifesto – a prelude to poetic destiny in which, as Sir Sidney Colvin has observed, 'the ardent novice communes intently with himself on his own hopes and ambitions . . . , possessed by the thrilling sense that everything in earth and air is full, as it were, of poetry in solution, [although] he has as yet no clearness as to the forms and modes in which these suspended elements will crystallise for him'.[1]

In the central section of the poem, having declared himself a dedicated (albeit largely untried) servant of Apollo –

> O Poesy! For thee I hold my pen
> That am not yet a glorious denizen
> Of thy wide heaven   [47–9]

– Keats turns [lines 63–84] to an enumeration of the kinds and varieties of poetry that he imagines himself writing in the future. There is a clear pattern, a clear ascent and progression, in this programme. Beginning with simple pastoral or rustic poetry, he intends to advance toward the treatment of some graver subject inspired by the 'Vistas of solemn beauty' haunting his imagination and leading him, through the inspired power of visionary insight, to reveal all that is permitted of the sacred mystery of human life and activity. If fate will grant him but ten years to 'overwhelm / Myself in poesy', he promises (with moving irony), then he will have time enough to accomplish 'the deed / That my own soul has to itself decreed' [96–8]. Imitating the Wordsworthian pattern of individual development in *Tintern Abbey*, he envisages his poetic career as an ascent through a period of unreflecting delight in natural beauty towards the attainment, eventually, of a profound and visionary understanding of the secret workings of the human soul. The first stage of the journey would be spent in the languorously pastoral realm of 'Flora and old Pan', where a simple and self-indulgent enjoyment of Nature suffices, and where the pampered poet can allow himself to

> sleep in the grass,
> Feed upon apples red and strawberries,
> And choose each pleasure that [his]fancy sees.   [102–4]

But at length, swept aloft by the power of imagination, Keats and those who, like him, aspire to become serious poets must bid such selfish joys farewell, must pass beyond them to

> a nobler life,
> Where I may find the agonies, the strife
> Of human hearts.   [123-5]

All of this, however, lies in the future. The vision of poetic destiny fades, tumbling him back into the painful reality of the habitual self – but leaving him, too, vowing to strive, against all doubtings, toward the promise of a future that he knows can be his if he consecrates himself to it unswervingly.

Later in the poem, after a long section lamenting the decline of English poetry since the Renaissance, Keats comes back to the personal theme once more [lines 270–312]. Freely confessing his own ignorance and immaturity, he feels impelled nonetheless to declare, as clearly as his understanding of it permits, the firm imaginative faith that sustains him on the threshold of his commitment to poetry:

> yet there ever rolls
> A vast idea before me, and I glean
> Therefrom my liberty. Thence too I've seen
> The end and aim of Poesy. 'Tis clear
> As anything most true: as that the year
> Is made of the four seasons; manifest
> As a large cross, some old cathedral's crest,
> Lifted to the white clouds.   [290-7]

While there is, of course, little in these vague analogies to clarify the 'vast idea' that drives him forward, Keats is not really interested in speculative precision, in sorting out to a clear conceiving those shadowy but powerful truths beckoning to him from somewhere deep in his inner being. For the moment, it is enough simply to respond to their call with emotional and imaginative commitment, trusting that wisdom and understanding will come in due course. Like Cortez in the sonnet *On First Looking into Chapman's Homer* (October 1816), who stands in silent amazement on a peak in Darien surveying the limitless expanse of the newly-discovered Pacific Ocean, Keats imagines himself on the near shore of his poetic career, gazing out across the waters of experience like an explorer preparing to set off into the unknown:

An ocean dim, sprinkled with many an isle,
Spreads awfully before me. How much toil,
How many days, what desperate turmoil,
Ere I can have explored its widenesses!
Ah, what a task!   [306–10]

He is tempted to draw back, tempted momentarily to unsay the solemn vows he has made – but 'no, impossible! Impossible!'

Although marked by many immaturities, *Sleep and Poetry* is a crucial document in the brief Keatsian canon. Both in substance and intention it prefigures and helps give shape to much that follows. Later poems and comments in Keats's letters, of course, refine its insights, investing them with a depth and a precision well beyond his grasp in the autumn of 1816; and yet, for all that, *Sleep and Poetry* provides an indispensable *terminus a quo* from which to trace the general pattern of his later achievement. When one considers its emphasis, for example, on a neo-Wordsworthian pattern of perceptual and imaginative growth [lines 101–54], it may be seen to anticipate Keats's actual growth from the Flora-and-old-Pan pastoralism of *Endymion* to the maturing exploration of the agonies and strife of human hearts in such later works as the two *Hyperion* poems – a growth to be measured chiefly, though not exclusively, in the series of narrative poems and fragments composed between the spring of 1817 and autumn of 1819. In a sense the great odes of May and September 1819, along with many of the shorter poems of this period, are spin-off pieces – at times almost relief-valves – nourished and made possible by the labour of sustained thought and creativity required for the composition of a long, demanding narrative work. To say this, of course, is not to denigrate in any way the quality of the odes and other short poems; it is merely to insist, rather, that they benefited in a substantial way from the efforts being expended concurrently, or almost so, on one or other of the narrative poems.

In mid-April 1817, little more than a month after the publication of his first volume of poems (in which *Sleep and Poetry* stands last, like a promise of things to come), Keats began work on *Endymion*: a poetic romance based on the Greek myth of the love of the Moon-Goddess (known variously as Selene or Phoebe or Cynthia) for a Latmian shepherd named Endymion. His intention in writing the poem, as he told his friend Benjamin Bailey (letter of 8 October 1817), was to 'make 4000 lines of one bare circumstance and fill them with Poetry'. He worked diligently, almost feverishly, at it through the summer and autumn of 1817, completing the first draft by the end of November. It was published in April 1818 by the London firm of Taylor and Hessey.

By far the longest work Keats was destined to complete, *Endymion* is neither an easy poem to read nor an easy poem to like. Matthew Arnold* (speaking for many) wished it might have been suppressed or lost, and tartly declared that he resented 'the space it occupies in the volume of Keats's poetry'. The earliest reviewers, as the extracts from J. G. Lockhart and J. W. Croker (*inter alia*) amply demonstrate, are even less charitable in their assessments.

Toward the end of the nineteenth century, however, there emerged a new and strongly positive critical approach arguing that *Endymion*, despite its mawkishness and saccharine immaturities, should be read as a serious attempt at Neoplatonic allegory – a parable of the adventures of the poetic soul (Endymion-Keats) questing after communion with the spirit of ideal Beauty (Cynthia). This view of the poem is vigorously defended, for example, by Sir Sidney Colvin in his important critical biography of Keats, and was further

---

* The absence of a source-reference for a critical comment cited in this Introduction signifies that the material is excerpted in the ensuing selection. The references appropriate to other material are either given in the text or specified in the Notes, p. 22 below.

developed, through the first three decades of present century, by such articulate exponents as John Middleton Murry in *Keats and Shakespeare* (1925) and Claude L. Finney in *The Evolution of Keats's Poetry* (1936). In the late 1940s a severe reaction to the allegorical school set in. Spearheaded by Newell Ford, a vocal phalanx of anti-allegorical critics flatly denied the existence in the poem of any consistency of thematic purpose. *Endymion*, Ford declared, is a simple romance, a rapturously disjointed hymn to feminine beauty energised by Keats's adolescent erotic fantasies. More recent commentators, seeking a middle ground between the extremes represented by Colvin and Ford, have generally chosen to approach the poem as an apprentice work, a 'long worksheet' – in W. J. Bate's words[2] – allowing that experimental 'stretch of inventive muscle' necessary to Keats in order for him to develop his ideas and strengthen his wings for later flight.

Endymion, then, is not so much a statement of meaning as it is a search for meaning and technique. According to Stuart Sperry, for example, who belongs to this same group of moderate critics, the poem is a broadly allegorical exploration of the creative process, neither wholly coherent nor remarkably successful except that it reflects the complex process of creative self-discovery and Keats's quickly maturing aesthetic perception.

With *Endymion* out of his system, Keats turned in the spring of 1818 to other ventures. His next long poem (nowhere near as long as *Endymion*, however) was *Isabella; or, The Pot of Basil*, begun probably in early March and completed by the end of April.

Based on a tale in Boccaccio's *Decameron*, poor *Isabella* has always been, as Louise Smith has said, 'the wallflower among Keats's narratives'. Although Charles Lamb thought highly of it, the poem has usually been ignored by later critics; or, when discussed, it has been curtly dismissed as superficial and sentimental: the distilled backwash, says one, of the weaknesses of *Endymion*, and, according to another, Keats's 'last poetic failure'.[3] Professor Smith, however, offers a spirited defence of *Isabella*, arguing that its juxtaposition of romance and realism (usually seen as a defect) exemplifies the 'new romance' which, eschewing mere escapism, seeks to balance romantic sensibility with realistic detachment. As such, *Isabella* marks an important stage in Keats's growth from simple pastoralism toward his mature treatment of 'the fierce dispute / Betwixt damnation and impassioned clay' in the later narratives and odes.

After finishing *Isabella*, Keats wrote almost no serious verse for close to six months, until the autumn of 1818, when he began work on *Hyperion* (which I shall consider later, together with *The Fall of Hyperion*). For a number of reasons, however, *Hyperion* did not proceed smoothly, and early in the new year (1819) he diverted his creative energies into a breathtaking series of poems, composed with astonishing speed and fluency in the space of less than five months. On a visit to Chichester in late January he wrote *The Eve of St Agnes*; in mid-February, back at Wentworth Place, Hampstead, he composed *The Eve of St Mark*, which was followed a few weeks later by *La Belle Dame sans Merci* (April) and all of the major odes (April–May), except *To Autumn* which belongs to September of that year. In the poems of these five months at the beginning of 1819, Keats assured himself a place in the company of England's greatest poets.

The Eve of St Agnes, a story of young love in a hostile world, drawing heavily on Shakespeare's *Romeo and Juliet* and the romanticised medievalism of Coleridge and Scott, has always been something of a favourite with Keats's readers. Among nineteenth-century critics (especially the pre-Raphaelites), who cheerfully proclaimed that the poem 'means next to nothing', it was prized for its delicate eroticism and sensuous richness of descriptive detail. 'A perfect and unsurpassable study in pure colour and clear melody', Swinburne declared rapturously in 1886.

In contrast, most twentieth-century commentators, cautiously distrustful of pure metaphor and the unseemly taint of *ars gratia artis*, have strongly resisted any temptation to sacrifice sense to sound in their analyses of *The Eve of St Agnes*. They have grounded themselves, as firmly as the terrain will

permit, on a study of the poem's *meaning*. A case in point is
E. R. Wasserman's elaborate interpretation in *The Finer Tone*
(1953), which is reprinted (in part) in Part Three below.
Applying to the poem a number of seminal theoretical
statements from Keats's letters,[4] Wasserman seeks to
demonstrate: (a) that Porphyro's upward progression through
the castle toward Madeline's chamber represents a spiritual
ascent or pilgrimage to heaven's bourne; (b) that Madeline's
awakening to find that her dream of Porphyro has come true is
a validation of the operation of the visionary imagination; and
(c) that the sexual union of the lovers is an enactment of one of
those 'intensities' of life destined to be repeated, divested of its
mutability, in a finer tone in heaven.

A growing number of more recent critics, however, led by
Jack Stillinger, have reacted strongly against Wasserman and
those other 'metaphysical critics' who, like him, have freighted
The Eve of St Agnes with a burden of philosophic interpretation
that its slender structure simply cannot bear. In an article of
central importance, which has prompted a general
reconsideration of the entire poem, Stillinger argues that *The
Eve of St Agnes*, far from being a perfumed affirmation of
romantic love or a case history of the visionary imagination, is
a tale of seduction. Porphyro, who deceives Madeline by 'a
stratagem', may trace his roots in such characters as the
knavish Iachimo in Shakespeare's *Cymbeline* or in Lovelace,
the unprincipled rake in Richardson's *Clarissa*; and sweet
innocent Madeline, the self-hoodwinked dreamer who
becomes the victim of her own superstitious conjuring,
demonstrates (as do most of Keats's major poems of 1819) that
individuals cannot wilfully ignore 'the realities of this world'
without grief and disaster. The rose, as Madeline learns a little
too late, cannot shut and be a bud again.

The brief and fragmentary *Eve of St Mark*, impressionistic,
muted in tone and colour, is a poem which Keats for some
reason set aside and never returned to. Although highly
praised by the pre-Raphaelites (whose manner it anticipates)
for its chaste artistry and 'astonishingly real medievalism',[5] the

poem has not attracted much attention among later commentators. In one of the few modern studies of it, Walter Houghton disputes the received assumption that *The Eve of St Mark* was intended as a companion piece for *The Eve of St Agnes*; and he argues, instead, that the poem (had Keats completed it) was to have been about the longing for ecstatic experience in a mundane world. That is to say, it is concerned not with popular superstitions about St Mark's Eve (as is often assumed) but with the medieval legend of St Mark's martyrdom: not with fairy-tale romance but with the sadly tragic spectacle of 'a modern girl in an English town reading medieval legends and dreaming of martyrdom'.

Properly speaking, *La Belle Dame sans Merci* is not, of course, a narrative poem at all. It is a literary ballad. Nevertheless, it does *imply* (even if it does not actually *tell*) a story; and, given its importance in the short Keats canon, it is neither possible nor desirable to leave it out of consideration here.

In a very real sense *La Belle Dame sans Merci*, hauntingly suggestive but elusive in meaning, is a poem beyond the reach of criticism. Challenging but then defying deductive analysis, it is (when all is said and done) pre-eminently a poem of impression. 'It provokes and unprovokes', as the Porter in *Macbeth* says (in quite another context), 'it provokes the desire, but it takes away the performance'. But this has not, of course, deterred critics from trying anyway.

Some, like David Perkins, are content to relate *La Belle Dame sans Merci* to the general Keatsian concern (expressed in many of the poems of 1819) with visionary insight and the inevitable sadness occasioned by its loss when the visionary is plunged back into cold reality. Others, like Mario D'Avanzo, propose more systematic readings – as that it is a poem about the poetic process itself – which threaten, sometimes, to reduce its delicate and fugitive symbolism into something approaching allegory. Individual readers must test these various readings on their own pulses, never taking anything for granted and examining the truth of even the most widely accepted interpretations.

After the flurry of shorter narratives and odes in the spring of 1819, Keats turned his hand to dramatic writing (*Otho the Great*) and to the composition, or reworking, of a number of long narrative pieces: *Lamia, Hyperion, The Fall of Hyperion.*

The romance-like tale of the serpent Lamia and her mortal lover Lycius, begun at the end of June and finished by the first week in September 1819, is based on a story (which Keats printed at the end of the poem) from Robert Burton's *Anatomy of Melancholy* [III 2 i]. Despite its mature style and compressed richness of expression, *Lamia* is a perplexing poem over which generations of readers have remained sorely divided.

For Leigh Hunt (and many after him) it is an argument for the triumph of thought over feeling, reason over imagination, the actual over the ideal. Other readers have insisted vehemently, however, that it is, rather, a satiric denunciation of 'philosophy' or, at least, of that particular strain of crabbed rationalism that must inevitably, because it denies the possibility of imaginative truth, attempt to unweave the rainbow and clip the angel wings of poesy. Neither of these extreme views has found unqualified support among most recent commentators on the poem. David Perkins, for example, points out that *Lamia* contains no clear-cut heroes or villains – a fact which, he maintains, demonstrates the essential ambiguity (not to say confusion) of Keats's own position. Perhaps too, though, it should be said that more than any other of his narrative poems, *Lamia* displays the impulse of the dramatic principle of 'disinterestedness' at work. Contrasting narrative and dramatic poets like himself with lyrical solipsists of the Wordsworthian school, Keats once observed that the 'poetical Character itself . . . has no self – it is every thing and nothing . . . [and] has as much delight in conceiving an Iago as an Imogen'.[6] It may be that *Lamia* is best read in the light of this statement, thus making Lamia and Lycius and even old Apollonius essentially 'dramatic' creations instead of (mere) counters in a Keatsian dialectic.

Hyperion and *The Fall of Hyperion*, both fragments, are parts of an epic scheme centring on the myth (from Hesiod's *Theogony*) of the displacement of the Titans by the Olympian gods. Keats began *Hyperion* in the autumn of 1818 and abandoned it in April of the following year; three months later, in July 1819, he picked it up again, attempting to rework it into a visionary dream-poem (*The Fall of Hyperion*), but this too he eventually abandoned in late September, although he continued to tinker with it until as late as December 1819. Keats published the fragment of *Hyperion* in his last volume of poems: *Lamia, Isabella, The Eve of St Agnes, and other Poems* (1820). *The Fall of Hyperion* appeared only posthumously, long after its author's death, in the *Miscellanies of the Philobiblion Society* (1856).

The imposing fragment *Hyperion*, a bold imitation of a Miltonic blank-verse epic, was highly praised by Keats's contemporaries, including Hunt and Shelley, and later by such poet-critics as Matthew Arnold and Dante Gabriel Rossetti. *The Fall of Hyperion*, on the other hand, less well known and less powerful in its immediate impact than *Hyperion*, was regarded as an inferior production by most nineteenth- and early twentieth-century critics, who lamented the alteration of form and structure in the remodelled version and, perhaps especially, its de-Miltonised and de-latinised style.[7] Modern critics, however, seeing no necessity to choose between the two versions, and recognising a marked advance in the thematic maturity of *The Fall of Hyperion*, have generally concerned themselves with analysing the complex interrelationship (including questions of meaning) between the two fragments.

Since it is impossible to do justice here to the diversity of critical issues addressed by these modern readers, I have reprinted in Part Three two of the most interesting and influential essays on the *Hyperion* poems. Kenneth Muir proposes that the primary meaning of both poems, *Hyperion* and *The Fall of Hyperion*, may be traced to Keats's theory of human progress, in which the new gods of achievement, more sensitive and vulnerable than their Titan predecessors, are victorious over the old gods of power. Paul Sheats in his valuable general article, which brings into balanced perspective much of the recent criticism on the two *Hyperion* poems, demonstrates convincingly that in the disciplined revision which produced *The Fall of Hyperion* Keats achieved a detached, almost anti-romantic style that, in contrast to the passionate intensity evoked in his earlier verse, 'neither displays nor encourages imaginative entanglements' with the physical world. By setting *The Fall of Hyperion* in its place in the chronology of Keats's development, Sheats shows how the last poems, more quiet and thoughtful than those written earlier, are less an ending than the 'final beginning' in a poetic career dedicated to seeking a deeper, and still deeper, understanding of the pain and vulnerability that Titans and men alike are heir to.

> And can I ever bid these joys farewell?
> Yes, I must pass them for a nobler life,
> Where I may find the agonies, the strife
> Of human hearts. . . .   [*Sleep and Poetry*, 121–5]

★

Finally, it should be said that the task of selecting the modern critical essays for this collection has been formidable. I am only too well aware of the many fine papers and book-chapters which it has been necessary to omit; some of these are listed in the Bibliography. In general, my choice of critical essays and passages to be reprinted has been governed by the needs of the undergraduate students for whom this work is primarily intended. For this reason, specialist and highly technical studies have been omitted.

NOTES

1. Sidney Colvin, *John Keats: His Life and Poetry, His Friends, Critics, and After-Fame* (London, 1917), p. 114.
2. Walter Jackson Bate, *John Keats* (Cambridge, Mass., 1964), p. 170.
3. Bernard Blackstone, *The Consecrated Urn: An Interpretation of Keats in Terms of Growth and Form* (London, 1959), pp. 266–7; Jack Stillinger, 'Keats and Romance', *Studies in English Literature*, 8 (1968), p. 593.
4. See especially Keats's letters to Benjamin Bailey (22 November 1817) and John Hamilton Reynolds (3 May 1818).
5. D. G. Rossetti in a letter (11 February 1880) to H. Buxton Forman.
6. Keats's letter to Richard Woodhouse (27 October 1818).
7. Colvin (above, note 1), p. 447.

PART ONE

Extracts from Keats's Letters

1. COMMENTS ON INDIVIDUAL POEMS

Endymion: A Poetic Romance

Composed April–November 1817; published April 1818.

TO B. R. HAYDON, 28 September 1817

. . . You will be glad to hear that within these last three weeks I have written 1000 lines–which are the third Book of my Poem. My ideas with respect to it I assure you are very low– and I would write the subject thoroughly again. but I am tired of it and think the time would be better spent in writing a new Romance which I have in my eye for next summer– Rome was not built in a Day. and all the good I expect from my employment this summer is the fruit of Experience which I hope to gather in my next Poem. . . . [p. 25]*

TO BENJAMIN BAILEY, 8 October 1817

. . . I am quite disgusted with literary Men and will never know another except Wordsworth–no not even Byron—Here

---

* Page references here and elsewhere in Part One are to the *Letters of John Keats*, ed. Robert Gittings (London, 1970). Spelling, punctuation, grammar etc. follow in essentials as closely as possible the manuscript original. Reference numbers in the text relate to editorial Notes at the end of each poem-section in Part One. Variations in the styling of poem-titles are retained as in the original sources in Parts One and Two; in Part Three they are standardised to a modern usage.

is an instance of the friendships of such—Haydon and Hunt[1] have known each other many years - now they live pour ainsi dire jealous Neighbours. Haydon says to me Keats dont show your Lines to Hunt on any account or he will have done half for you—so it appears Hunt wishes it to be thought. When he met Reynolds in the Theatre John[2] told him that I was getting on to the completion of 4000 Lines. Ah! says Hunt, had it not been for me they would have been 7000! If he will say this to Reynolds what would he to other People? Haydon received a Letter a little while back on this subject from some Lady—which contains a caution to me through him on this subject—Now is not all this a most paultry thing to think about? You may see the whole of the case by the following extract from a Letter I wrote to George in the spring[3] 'As to 'what you say about my being a poet, I can retu[r]n no answer 'but by saying that the high Idea I have of poetical fame makes 'me think I see it towering to[o] high above me. At any rate I 'have no right to talk until Endymion is finished—it will be a 'test, a trial of my Powers of Imagination and chiefly of my 'invention which is a rare thing indeed—by which I must make '4000 Lines of one bare circumstance and fill them with Poetry; 'and when I consider that this is a great task, and that when 'done it will take me but a dozen paces towards the Temple of 'Fame—it makes me say—God forbid that I should be without 'such a task! I have heard Hunt say and may be asked—why 'endeavour after a long Poem? To which I should answer—Do 'not the Lovers of Poetry like to have a little Region to wander 'in where they may pick and choose, and in which the images 'are so numerous that many are forgotten and found new in a 'second Reading: which may be food for a Week's stroll in the 'Summer? Do not they like this better than what they can read 'through before Mrs Williams comes down stairs? a Morning 'work at most. Besides a long Poem is a test of Invention which 'I take to be the Polar Star of Poetry, as Fancy is the Sails, and 'Imagination the Rudder. Did our great Poets ever write short 'Pieces? I mean in the shape of Tales—This same invention 'seems indeed of late Years to have been forgotten as a Poetical 'excellence. But enough of this, I put on no Laurels till I shall 'have finished Endymion, and I hope Apollo is not angered at 'my having made a Mockery of him at Hunts'⁴ . . .   [pp. 26–7]

TO JOHN TAYLOR, 27 February 1818

. . . It is a sorry thing for me that any one should have to overcome Prejudices in reading my Verses–that affects me more than any hypercriticism on any particular Passage. In *Endymion* I have most likely but moved into the Go-cart from the leading strings. In Poetry I have a few Axioms, and you will see how far I am from their Centre. 1st I think Poetry should surprise by a fine excess and not by Singularity–it should strike the Reader as a wording of his own highest thoughts, and appear almost a Remembrance—2nd Its touches of Beauty should never be half way therby making the reader breathless instead of content: the rise, the progress, the setting of imagery should like the Sun come natural natural too him – shine over him and set soberly although in magnificence leaving him in the Luxury of twilight–but it is easier to think what Poetry should be than to write it–and this leads me on to another axiom. That if Poetry comes not as naturally as the Leaves to a tree it had better not come at all. However it may be with me I cannot help looking into new countries with 'O for a Muse of fire to ascend!'—If Endymion serves me as a Pioneer perhaps I ought to be content. I have great reason to be content, for thank God I can read and perhaps understand Shakspeare to his depths, and I have I am sure many friends, who, if I fail, will attribute any change in my Life and Temper to Humbleness rather than to Pride–to a cowering under the Wings of great Poets rather than to a Bitterness that I am not appreciated. I am anxious to get Endymion printed that I may forget it and proceed. . . .   [pp. 69–70]

TO J. H. REYNOLDS, 9 April 1818

. . . Since you all agree that the thing⁵ is bad, it must be so-
though I am not aware there is any thing like Hunt in it, (and
if there is, it is my natural way, and I have something in
common with Hunt) look it over again and examine into the
motives, the seeds from which any one sentence sprung—I
have not the slightest feel of humility towards the Public–or to
any thing in existence,–but the eternal Being, the Principle of
Beauty,–and the Memory of great Men—When I am writing
for myself for the mere sake of the Moment's enjoyment,
perhaps nature has its course with me–but a Preface is written
to the Public; a thing I cannot help looking upon as an Enemy,
and which I cannot address without feelings of Hostility—If I
write a Preface in a supple or subdued style, it will not be in
character with me as a public speaker—I woᵈ be subdued
before my friends, and thank them for subduing me–but
among Multitudes of Men–I have no feel of stooping, I hate
the idea of humility to them–
     I never wrote one single Line of Poetry with the least
Shadow of public thought. . . .   [pp. 84–5]

TO J. A. HESSEY, 8 October 1818

. . . Praise or blame has but a momentary effect on the man
whose love of beauty in the abstract makes him a severe critic
on his own Works. My own domestic criticism has given me
pain without comparison beyond what Blackwood or the
Quarterly could possibly inflict.   and also when I feel I am
right, no external praise can give me such a glow as my own
solitary reperception & ratification of what is fine. J. S.⁶ is
perfectly right in regard to the slipshod Endymion. That it is so
is no fault of mine.—No!–though it may sound a little

paradoxical. It is as good as I had power to make it—by myself—Had I been nervous about its being a perfect piece, & with that view asked advice, & trembled over every page, it would not have been written; for it is not in my nature to fumble—I will write independantly.—I have written independently *without Judgment*—I may write independently *& with judgment* hereafter.—The Genius of Poetry must work out its own salvation in a man: It cannot be matured by law & precept, but by sensation & watchfulness in itself—That which is creative must create itself—In Endymion, I leaped headlong into the Sea, and thereby have become better acquainted with the Soundings, the quicksands, & the rocks, than if I had stayed upon the green shore, and piped a silly pipe, and took tea & comfortable advice.—I was never afraid of failure; for I would sooner fail than not be among the greatest—But I am nigh getting into a rant. . . .   [pp. 155–6]

TO GEORGE AND GEORGIANA KEATS, 19 February 1819

. . . I have not said in any Letter yet a word about my affairs—in a word I am in no despair about them—my poem has not at all succeeded–in the course of a year or so I think I shall try the public again—in a selfish point of view I should suffer my pride and my contempt of public opinion to hold me silent–but for your's and fanny's sake [i.e. Keats's sister Fanny] I will pluck up a spirit, and try again—I have no doubt of success in a course of years if I persevere – but it must be patience–for the Reviews have enervated and made indolent mens minds–few think for themselves—These Reviews too are getting more and more powerful and especially the Quarterly—They are like a superstition which the more it prostrates the Crowd and the longer it continues the more powerful it becomes just in proportion to their increasing weakness—I was in hopes that when people saw, as they must do now, all the trickery and iniquity of these Plagues they would scout them, but no they are like the spectators at the Westminster cock-pit–they like the battle and do not care who wins or who looses– . . .   [p. 216]

NOTES ON 'ENDYMION' LETTERS

1. Benjamin Robert Haydon (1786–1846), the painter, and Leigh Hunt (1784–1859), poet and journalist, were friends of Keats.

2. John Hamilton Reynolds (1796–1852) was another of Keats's friends.

3. This letter of Spring 1817 to George Keats (the poet's brother, then living in America) is lost.

4. In the early Spring of 1817 Keats and Leigh Hunt, in a moment of post-prandial levity, exchanged laurel crowns in the manner of the elder poets. The incident was remembered by Keats with acute embarrassment.

5. The original preface to *Endymion* is 'the thing' referred to. Keats did subsequently abandon it, and write another.

6. This refers to a review of *Endymion* by 'J.S.' – probably John Scott (1783–1821), a schoolmate of Byron's in Aberdeen. It had appeared in the *Morning Chronicle* (3 Oct. 1818).

Isabella; or, The Pot of Basil

Composed March–April 1818; published July 1820.

TO GEORGE AND GEORGIANA KEATS, 14 October 1818

. . . Reynolds has returned from a six weeks enjoyment in Devonshire, he is well and persuades me to publish my pot of Basil as an answer to the attacks made on me in Blackwood's Magazine and the Quarterly Review. There have been two Letters in my defence in the Chronicle and one in the Examiner, coppied from the Alfred Exeter paper, and written by Reynolds–I do not know who wrote those in the chronicle—This is a mere matter of the moment–I think I shall be among the English Poets after my death. Even as a Matter of present interest the attempt to crush me in the Quarterly has only brought me more into notice and it is a common expression among book men 'I wonder the Quarterly should cut its own throat.' . . .   [p. 161]

TO RICHARD WOODHOUSE, 22 September 1819

. . . I will give you a few reasons why I shall persist in not publishing The Pot of Basil—It is too smokeable[1]–I can get it smoak'd at the Carpenters shaving chimney much more cheaply—There is too much inexperience of live [*for* life], and simplicity of knowledge in it–which might do very well after one's death–but not while one is alive. There are very few would look to the reality. I intend to use more finesse with the Public. It is possible to write fine things which cannot be laugh'd at in any way. Isabella is what I should call were I a reviewer 'A weak-sided Poem' with an amusing sober-sadness about it. Not that I do not think Reynolds and you are quite right about it–it is enough for me. But this will not do to be public—If I may say so, in my dramatic capacity I enter fully into the feeling: but in Propria Persona I should be apt to quiz it myself—There is no objection of this kind to Lamia—A good deal to St Agnes Eve–only not so glaring– . . .   [p. 298]

NOTE ON 'ISABELLA' LETTERS

1. 'Smokeable' – open to sarcastic criticism [Gittings's note].

Hyperion. A Fragment
The Fall of Hyperion. A Dream

Hyperion was begun in the Autumn of 1818 and finally abandoned in April 1819; published in 1820. *The Fall of Hyperion*, a reconstruction of the earlier poem, was composed in July–September 1819; not published until 1856.

TO B. R. HAYDON, 23 January 1818

. . .–in Endymion I think you may have many bits of the deep and sentimental cast–the nature of *Hyperion* will lead me to treat it in a more naked and grecian Manner–and the march of passion and endeavour will be undeviating–and one great contrast between them will be–that the Hero of the written tale[1] being mortal is led on, like Buonaparte, by circumstance; whereas the Apollo in Hyperion being a fore-seeing God will shape his actions like one. . . .   [p. 51]

TO J. H. REYNOLDS, 21 September 1819

. . . I always somehow associate Chatterton with autumn. He is the purest writer in the English Language. He has no French idiom, or particles like Chaucer–'tis genuine English Idiom in English words. I have given up Hyperion[2]–there were too many Miltonic inversions in it–Miltonic verse cannot be written but in an artful or rather artist's humour. I wish to give myself up to other sensations.[3] English ought to be kept up. It may be interesting to you to pick out some lines from Hyperion and put a mark × to the false beauty proceeding from art, and one

‖ to the true voice of feeling. Upon my soul 'twas imagination I cannot make the distinction—Every now & then there is a Miltonic intonation—But I cannot make the division properly. . . .   [p. 292]

NOTES ON THE 'HYPERION' LETTERS

1. I.e., *Endymion*.
2. I.e., *The Fall of Hyperion*.
3. There is a similar statement in a letter (17–27 September 1819) to the George Keatses in America: 'I have but lately stood on my guard against Milton. Life to him would be death to me. Miltonic verse cannot be written but [in] the vein of art – I wish to devote myself to another sensation –' (*Letters*, pp. 325–6).

The Eve of St Agnes

Composed January–February 1819; published July 1820.

TO GEORGE AND GEORGIANA KEATS, 14 February 1819

. . . I believe I told you I was going thither [i.e. to Chichester] –I was nearly a fortnight at Mr John Snook's and a few days at old Mr Dilke's—Nothing worth speaking of happened at either place—I took down some of the thin paper and wrote on it a little Poem call'd 'St Agnes Eve'–which you shall have as it is. . . .   [p. 211]

TO JOHN TAYLOR, 17 November 1819

. . . I have come to a determination not to publish any thing I have now ready written; but for all that to publish a Poem before long and that I hope to make a fine one. As the marvellous is the most enticing and the surest guarantee of harmonious numbers I have been endeavouring to persuade myself to untether Fancy and let her manage for herself–I and myself cannot agree about this at all. Wonders are no wonders to me. I am more at Home amongst Men and women. I would rather read Chaucer than Ariosto—The little dramatic skill I may as yet have however badly it might show in a Drama would I think be sufficient for a Poem—I wish to diffuse the colouring of St Agnes eve throughout a Poem in which Character and Sentiment would be the figures to such drapery—Two or three such Poems, if God should spare me, written in the course of the next six years, would be a famous gradus ad Parnassum altissimum[1]—I mean they would nerve me up to the writing of a few fine Plays–my greatest ambition–when I do feel ambitious. . . .   [pp. 340–1]

NOTE ON 'THE EVE OF ST AGNES' LETTERS
    1. Translation: 'step toward the highest Parnassus'.

The Eve of St Mark

Composed February 1819; published 1848.

TO GEORGE AND GEORGIANA KEATS, 20 September 1819

. . . The great beauty of Poetry is, that it makes every thing every place interesting–The palatine venice and the abbotine Winchester are equally interesting—Some time since I began a Poem call'd "the Eve of St Mark quite in the spirit of Town quietude. I th[i]nk it will give you the sensation of walking about an old country Town in a coolish evening. I know not yet whether I shall ever finish it–I will give it as far as I have gone. . . .   [p. 315]

Lamia

Composed June–September 1819; published July 1820.

TO J. H. REYNOLDS, 11 July 1819

. . . You will be glad to hear . . . how diligent I have been, & am being. I have finish'd the Act[1] and in the interval of beginning the 2d have proceeded pretty well with Lamia, finished the 1st part which consists of about 400 lines. I have great hopes of success, because I make use of my Judgment more deliberately than I yet have done; but in Case of failure with the world, I shall find my content. . . .   [pp. 267–8]

TO GEORGE AND GEORGIANA KEATS, 18 September 1819

. . . I have been reading over a part of a short poem I have composed lately call'd 'Lamia'–and I am certain there is that sort of fire in it which must take hold of people in some way–give them either pleasant or unpleasant sensation. What they want is a sensation of some sort. . . .   [p. 308]

NOTE ON 'LAMIA' LETTERS

1. Act I of *Otho the Great*, which Keats was writing in collaboration with his friend Charles Brown.

2. GENERAL COMMENTS

TO GEORGE AND GEORGIANA KEATS, 14 February 1819

. . . In my next Packet as this is one by the way, I shall send you the Pot of Basil, St Agnes eve, and if I should have finished it a little thing call'd the 'eve of St Mark' you see what fine mother Radcliff[1] names I have–it is not my fault–I did not search for them—I have not gone on with Hyperion–for to tell the truth I have not been in great cue for writing lately–I must wait for the sp[r]ing to rouse me up a little– . . .   [p.214]

TO PERCY BYSSHE SHELLEY, 16 August 1820

. . . I am glad you take any pleasure in my poor Poem;[2]—which I would willingly take the trouble to unwrite, if possible, did I care so much as I have done about Reputation. I received a copy of the Cenci, as from yourself from Hunt. There is only one part of it I am judge of; the Poetry, and dramatic effect, which by many spirits now a days is considered the mammon. A modern work it is said must have a purpose, which may be the God—*an artist* must serve Mammon – he must have 'self concentration' selfishness perhaps. You I am sure will forgive me for sincerely remarking that you might curb your magnanimity and be more of an artist, and 'load every rift' of your subject with ore[3] The thought of such discipline must fall like cold chains upon you, who perhaps never sat with your wings furl'd for six Months together. And is not this extraordina[r]y talk for the writer of Endymion? whose mind was like a pack of scattered cards—I am pick'd up and sorted to a pip. My Imagination is a Monastry and I am its Monk—you must explain my metap^{cs} [metaphysics] to yourself. I am in expectation of Prometheus[4] every day. Could I have my own wish for its interest effected you would have it still in manuscript—or be but now putting an end to the second act. I remember you advising me not to publish my first-blights, on Hampstead heath—I am returning advice upon your hands. Most of the Poems in the volume[5] I send you have been written above two years, and would never have been publish'd but from a hope of gain; so you see I am inclined enough to take your advice now. . . .   [pp. 389–90]

TO CHARLES BROWN, August (?) 1820

. . . The sale of my book[6] is very slow, though it has been very highly rated. One of the causes, I understand from different quarters, of the unpopularity of this new book, and the others also, is the offence the ladies take at me. On thinking the matter over, I am certain that I have said nothing in a spirit to displease any woman I would care to please: but still there is a tendency to class women in my books with roses and sweetmeats, –they never see themselves dominant. . . .   [pp. 390–1]

NOTES

1. 'mother Radcliff: an allusion to Mrs Ann Radcliffe (1764–1823), the popular writer of terror and mystery tales (e.g., *The Mysteries of Udolpho* and *The Italian*).
2. In a letter to Keats of 27 July 1820, Shelley had written: 'I have lately read your *Endymion* again & ever with a new sense of the treasures of poetry it contains, though treasures poured forth with indistinct profusion'.
3. Spenser, *The Faerie Queene*, 2 VII xxviii 5.
4. Shelley's *Prometheus Unbound* (1820).
5. Keats's *Lamia, Isabella, The Eve of St Agnes, and Other Poems* (July 1820).
6. The same.

PART TWO

Nineteenth-Century Viewpoints

1. *ENDYMION: A POETIC ROMANCE*

John Gibson Lockhart   (1818)

Of all the manias of this mad age, the most incurable, as well
as the most common, seems to be no other than the *Metromanie*.
The just celebrity of Robert Burns and Miss Baillie has had the
melancholy effect of turning the heads of we know not how
many farm-servants and unmarried ladies; our very footmen
compose tragedies, and there is scarcely a superannuated
governess in the island that does not leave a roll of lyrics
behind her in her band-box. To witness the disease of any
human understanding, however feeble, is distressing; but the
spectacle of an able mind reduced to a state of insanity is of
course ten times more afflicting. It is with such sorrow as this
that we have contemplated the case of Mr John Keats. This
young man appears to have received from nature talents of an
excellent, perhaps even of a superior order – talents which,
devoted to the purposes of any useful profession, must have
rendered him a respectable, if not an eminent citizen. His
friends, we understand, destined him to the career of
medicine, and he was bound apprentice some years ago to a
worthy apothecary in town. But all has been undone by a
sudden attack of the malady to which we have alluded.
Whether Mr John had been sent home with a diuretic or
composing draught to some patient far gone in the poetical
mania, we have not heard. This much is certain, that he has
caught the infection, and that thoroughly. For some time we
were in hopes, that he might get off with a violent fit or two;
but of late the symptoms are terrible. The phrenzy of the
Poems[1] was bad enough in its way; but it did not alarm us half
so seriously as the calm, settled, imperturbable drivelling
idiocy of *Endymion*. We hope, however, that in so young a

person, and with a constitution originally so good, even now the disease is not utterly incurable. Time, firm treatment, and rational restraint, do much for many apparently hopeless invalids; and if Mr Keats should happen, at some interval of reason, to cast his eye upon our pages, he may perhaps be convinced of the existence of his malady, which, in such cases, is often all that is necessary to put the patient in a fair way of being cured. . . .

Before giving any extracts, we must inform our readers, that this romance is meant to be written in English heroic rhyme. To those who have read any of [Leigh] Hunt's poems, this hint might indeed be needless. Mr Keats has adopted the loose, nerveless versification, and Cockney rhymes of the poet of *Rimini*;[2] but in fairness to that gentleman, we must add, that the defects of the system are tenfold more conspicuous in his disciple's work than in his own. Mr Hunt is a small poet, but he is a clever man. Mr Keats is a still smaller poet, and he is only a boy of pretty abilities, which he has done every thing in his power to spoil. . . .

And now, good-morrow to 'the Muses' son of Promise'; as for 'the feats he yet may do', as we do not pretend to say, like himself, 'Muse of my native land am I inspired', we shall adhere to the safe old rule of *pauca verba*. We venture to make one small prophecy, that his bookseller will not a second time venture £50 upon any thing he can write. It is a better and a wiser thing to be a starved apothecary than a starved poet; so back to the shop Mr John, back to 'plasters, pills, ointment boxes', &c. But, for Heaven's sake, young Sangrado,[3] be a little more sparing of extenuatives and soporifics in your practice than you have been in your poetry.

SOURCE: excerpted from a review signed 'Z' in *Blackwood's Edinburgh Review*, III (August 1818), pp. 519–24.

NOTES

1. Keats's first publication, *Poems* (March 1817).
2. Leigh Hunt's *The Story of Rimini* (1816).
3. In Alain-René Le Sage's picaresque romance *Gil Blas* (1715–35), Dr

Sangrado is a quack physician who employs the same remedies for all disorders.

John Wilson Croker   (1818)

Reviewers have been sometimes accused of not reading the works which they affected to criticise. On the present occasion we shall anticipate the author's complaint, and honestly confess that we have not read his work. Not that we have been wanting in our duty – far from it – indeed, we have made efforts almost as superhuman as the story itself appears to be, to get through it; but with the fullest stretch of our perseverance, we are forced to confess that we have not been able to struggle beyond the first of the four books of which this Poetic Romance consists. We should extremely lament this want of energy, or whatever it may be, on our parts, were it not for one consolation – namely, that we are no better acquainted with the meaning of the book through which we have so painfully toiled, than we are with that of the three which we have not looked into. . . .

This author is a copyist of Mr Hunt, but he is more unintelligible, almost as rugged, twice as diffuse, and ten times more tiresome and absurd than his prototype, who, though he impudently presumed to seat himself in the chair of criticism, and to measure his own poetry by his own standard, yet generally had a meaning. But Mr Keats had advanced no dogmas which he was bound to support by examples; his nonsense therefore is quite gratuitous; he writes for its own sake, and, being bitten by Mr Leigh Hunt's insane criticism, more than rivals the insanity of his poetry. . . .[1]

Of the story we have been able to make out but little; it seems to be mythological, and probably relates to the loves of Diana and Endymion; but of this, as the scope of the work has altogether escaped us, we cannot speak with any degree of certainty; and must therefore content ourselves with giving some instances of its diction and versification: – and here again we are perplexed and puzzled. – At first it appeared to us, that Mr Keats had been amusing himself and wearying his readers with an immeasurable game at *bouts-rimés*; but, if we recollect rightly, it is an indispensable condition at this play, that the rhymes when filled up shall have a meaning; and our author, as we have already hinted, has no meaning. He seems to us to write a line at random, and then he follows not the thought excited by this line, but that suggested by the *rhyme* with which it concludes. There is hardly a complete couplet inclosing a complete idea in the whole book. He wanders from one subject to another, from the association, not of ideas but of sounds, and the work is composed of hemistichs which, it is quite evident, have forced themselves upon the author by the mere force of the catchwords on which they turn. . . .

SOURCE: excerpted from unsigned review in the *Quarterly Review*, XIX (September 1818), pp. 204–8.

NOTE

1. More than one reviewer protested at Croker's harsh, *ad hominem* and politically motivated attack on Keats as a disciple of Leigh Hunt. Writing in the *Morning Chronicle* (3 Oct. 1818), for example, 'J.S.' – probably John Scott – declared: 'Mr L. Hunt, it appears, has thought highly of the poetical talents of Mr Keats; hence Mr K. is doomed to feel the merciless tomahawk of the Reviewers, termed Quarterly, I presume from the modus operandi'.

Francis Jeffrey   (1820)

. . . The thin and scanty tissue of his story is merely the light frame work on which his florid wreaths are suspended; and while his imaginations go rambling and entangling themselves everywhere, like wild honeysuckles, all idea of sober reason, and plan, and consistency, is utterly forgotten, and are 'strangled in their waste fertility'. A great part of the work indeed, is written in the strangest and most fantastical manner that can be imagined. It seems as if the author had ventured everything that occurred to him in the shape of a glittering image or striking expression – taken the first word that presented itself to make up a rhyme, and then made that word the germ of a new cluster of images – a hint for a new excursion of the fancy – and so wandered on, equally forgetful whence he came, and heedless whither he was going, till he had covered his pages with an interminable arabesque of connected and incongruous figures, that multiplied as they extended, and were only harmonized by the brightness of their tints, and the graces of their forms. In this rash and headlong career he has of course many lapses and failures. There is no work, accordingly, from which a malicious critic could cull more matter for ridicule, or select more obscure, unnatural, or absurd passages. But we do not take *that* to be our office; – and just beg leave, on the contrary, to say, that any one who, on this account, would represent the whole poem as despicable, must either have no notion of poetry, or no regard to truth.

SOURCE: excerpted from a review in *Edinburgh Review*, XXXIV (August 1820), pp. 203–13.

Percy Bysshe Shelley   (1820, 1821)

I

. . . I am aware that the first duty of a Reviewer is towards the public, and I am willing to confess that the Endymion is a poem considerably defective, & that perhaps it deserved as much censure as the pages of your review record against it. But not to mention that there is a certain contemptuousness of phraseology from which it is difficult for a critic to abstain, in the Review of Endymion, – I do not think that the writer has given it its due praise. Surely the poem with all its faults is a very remarkable production for a man of Keats's age and the promise of ultimate excellence is such as has rarely been afforded even by such as have afterwards attained high literary eminence. Look at Book 2. line 833 &c. & Book 3. line 113. to 120 – read down that page & then again from line 193 – I could cite many other passages to convince you that it deserved milder usage. Why it should have been reviewed at all, excepting for the purpose of bringing its excellencies into notice I cannot conceive, for it was very little read, & there was no danger that it should become a model to the age of that false taste with which I confess that it is replenished – . . .

SOURCE: excerpted from a letter of Shelley's to the Editor of the *Quarterly Review* (? November 1820); reproduced in *Letters of Percy Bysshe Shelley*, ed. F. L. Jones, 2 vols (Oxford, 1964), II, p. 252.

II

. . . The genius of the lamented person to whose memory I have dedicated these unworthy verses was not less delicate and fragile than it was beautiful; and where canker-worms abound, what wonder if its young flower was blighted in the bud? The savage criticism on his *Endymion*, which appeared in the *Quarterly Review*, produced the most violent effect on his susceptible mind; the agitation thus originated ended in the rupture of a blood-vessel in the lungs; a rapid consumption ensued, and the succeeding acknowledgements from more candid critics of the true greatness of his powers were ineffectual to heal the wound thus wantonly inflicted.

It may be well said that these wretched men know not what they do. They scatter their insults and their slanders without heed as to whether the poisoned shaft lights on a heart made callous by many blows or one like Keats's composed of more penetrable stuff. One of their associates is, to my knowledge, a most base and unprincipled calumniator. As to *Endymion*, was it a poem, whatever might be its defects, to be treated contemptuously by those who had celebrated, with various degrees of complacency and panegyric, *Paris*, and *Woman*, and a *Syrian Tale*, and Mrs Lefanu, and Mr Barrett, and Mr Howard Payne, and a long list of the illustrious obscure? Are these the men who in their venal good nature presumed to draw a parallel between the Rev. Mr Milman and Lord Byron? What gnat did they strain at here, after having swallowed all those camels? Against what woman taken in adultery dares the foremost of these literary prostitutes to cast his opprobrious stone? Miserable man! you, one of the meanest, have wantonly defaced one of the noblest specimens of the workmanship of God. Nor shall it be your excuse, that, murderer as you are, you have spoken daggers, but used none. . . .

SOURCE: excerpted from the Preface to *Adonais* (July 1821); reproduced in *The Complete Poetical Works of Percy Bysshe Shelley*, ed. Thomas Hutchinson (London and New York, 1905; reprinted 1961), p. 431.

Lord Byron   (1821)

. . . Are you aware that Shelley has written an elegy on Keats, and accuses the *Quarterly* of killing him?

> 'Who killed John Keats?'
> 'I', says the Quarterly,
> So savage and Tartarly;
> ''Twas one of my feats.'

'Who shot the arrow?'
'The poet-priest Milman
(So ready to kill man),
Or Southey or Barrow.'

You know very well that I did not approve of Keats's poetry, or principles of poetry, or of his abuse of Pope;[1] but, as he is dead, omit *all* that is said *about him* in any *MSS.* of mine, or publication. His *Hyperion* is a fine monument, and will keep his name. I do not envy the man who wrote the article: your review people have no more right to kill than any other foot pads. However, he who would die of an article in a review would probably have died of something else equally trivial. . . .

SOURCE: excerpted from a letter of Byron's to his publisher, John Murray (30 July 1821); reproduced in *Byron: A Self-Portrait*, ed. P. Quennell, 2 vols (London, 1950; reprinted 1967), II, p. 661.

NOTE

1. Byron's position is amplified in Thomas Medwin's *Conversations of Lord Byron* (1824), where Byron is reported as having said: 'I am always battling with *the Snake* [i.e. Shelley] about Keats, and wonder what he finds to make a god of, in that idol of the Cockneys. . . . He will, like me, return some day to admire Pope, and think *The Rape of the Lock* and its sylphs worth fifty *Endymions*, with their faun and satyr machinery!' – quoted in *Keats: The Critical Heritage*, ed. G. M. Matthews (London, 1971), p. 132.

William Hazlitt   (1822)

. . . I cannot help thinking that the fault of Mr Keats's poems was a deficiency in masculine energy of style. He had beauty, tenderness, delicacy, in an uncommon degree, but there was a want of strength and substance. His Endymion is a very delightful description of the illusions of a youthful imagination, given up to airy dreams – we have flowers, clouds, rainbows, moonlight, all sweet sounds and smells, and Oreads and Dryads flitting by – but there is nothing tangible in it, nothing marked or palpable – we have none of the hardy spirit or rigid forms of antiquity. He painted his own thoughts and character; and did not transport himself into the fabulous and heroic ages. There is a want of action, of character, and so far, of imagination, but there is exquisite fancy. All is soft and fleshy, without bone or muscle. We see in him the youth, without the manhood of poetry. His genius breathed 'vernal delight and joy'. – 'Like Maia's son he stood and shook his plumes', with fragrance filled. His mind was redolent of spring. He had not the fierceness of summer, nor the richness of autumn, and winter he seemed not to have known, till he felt the icy hand of death!

SOURCE: excerpted from Essay XXV in *Table-Talk: or, Original Essays* (1822); reproduced in *The Complete Works of William Hazlitt*, ed. P. P. Howe, 21 vols (London, 1930–34), reprinted (New York, 1967), VIII, pp. 254–5.

D. M. Moir (1851)

. . . in the following year appeared his *Endymion*, a poetic romance. It would be difficult to point out anywhere a work more remarkable for its amount of beauties and blemishes, inextricably entertwined. . . . We are entranced with the prodigal profusion of imagery, and the exquisite variety of metres sweeping along with an Æolian harmony, at once so refined and yet seemingly so inartificial. All is, however, a wild luxurious revel merely, where Imagination laughs at Taste, and bids defiance to Judgment and Reason. There is no discrimination, no selection – even the very rhymes seem sometimes to have suggested the thoughts that follow; and whatever comes uppermost comes out, provided it be florid, gorgeous, or glittering. The work is a perfect mosaic of bright tints and graceful forms, despotically commingled, almost without regard to plan or congruity; so that we often lose the thin thread of story altogether in the fantastic exuberance of ornament and decoration. Ever and anon, however, we come to bits of exquisite beauty – patches of deep, serene blue sky, amid the rolling clouds, which compel us to pause in admiration – glimpses of nature full of tenderness and truth – touches of sentiment deep as they are delicate. His opening line, 'A thing of beauty is a joy for ever', conveys a fine philosophic sentiment, and is the key-note to the whole body of his poetry. Crude, unequal, extravagant, nay, absurd as he sometimes is – for there is scarcely an isolated page in *Endymion* to which one or more of these harsh epithets may not in some degree be justly applied – yet, on the other hand, it would be difficult to point out twenty lines in sequence unredeemed by some happy turn of thought, some bright image, or some eloquent expression. . . .

SOURCE: excerpted from *Sketches of the Poetical Literature of the Past Half-Century* (1851), pp. 215–21.

Matthew Arnold   (1887)

. . . What is good in *Endymion* is not as good as you say,[1] and the poem as a whole I could wish to be suppressed and lost. I really resent the space it occupies in the volume of Keats's poetry. . . .

SOURCE: excerpted from a letter of Arnold's to Sidney Colvin (26 June 1887); reproduced in E. V. Lucas, *The Colvins and their Friends* (London, 1928), p. 193.

NOTE

1. For Colvin on *Endymion*, see ch. 5 of his *Keats* (London, 1889), or his fuller account in chs 6 and 7 of his *John Keats: His Life and Poetry, His Friends, Critics, and After-Fame* (London, 1917) – see the excerpt in Part Three, below.

2. ISABELLA; OR, THE POT OF BASIL

Charles Lamb   (1820)

. . . The finest thing in the volume [i.e., Keats's *Poems* (1820)] is the paraphrase of Boccaccio's story of the Pot of Basil. Two Florentines, merchants, discovering that their sister Isabella has placed her affections upon Lorenzo, a young factor in their employ, when they had hopes of procuring for her a noble match, decoy Lorenzo, under pretence of a ride, into a wood, where they suddenly stab and bury him. The anticipation of the assassination is wonderfully conceived in one epthet, in the narration of the ride –

> So the two brothers, and their *murder'd* man,
>   Rode past fair Florence, to where Arno's stream
> Gurgles –

Returning to their sister, they delude her with a story of their having sent Lorenzo abroad to look after their merchandises; but the spirit of her lover appears to Isabella in a dream, and discovers how and where he was stabbed, and the spot where they have buried him. To ascertain the truth of the vision, she sets out to the place, accompanied by her old nurse, ignorant as yet of her wild purpose. Her arrival at it, and digging for the body, is described in the following stanzas, than which there is nothing more awfully simple in diction, more nakedly grand and moving in sentiment, in Dante, in Chaucer, or in Spenser: – [quotes *Isabella*, stanzas 46–8]. . . .

SOURCE: excerpted from unsigned review in the *New Times*, No. 6210 (19 July 1820).

John Scott   (1820)

. . . There are some stanzas introduced into his delicious tale of 'Isabel – poor simple Isabel' . . . which, we think, dreadfully mar the musical tenderness of its general strain. They are no better than extravagant school-boy vituperation of trade and traders; just as if lovers did not trade, – and that, often in stolen goods – or had in general any higher object than a barter of enjoyment! These stanzas in Mr Keats's poem, when contrasted with the larger philosophy of Boccaccio, and his more genial spirit, as exemplified with reference to the very circumstances in question, are additionally offensive. Instead of tirading against the brothers as 'money-bags,' 'Baalites of pelf,' 'ledger-men', – and asking, 'why, in the name of glory, were they proud?' Boccaccio describes the honour of the family as actually injured by Lorenzo, whom they employed – he shows us the elder brother, on discovering his sister's dishonour, afflicted with grief and perplexity, and passing a sleepless night on his bed – he even compliments the discretion of this member of the family – and it is thus naturally, and faithfully, and feelingly introduced, that he leads up the dreadful catastrophe to its consummation in Italian revenge, and the broken-heartedness of widowhood. Does the pathos of the tale suffer by thus looking fairly into the face of human nature? Do we pity the lovers less; do we sympathize less with Isabel's bitter tears, because we have both sides of the case thus placed before us? No – our sympathies, being more fairly excited, are more keenly so: the story is in fine keeping, as a painter would say: the effect of truth overpowers us: we weep the more because we feel that human frailty provides for human suffering, and that the best impulses of the heart are not removed from the liability of producing the extremities of agony and of crime. Mr Keats, we are sure, has a sensibility sufficiently delicate to feel this beauty in Boccaccio: why then has he substituted for it, in his own composition, a boisterous rhapsody, which interrupts the harmony of the sorrowful tale,

– repels sympathy by the introduction of caricature, – and suggests all sorts of dissenting, and altercating prejudices and opinions? His device is a clumsy one: Boccaccio's delicate and true. . . .

SOURCE: excerpted from an unsigned review in Baldwin's *London Magazine*, II (September 1820), pp. 315–21.

Matthew Arnold   (1853)

. . . The poem of Isabella, then, is a perfect treasure-house of graceful and felicitous words and images: almost in every stanza there occurs one of those vivid and picturesque turns of expression, by which the object is made to flash upon the eye of the mind, and which thrill the reader with a sudden delight. This one short poem contains, perhaps, a greater number of happy single expressions which one could quote than all the extant tragedies of Sophocles. But the action, the story? The action in itself is an excellent one; but so feebly is it conceived by the Poet, so loosely constructed, that the effect produced by it, in and for itself, is absolutely null. Let the reader, after he has finished the poem of Keats, turn to the same story in the Decameron [of Boccaccio]: he will then feel how pregnant and interesting the same action has become in the hands of a great artist, who above all things delineates his object; who subordinates expression to that which it is designed to express. . . .

SOURCE: excerpted from the Preface to *Poems* (1853); reproduced in *Arnold: Poetical Works*, ed. C. B. Tinker and H. F. Lowry (London and New York, 1950; reprinted 1966), p. *xxvi*.

Algernon Charles Swinburne (1886)

. . . *Isabella*, feeble and awkward in narrative to a degree almost incredible in a student of Dryden and a pupil of Leigh Hunt, is overcharged with episodical effects of splendid and pathetic expression beyond the reach of either. . . .

SOURCE: excerpted from *Miscellanies* (1886); reproduced in *The Complete Works of Algernon Charles Swinburne*, ed. E. Gosse and T. J. Wise, 20 vols (London, 1925; reprinted New York, 1968), IV, p. 298.

3. HYPERION. A FRAGMENT

Leigh Hunt   (1820)

. . . The *Hyperion* is a fragment, – a gigantic one, like a ruin in the desert, or the bones of the mastodon. It is truly of a piece with its subject, which is the downfall of the elder gods. It opens with Saturn, dethroned, sitting in a deep and solitary valley, benumbed in spite of his huge powers with the amazement of the change. . . . The fragment ends with the deification of Apollo. It strikes us that there is something too effeminate and human in the way in which Apollo receives the exaltation which his wisdom is giving him. He weeps and wonders somewhat too fondly; but his powers gather nobly on him as he proceeds. . . .

If any living poet could finish this fragment, we believe it is the author himself. But perhaps he feels that he ought not. A story which involves passion, almost of necessity involves speech; and though we may well enough describe beings greater than ourselves by comparison, unfortunately we cannot make them speak by comparison. Mr Keats, when he first introduces Thea consoling Saturn, says that she spoke

> Some mourning words, which in our feeble tongue
> Would come in these like accents; O how frail
> To that large utterance of the early Gods!

This grand confession of want of grandeur is all that he could do for them. Milton could do no more. Nay, he did less, when according to Pope he made

> God the father turn a school divine.

The moment the Gods speak, we forget that they did not speak like ourselves. The fact is, they feel like ourselves; and the poet would have to make them feel otherwise, even if he could make them speak otherwise, which he cannot, unless he venture upon an obscurity which would destroy our sympathy: and what is sympathy with a God, but turning him into a man? We allow, that superiority and inferiority are, after all, human terms, and imply something not so truly fine and noble as the levelling of a great sympathy and love; but poems of the present nature, like *Paradise Lost*, assume a different principle; and fortunately perhaps, it is one which it is impossible to reconcile with the other. . . .

SOURCE: excerpted from a review in the *Indicator*, XLIII (2 August 1820), pp. 337–44.

Percy Bysshe Shelley   (1821)

. . . Among your anathemas of the modern attempts in poetry, do you include Keats's 'Hyperion'? I think it is very fine. His other poems are worth little; but if the 'Hyperion' be not grand poetry, none has been produced by our contemporaries. . . .

SOURCE: excerpted from a letter of Shelley's to Thomas Love Peacock (15 February 1821); reproduced in *Complete Poetical Works*, op. cit., p. 262.

George Gilfillan   (1845)

. . . *Hyperion* is the greatest of poetical Torsos. 'Left untold', like *Cambuscan*[1] and *Christabel*, and Burns's speech of Liberty, it is perhaps better that it remains a fragment. Had only the two first Books of *Paradise Lost* come down to us, we question if they had not impressed us with a higher opinion of the author's powers than the complete work. Such magnificent mutilations are regarded with a complex emotion, composed of admiration, expectation, and regret. Short and sustained, they seldom tire or disappoint. And the poem itself is so bold in its conception, so true to the genuine classical spirit, so austerely statuesque in its still or moving figures, so antique to awfulness in its spirit, and, above all, indicates a rise so rapid and so great from his other works, as from Richmond-hill to an Alp, that those who love not Keats are compelled to admire *Hyperion*. It is, says Byron, 'as sublime as Eschylus'. . . .

SOURCE: excerpted from *A Gallery of Literary Portraits* (1845), pp. 372–85.

NOTE

1. In Chaucer's *Squire's Tale*.

4. *THE EVE OF ST AGNES*

Richard Woodhouse (1819)

. . . [Keats] wanted I believe to publish the Eve of St Agnes & Lamia *immediately*: but Hessey[1] told him it could not answer to do so now. I wondered why he said nothing of Isabella: & assured him it would please more [than] the Eve of St Agnes – He said he could not bear the former now. It appeared to him mawkish. This certainly cannot be so. . . . The feeling of mawkishness seems to me to be that which comes upon us where any thing of great tenderness & excessive simplicity is met with when we are not in a sufficiently tender & simple frame of mind to bear it: when we experience a sort of revulsion, or resiliency (if there be such a word) from the sentiment or expression. Now I believe there is nothing in any of the most passionate parts of Isabella to excite this feeling. It may, as may Lear, leave the reader far behind: but there is none of that sugar & butter sentiment, that cloys & disgusts. – He had the Eve of St A. copied fair: He has made trifling alterations. . . . There was [one] alteration, which I abused for 'a full hour by the *Temple* clock'. You know if a thing has a decent side, I generally look no further – As the Poem was origy written, *we* innocent ones (ladies & myself) might very well have supposed that Porphyro, when acquainted with Madeline's love for him, & when 'he arose, Etherial flushd' &c. &c. (turn to it) set himself at once to persuade her to go off with him, & succeeded & went over the 'Dartmoor black' (now changed for some other place) to be married, in right honest chaste & sober wise. But, as it is now altered, as soon as M. has confessed her love, P. winds by degrees his arm round her, presses breast to breast, and acts all the acts of a bonâ fide husband, while she fancies she is only playing the part of a Wife in a dream. This alteration is of about 3 stanzas; and tho' there are no improper expressions but all is left to inference, and tho' profanely speaking, the Interest on the reader's imagination is greatly heightened, yet I do apprehend it will render the poem unfit for ladies, & indeed scarcely to be mentioned to them among the 'things that are'. − He says he does not want ladies to read his poetry: that he writes for men, & that if in the former poem there was an opening for a doubt what took place, it was his fault for not writing clearly & comprehensibly − that he sh^d despise a man who would be such an eunuch in sentiment as to leave a maid, with that Character about her, in such a situation: & sho^d despise himself to write about it &c &c &c − and all this sort of Keats-like rhodomontade. . . . [2]

SOURCE: excerpted from a letter of Woodhouse's to John Taylor (20 September 1819); reproduced in *The Keats Circle*, ed. H. E. Rollins, 2 vols. (Cambridge, Mass. and Oxford, 1948; 2nd edn 1965), I, pp. 90–2.

   Richard Woodhouse (1788–1834), a lawyer, was a devoted admirer of Keats. John Taylor (1781–1864) was the publisher of *Endymion* and *Poems* (1820).

NOTES

   1. James Hessey (1785–1870) was John Taylor's partner in the publishing firm of Taylor & Hessey.
   2. The sexual 'indelicacy' of *The Eve of St Agnes* was a source of concern to a number of Keats's friends.

Leigh Hunt   (1820)

. . . 'The Eve of St Agnes', which is rather a picture than a story, may be analysed in a few words. It is an account of a young beauty, who going to bed on the eve in question to dream of her lover, while her rich kinsmen, the opposers of his

love, are keeping holiday in the rest of the house, finds herself
waked by him in the night, and in the hurry of the moment
agrees to elope with him. The portrait of the heroine,
preparing to go to bed, is remarkable for its union of extreme
richness and good taste; not that those two properties of
description are naturally distinct; but that they are too often
separated by very good poets, and that the passage affords a
striking specimen of the sudden and strong maturity of the
author's genius. When he wrote *Endymion* he could not have
resisted doing too much. To the description before us, it would
be a great injury either to add or diminish. It falls at once
gorgeously and delicately upon us, like the colours of the
painted glass. Nor is Madeline hurt by all her encrusting
jewelry and rustling silks. Her gentle, unsophisticated heart is
in the midst, and turns them into so many ministrants to her
loveliness. [Quotes stanzas 24–7 of *The Eve of St Agnes*.] . . .[1] Is
not this perfectly beautiful? . . .

SOURCE: excerpted from a review in the *Indicator*, XLIII (2
August 1820), pp. 337–44.

NOTE

1. In 1835 Leigh Hunt published in his *London Journal* (21 Jan. 1835) a
sensitive and systematic commentary on *The Eve of St Agnes*, which is,
unfortunately, too long to reproduce here. See *Critical Heritage*, ed.
Matthews, op. cit., pp. 275–80.

Alexander Smith   (1857)

. . . The same wonderful artistic sense is exhibited in the 'Eve
of St Agnes'. It is rich in colour as the stained windows of a
Gothic cathedral, and every verse bursts into picturesque and
graceful fancies; yet all this abundance is so subdued and
harmonized in such wonderful keeping with the story and the

mediaeval period, as to render it a perfect chrysolite – a precious gem of art. . . .

SOURCE: excerpted from signed article in the *Encyclopaedia Britannica*, 8th edn (1857), XIII, pp. 56–7.

Algernon Charles Swinburne   (1886)

. . . *The Eve of St Agnes,* aiming at no doubtful success, succeeds in evading all casual difficulty in the line of narrative; with no shadow of pretence to such interest as may be derived from stress of incident or depth of sentiment, it stands out among all other famous poems as a perfect and unsurpassable study in pure colour and clear melody – a study in which the figure of Madeline brings back upon the mind's eye, if only as moonlight recalls a sense of sunshine, the nuptial picture of Marlowe's Hero and the sleeping presence of Shakespeare's Imogen. Beside this poem should always be placed the less famous but not less precious *Eve of St Mark*, a fragment unexcelled for the simple perfection of its perfect simplicity, exquisite alike in suggestion and in accomplishment. . . .

SOURCE: excerpted from *Miscellanies* (1886); reproduced in *Complete Works*, op. cit., IV, p. 298.

William Michael Rossetti   (1887)

'Isabella' is written in the octave stanza; 'The Eve of St Agnes' in the Spenserean. This difference of metre corresponds very closely to the difference of character between the two poems.

'Isabella' is a narrative poem of event and passion, in which the incidents are presented so as chiefly to subserve purposes of sentiment; 'The Eve of St Agnes', though it assumes a narrative form, is hardly a narrative, but rather a monody of dreamy richness, a pictured and scenic presentment, which sentiment again permeates and over-rules. I rate it far above 'Isabella' – and indeed above all those poems of Keats, not purely lyrical, in which human or quasi-human agents bear their part, except only the ballad 'La Belle Dame sans Merci', and the uncompleted 'Eve of St Mark'. 'Hyperion' stands aloof in lone majesty; but I think that, in the long run, even 'Hyperion' represents the genius of Keats less adequately, and past question less characteristically, than 'The Eve of St Agnes'. The story of this fascinating poem is so meagre as to be almost nugatory. There is nothing in it but this – that Keats took hold of the superstition proper to St Agnes' Eve, the power of a maiden to see her absent lover under certain conditions, and added to it that a lover, who was clandestinely present in this conjuncture of circumstances, eloped with his mistress. This extreme tenuity of constructive power in the poem, coupled with the rambling excursiveness of 'Endymion', and the futility of 'The Cap and Bells', might be held to indicate that Keats had very little head for framing a story – and indeed I infer that, if he possessed any faculty in that direction, it remained undeveloped up to the day of his death. One of the few subsidiary incidents introduced into 'The Eve of St Agnes' is that the lover Porphyro, on emerging from his hiding-place while his lady is asleep, produces from the cupboard and marshals to sight a large assortment of appetizing eatables. Why he did this no critic and no admirer has yet been able to divine; and the incident is so trivial in itself, and is made so much of for the purpose of verbal or metrical embellishment, as to reinforce our persuasion that Keats's capacity for framing a story out of successive details of a suggestive and self-consistent kind was decidedly feeble. The power of 'The Eve of St Agnes' lies in a wholly different direction. It lies in the delicate transfusion of sight and emotion into sound; in making pictures out of words, or turning words into pictures; of giving a visionary beauty to the closest items of description; of holding all the materials of the poem in a long-drawn suspense of music and reverie. 'The Eve of St Agnes' is *par excellence* the poem of 'glamour'. It means next to nothing; but means that little so exquisitely, and in so rapt a mood of musing or of trance, that it tells as an intellectual no less than a sensuous restorative. Perhaps no reader has ever risen from 'The Eve of St Agnes' dissatisfied. After a while he can question the grounds of his satisfaction, and may possibly find them wanting; but he has only to peruse the poem again, and the same spell is upon him. . . .

SOURCE: excerpted from W. M. Rossetti, *Life of John Keats* (London, 1887), pp. 182–4.

5. *LA BELLE DAME SANS MERCI*

Coventry Patmore   (1848)

. . . The only striking proof of the existence of true metrical power in Keats, seems to us to occur in the measure of a little, and almost unknown poem, called 'La belle Dame sans merci', which appeared first in one of Mr Leigh Hunt's publications, and is reprinted now in the *Remains*.[1] This poem is, indeed, among the most mark-worthy of the productions of Keats; besides being good and original in metre, it is simple, passionate, sensuous,[2] and, above all, truly musical. . . .

> SOURCE: excerpted from unsigned review in the *North British Review*, X (November 1848), pp. 69–76.

> NOTES

> 1. Richard Monckton Milnes, *The Life, Letters and Literary Remains of John Keats*, 2 vols (London, 1848).
> 2. Patmore here alludes to Milton's description of poetry in *Of Education* (1644) as being 'lesse suttle and fine [than rhetoric], but more simple, sensuous and passionate'.

William Michael Rossetti   (1887)

. . . Passing from the long compositions, we find the cream of Keats's poetry in the ballad of 'La Belle Dame sans Merci', and in the five odes. . . . 'La Belle Dame sans Merci' may possibly have been written later than any of the odes, but this point is uncertain. I give it here as marking the highest point of romantic imagination to which Keats attained in dealing with human or quasi-human personages, and also his highest level of simplicity along with completeness of art. [Quotes *La Belle Dame sans Merci* in full.] . . . This is a poem of *impression*. The impression is immediate, final, and permanent; and words would be more than wasted upon pointing out to the reader that such and such are the details which have conduced to impress him. . . .

> SOURCE: excerpted from *Life of Keats*, op. cit., pp. 192–4.

6. *LAMIA*

Charles Lamb (1820)

. . . More exuberantly rich in imagery and painting is the story of the Lamia. It is of as gorgeous stuff as ever romance was composed of. Her first appearance in serpentine form –

> – a beauteous wreath with melancholy eyes –

her dialogue with Hermes, the *Star of Lethe*, as he is called by one of those prodigal phrases which Mr Keats abounds in, which are each a poem in a word, and which in this instance lays open to us at once, like a picture, all the dim regions and their inhabitants, and the sudden coming of a celestial among them; the charming of her into woman's shape again by the God; her marriage with the beautiful Lycius; her magic palace, which those who knew the street, and remembered it complete from childhood, never remembered to have seen before; the few Persian mutes, her attendants,

> – who that same year
> Were seen about the markets: none knew where
> They could inhabit; –

the high-wrought splendours of the nuptial bower, with the fading of the whole pageantry, Lamia, and all, away, before the glance of Apollonius, – are all that fairy land can do for us. They are for younger impressibilities. To *us* an ounce of feeling is worth a pound of fancy; and therefore we recur again, with a warmer gratitude, to the story of Isabella and the pot of basil, and those never-cloying stanzas which we have cited, and which we think should disarm criticism, if it be not in its nature cruel; if it would not deny to honey its sweetness, nor to roses redness, nor light to the stars in Heaven; if it would not bay the moon out of the skies, rather than acknowledge she is fair. . . .

SOURCE: excerpted from unsigned review in the *New Times*, No. 6210. (For Lamb on *Isabella*, see section 2 of this Part Two, above.)

Leigh Hunt   (1820)

. . . Mr Keats has departed as much from common-place in the character and moral of this story, as he has in the poetry of it. He would see fair play to the serpent, and makes the power of the philosopher an ill-natured and disturbing thing. Lamia though liable to be turned into painful shapes had a soul of humanity; and the poet does not see why she should not have her pleasures accordingly, merely because a philosopher saw that she was not a mathematical truth. This is fine and good. It is vindicating the greater philosophy of poetry. At the same time, we wish that for the purpose of his story he had not appeared to give in to the common-place of supposing that Apollonius's sophistry must always prevail, and that modern experiment has done a deadly thing to poetry by discovering the nature of the rainbow, the air, &c.: that is to say, that the knowledge of natural history and physics, by shewing us the nature of things, does away the imaginations that once adorned them. This is a condescension to a learned vulgarism, which so excellent a poet as Mr Keats ought not to have made. The world will always have fine poetry, as long as it has events, passions, affections, and a philosophy that sees deeper than this philosophy. There will be a poetry of the heart, as long as there are tears and smiles: there will be a poetry of the imagination, as long as the first causes of things remain a mystery. A man who is no poet, may think he is none, as soon as he finds out the physical cause of the rainbow; but he need not alarm himself: – he was none before. The true poet will go deeper. He will ask himself what is the cause of that physical cause; whether truths to the senses are after all to be taken as truths to the imagination; and whether there is not room and mystery enough in the universe for the creation of infinite things, when the poor matter-of-fact philosopher has come to the end of his own vision. It is remarkable that an age of poetry has grown up with the progress of experiment; and that the very poets, who seem to countenance these notions, accompany them by some of their finest effusions. Even if there were nothing new to be created, – if philosophy, with its line and rule, could even score the ground, and say to poetry 'Thou shalt go no further', she would look back to the old world, and still find it inexhaustible. The crops from its fertility are endless. But these alarms are altogether idle. The essence of poetical enjoyment does not consist in belief, but in a voluntary power to imagine. . . .

SOURCE: excerpted from a review in the *Indicator*, XLIII (2 August 1820), pp. 337–44.

PART THREE

Twentieth-Century Studies

Sir Sidney Colvin 'Endymion: A Neo-Elizabethan Allegory' (1917)

. . . *Endymion* . . . is a joint outcome of [Keats's] intense, his abnormal susceptibility to the spell of moonlight and of his pleasure in the ancient myth of the loves of the moon-goddess Cynthia and the shepherd-prince Endymion as made known to him through the earlier English poets.

The moon was to Keats a power very different from what she has always been to popular astrology and tradition. Traditionally and popularly she was the governess of floods, the presiding planet of those that ply their trade by sea, river or canal, also of wanderers and vagabonds generally: the disturber and bewilderer withal of mortal brains and faculties, sending down upon men under her sway that affliction of lunacy whose very name was derived from her. For Keats it was her transmuting and glorifying power that counted, not her pallor but her splendour, the magic alchemy exercised by her light upon the things of earth, the heightened mystery, poetry, and withal unity of aspect which she sheds upon them. He can never keep her praises long out of his early poetry, and we [see], in *I stood tip-toe*, what a range of beneficent activities he attributes to her. Now, as he settles down to work on *Endymion*, we shall find her, by reason of that special glorifying and unifying magic of her light, become for him, at first perhaps instinctively and unaware, but more and more consciously as he goes on, a definite symbol of Beauty itself – what he calls in a letter 'the principle of Beauty in all things', the principle which binds in a divine community all such otherwise unrelated matters as those we shall find him naming together as things of beauty in the exordium of his poem. Hence the tale of the loves of the Greek shepherd-prince and the moon-goddess turns under his hand into a parable of the adventures of the poetic soul striving after full communion with this spirit of essential Beauty.

As to the literary associations which drew Keats to the

Endymion story, there is scarce one of our Elizabethan poets but touches on it briefly or at length. Keats was no doubt acquainted with the *Endimion* of John Lyly, an allegorical court comedy in sprightly prose which had been among the plays edited, as it happened, by one of his new Hampstead friends, Charles Dilke: but in it he could have found nothing to his purpose. Marlowe is likely to have been in his mind, with

> – that night-wandering, pale, and watery star,
> When yawning dragons draw her thirling car
> From Latmus' mount up to the gloomy sky,
> Where, crowned with blazing light and majesty,
> She proudly sits.

So will Shakespeare have been certainly, with the call

> Peace, ho! the moon sleeps with Endymion,
> And would not be awaked,

uttered by Portia at the close of the most enchanting moonlight scene in all literature. Scarcely less familiar to Keats will have been the invocation near the end of Spenser's *Epithalamion*, or the reference to 'pale-changeful Cynthia' and her Endymion in Browne's *Britannia's Pastorals*; or those that recur once and again in the sonnets of Drummond of Hawthornden, or those he would have remembered from the masque in the *Maid's Tragedy* of Beaumont and Fletcher, or in translations of the love-elegies and heroical epistles of Ovid. But the two Elizabethans, I think, who were chiefly in his conscious or unconscious recollection when he meditated his theme are Fletcher and Michael Drayton. Here is the fine Endymion passage, delightfully paraphrased from Theocritus, and put into the mouth of the wanton Cloe, by Fletcher in the *Faithful Shepherdess*, that tedious, absurd, exquisitely written pastoral of which the measures caught and charmed Keats's ear in youth as they had caught and charmed the ear of Milton before him.

Shepherd, I pray thee stay, where hast thou been?
Or whither go'st thou? Here be Woods as green
As any, air likewise as fresh and sweet,
As where smooth *Zephyrus* plays on the fleet
Face of the curled Streams, with Flowers as many
As the young Spring gives, and as choise as any;
Here be all new Delights, cool Streams and Wells,
Arbors o'rgrown with Woodbinds, Caves, and Dells,
Chuse where thou wilt, whilst I sit by, and sing,
Or gather Rushes to make many a Ring
For thy long fingers; tell thee tales of Love,
How the pale *Phoebe* hunting in a Grove,
First saw the Boy *Endymion*, from whose Eyes
She took eternal fire that never dyes:
How she convey'd him softly in a sleep,
His temples bound with poppy, to the steep
Head of old Latmus, where she stoops each night,
Gilding the Mountain with her Brothers light,
To kiss her sweetest.

In regard to Drayton's handling of the story there is more to note. In early life he wrote a poem in heroic couplets called *Endimion and Phoebe*. This he never reprinted, but introduced passages from it into a later piece in the same metre called the *Man in the Moone*. The volume containing Drayton's earlier *Endimion and Phoebe* became so rare that when Payne Collier reprinted it in 1856 only two copies were known to exist. It is unlikely that Keats should have seen either of these. But he possessed of his own a copy of Drayton's poems in Smethwick's edition of 1636 (one of the prettiest of seventeenth century books). *The Man in the Moone* is included in that volume, and that Keats was familiar with it is evident. In it, as in the earlier version, but with a difference, the poet, having enthroned his shepherd-prince beside Cynthia in her kingdom of the moon, weaves round him a web of mystical disquisition and allegory, in which popular fancies and superstitions are queerly jumbled up with the then current conceptions of the science of astronomy and the traditions of mediaeval theology as to the number and order of the celestial hierarchies. In Drayton's earlier poem all this is highly serious and written in a rich and decorated vein of poetry intended, it might seem, to rival Marlowe's *Hero and Leander*: in his later, where the tale is told by a shepherd to his mates at the feast of Pan, the narrator lets down his theme with a satiric close in the vein of Lucian, recounting the human delinquencies nightly espied by Cynthia and her lover from their sphere.

The particular points in Keats's *Endymion* where I seem to find suggestions from Drayton's *Man in the Moone* are these. First the idea of introducing the story with the feast of Pan: but as against this it may be said with truth that feasts of Pan are stock incidents in Elizabethan masques and pastorals generally. Second, his sending his hero on journeys beside or in pursuit of his goddess through manifold bewildering regions of the earth and air: for this antiquity affords no warrant, and the hint may have been partly due to the following passage in Drayton (which is also interesting for its exceptionally breathless and trailing treatment of the verse):

> Endymion now forsakes
> All the delights that shepherds do prefer,
> And sets his mind so gen'rally on her
> That, all neglected, to the groves and springs,
> He follows Phoebe, that him safely brings
> (As their great queen) unto the nymphish bowers,
> Where in clear rivers beautified with flowers
> The silver Naiades bathe them in the brack.
> Sometime with her the sea-horse he doth back,
> Amongst the blue Nereides; and when,
> Weary of waters, goddess-like again
> She the high mountains actively assays,
> And there amongst the light Oriades,
> That ride the swift roes, Phoebe doth resort;
> Sometimes amongst those that with them comport,
> The Hamadriades, doth the woods frequent;
> And there she stays not; but incontinent
> Calls down the dragons that her chariot draw,
> And with Endymion pleased that she saw,
> Mounteth thereon, in twinkling of an eye,
> Stripping the winds, beholding from the sky
> The Earth in roundness of a perfect ball, . . .

(The sequel is irrelevant, and the passage so loose in grammar and construction that it matters not where it is broken off.)

Thirdly, we have the curious invention of the magic robe of

Glaucus in Keats's third book. In it, we are told, all the rulers and all the denizens of ocean are figured and indued with magic power to dwindle and dilate before the beholder's eyes. Keats describes this mystic garment in a dozen lines [III 196–209] which can scarcely be other than a summary and generalised recollection of a long passage of eighty in which Drayton describes the mantle of Cynthia herself, inwoven with figures of sea and storm and shipwreck and sea-birds and of men fishing and fowling (crafts supposed to be subject to the planetary influence of the moon) in tidal or inland waters. And lastly, Keats in his second book has taken a manifest hint from Drayton where he makes Venus say archly how she has been guessing in vain which among the Olympian goddesses is Endymion's lover [II 569–72, 908–16].

Not merely by delight in particular poets and familiarity with favourite passages, but by rooted instinct and by his entire self-training, Keats was beyond all his contemporaries – and it is the cardinal fact to be borne in mind about him – the lineal descendant and direct heir of the Elizabethans. The spirit of Elizabethan poetry was born again in him with its excesses and defects as well as its virtues. One general characteristic of this poetry is its prodigality and confusion of incidental, irrelevant and superfluous beauties, its lack, however much it may revel in classical ideas and associations, of the classical instinct for clarity, simplicity and selection. Another (I speak especially of narrative poetry) is its habitual wedding of allegory and romance, its love of turning into parable every theme, other than mere chronicle, which it touches. All the masters with whom Keats was at this time most familiar – Spenser of course first and foremost, William Browne and practically all the Spenserians – were men apt to conceive alike of Grecian myth and mediaeval romance as necessarily holding moral and symbolic under-meanings in solution. Again, it was from Ovid's *Metamorphoses*, as Englished by that excellent Jacobean translator, George Sandys, that Keats, more than from any other source, made himself familiar with the details of classic fable; and Sandys, in the fine Oxford folio edition of his book which we know Keats used, must needs conform to a fixed mediaeval and

Renaissance tradition by 'mythologising' his text, as he calls it, with a commentary full not only of illustrative parallel passages but of interpretations half rationalist, half ethical, which Ovid never dreamt of. Neither must it be forgotten that among Keats's own contemporaries Shelley had in his first important poem, *Alastor*, set the example of embarking on an allegoric theme, and one shadowing forth, as we shall find that *Endymion* shadows forth though on different lines, the adventures and experiences of the poetic soul in man.

The bewildering redundance and intricacy of detail in *Endymion* are obvious, the presence of an underlying strain of allegoric or symbolic meaning harder to detect. Keats's letters referring to his poem contain only the slightest and rarest hints of the presence of such ideas in it, and in the execution they are so little obtruded or even made clear that they were wholly missed by two generations of his earlier readers. It is only of late years that they have yielded themselves, and even now none too definitely, to the scrutiny of students reading and re-reading the poem by the light of incidental utterances in his earlier and later poetry and in his miscellaneous letters. But the ideas are certainly there: they account for and give interest to much that, taken as mere narrative, is confusing or unpalatable: and the best way of finding a clue through the mazes of the poem is by laying and keeping hold upon them wherever we can.

For such a clue to serve the reader, he must have it in his hand from the beginning. Let it be borne in mind, then, that besides the fundamental idea of treating the passion of Endymion for Cynthia as a type of the passion of the poetic soul for essential Beauty, Keats wrote under the influence of two secondary moral ideas or convictions, inchoate probably in his mind when he began but gaining definiteness as he went on. One was that the soul enamoured of and pursuing Beauty cannot achieve its quest in selfishness and isolation, but to succeed must first be taken out of itself and purified by active sympathy with the lives and sufferings of others: the other, that a passion for the manifold separate and dividual beauties of things and beings upon earth is in its nature identical with the passion for that transcendental and essential Beauty: hence the

various human love-adventures which befall the hero in
dreams or in reality, and seem to distract him from his divine
quest, are shown in the end to be in truth no infidelities but
only attractions exercised by his celestial mistress in disguise.

In devising the adventures of his hero in accordance with
these leading ideas, Keats works in part from his own mental
experience. He weaves into his tale, in terms always of
concrete imagery, all the complex fluctuations of joy and
despondency, gleams of confident spiritual illumination
alternating with faltering hours of darkness and self-doubt,
which he had himself been undergoing since the ambition to be
a great poet seized him. He cannot refrain from also weaving
in a thousand and one irrelevant matters which the activity
and ferment of his young imagination suggest, thus
continually confusing the main current of his narrative and
breaking the coherence of its symbolism. He draws out 'the
one bare circumstance', to use his own phrase, of the story into
an endless chain of intricate and flowery narrative, leading us
on phantasmagoric journeyings under the bowels of the earth
and over the floor of ocean and through the fields of air. The
scenery, indeed, is often not merely of a Gothic vastness and
intricacy: there is something of Oriental bewilderment – an
Arabian Night's jugglery with space and time – in the vague
suddenness with which its changes are effected. . . .

SOURCE: excerpted from *John Keats: His Life and Poetry, His
Friends, Critics, and After-Fame* (London, 1917), pp. 166–73.

Newell F. Ford 'Endymion and the Holiness of the Heart's Affections' (1951)

. . . The substance of *Endymion* is love, 'holy' but passionate, and given such 'young minded' Keatsian turns as these: 1. The happiness from love excels all other types of happiness (the 'pleasure thermometer' is but one of several proofs). 2. Love 'bless[es] / The world with benefits unknowingly'. 3. Devoted, ardent, faithful lovers can earn 'an immortality of passion' for themselves, either by being apotheosised (like Endymion) or by being resurrected to eternal bliss (like the legions of dead lovers). 4. The happy dreams of lovers, like the cherished imaginings of poets, are prefiguratively veracious: their 'beauty must be truth' (though occasional moments of scepticism invert this faith).

These conclusions are in harmony with Keats's first trial of the Endymion story, *I stood tip-toe*. The wind-up of that poem describes a miracle almost as wonderful as those in the longer poem:

> Cynthia! I cannot tell the greater blisses,
> That follow'd thine, and thy dear shepherd's kisses.   [239–40]

Almost speechless at the thought of such amorous rapture, Keats could only report that 'no lover did of anguish die', that sorrowing lovers were suddenly healed and rushed immediately, 'nigh foolish with delight', into each other's arms, and that lovers' vows 'made silken ties, that never may be broken' [236, 228, 238]. And why did this miracle happen? Simply because 'a Poet, sure a lover too', 'wept that such beauty [Cynthia's] should be desolate' (i.e., celibate) and 'in fine wrath' chose to memorialise poetically her 'bridal night' [193, 202, 203, 210].

Keats was a better poet, in selected passages at least, when he composed his second *Endymion*. But traces of 'mawkishness', 'great inexperience', and 'immaturity' were to be found there, as he candidly confessed in his Preface. For the poem was the product of a 'space of life between' boyhood and manhood – adolescence, in short – in which 'the soul is in a ferment' (Preface). This ferment was largely responsible for his frequent lapses of taste, and it was inseparable from his adulation of passionate love and the spell that this cast upon him. Cynthia's farewell to chastity, coupled with the immortalisation of her earthly lover, seemed to him the *summum bonum* and filled him with ineffable enthusiasm.

Thus his poem, though part of its drama occurs in heaven, can hardly be called an allegory of Heavenly Love, any more than the *Song of Songs* or *Venus and Adonis* or *The Eve of St Agnes* is such an allegory. Keats's shepherd-lover is not, like the Poet in Shelley's *Alastor*, in search of the Absolute, nor does he seek a mystic salvation in a quest of the infinite, like Novalis and the Germans in their emblem of the Blue Flower. As to the allegories which have been proposed for the poem since 1880, their gratuitousness may be a corollary of the fact that they did not originate until more than half a century after the poet's death, and that neither Keats nor any of his friends or contemporaries left the slightest hint of an allegorical purpose.

Let us freely admit that *Endymion* is, or contains, many elements which a description of its theme and plot leaves out of account. As many readers have felt, the poem is a kind of amiable miscellany, a paradise of dainty devices mingling myth and nature and passion, a garden of rambling honeysuckles and mazy journeys, a storied framework for clustered 'things of beauty', earthly, subterranean, submarine, aerial – 'a little region to wander in', as Keats himself described it. For these qualities it will continue to be read as a generous and zestful illustration of its celebrated opening line, and as a fervent and fruitful outpouring of a youthful imagination kindled by the manifold beauties of the world.

Granted all this – and we readily grant it and rejoice in it – we can hardly deny that in so far as the poem has a primary theme and a plot, this theme and plot are indissociable from the ardors and pleasures of youthful love and from the 'favorite speculation' of [his letter to Bailey].[1] Why should it be needful to 'spiritualise' Keats's interest in the most stirring of human emotions? No one is embarrassed by, or seeks to allegorise, *The Eve of St Agnes*. May it not be that the 'perfection of loveliness' in the language of the later poem – not to speak of its more skillful narrative, its pictorial richness, and the compressed, tense, suspensive drama of it – allow us to accept it without a thought of veiling the passion and the passion's consummation? Will not Hazlitt's defense of Juliet express Keats's state of mind in both *Endymion* and *St Agnes*, the almost religious fervor of his love, in such a way as to make all allegories and 'spiritualisations' needless: 'the feelings of the heart sanctify, without disguising, the impulses of nature'.

'The holiness of the heart's affections' was the very cornerstone of Keats's aesthetic. Out of this holiness grew his faith in 'the truth of imagination', and thus he turned to other poets for confirmation of his 'favourite speculation' (Adam's dream in *Paradise Lost* and the 'immortal freemasonry' of Shakespeare's verse), while he evolved his own argument and illustration in [the letter to Bailey] and in *Endymion*. What is more normal and natural than that his youthful imagination should fall rapturously in love with feminine beauty, and that like the youthful Shakespeare and Milton he should sing his hymn to love?

> And when Love speaks, the voice of all the gods
> Makes Heaven drowsy with the harmony.
> Never durst poet touch a pen to write
> Until his ink were tempered with Love's sighs.
> [*Love's Labour's Lost*, III iii 344–7]

SOURCE: excerpted from *The Prefigurative Imagination of John Keats: A Study of the Beauty-Truth Identification and its Implication* (Stanford, Cal., 1951; reprinted Hamden, Conn., 1966), pp. 84–6 (of reprint).

NOTE

1. [Ed.] See Keats's letter to Benjamin Bailey of 22 November 1817: *Letters*, ed. Gittings (1970), pp. 36–9.

Stuart M. Sperry Jnr   The Allegory of *Endymion*   (1962)

Endymion presents particular challenges to the critic. The poem is by far the longest Keats wrote and has, among his longer pieces, the notable advantage of completeness. He devoted almost a year of his brief career to it and learned much from its composition. It seems to merit the fullest critical attention. Yet the poem is labyrinthine and overgrown, a little wilderness amid whose tangles one can wander happily but at the risk of becoming lost. Keats was himself aware both of the fascinations and the dangers of the longer work. 'I have heard Hunt say and may be asked', he wrote George at about the time he began *Endymion*, 'why endeavour after a long Poem? To which I should answer – Do not the Lovers of Poetry like to have a little Region to wander in where they may pick and choose, and in which the images are so numerous that many are forgotten and found new in a second Reading: which may be food for a week's stroll in the Summer?' [I, p. 170].[1] A long poem could provide the reader with room to move about in, 'full of Symbols for his spiritual eye, of softness for his spiritual touch, of space for his wandering of distinctness for his Luxury', as he later put it [I, p. 232]. Nevertheless certain further guidelines and objectives were, if only by implication, necessary. 'Besides', he went on to George, 'a long Poem is a test of Invention which I take to be the Polar Star of Poetry, as Fancy is the Sails, and Imagination the Rudder' [I, p. 170]. Not long earlier he had pictured himself drifting on the stream of rhyme 'With shatter'd boat, oar snapt, and canvass rent'. It remained to be seen what navigational skill he could bring to the task of piloting the skip of poetry on a substantial voyage of conception'.

Such different needs – the desire for imaginative flexibility and amplitude together with the concern for some emerging pattern of realisation – were ones Keats sought to reconcile within the broader outlines of romance. (When it appeared, his poem was subtitled 'A Poetic Romance'.) They go far toward explaining the considerable disagreement that has, over the years, separated critics who have sought to define more exactly the category of romance to which the poem belongs. One need only return to such older critics of the poem as Sir Sidney Colvin, Robert Bridges and Ernest de Selincourt to recall that for many years it was traditional to read the work as a deliberate allegory, conceived more or less upon Platonic lines, of the poet's longing for and eventual union with the spirit of ideal beauty.[2] While differing with respect to minor points of interpretation, these critics resolved the action of the poem into a series of gradually ascending stages of human development, beginning with the love of sensuous beauty, leading in time to humanitarian service and active sympathy for fellow man, and ending with the recognition that these, rightly perceived, are one with the ideal. The argument of the poem was both sustained and coherent in development, essentially a dramatic working-out, culminating in the union of Cynthia and the Indian Maiden, of the conviction Keats expressed the very month he put an end to his first draft: 'I am certain of nothing but of the holiness of the Heart's affections and the truth of Imagination – What the imagination seizes as Beauty must be truth' [I, p. 184].

More recently the allegorical interpretation of the poem has come increasingly under attack. Critics like Newell Ford and E. C. Pettet have drawn attention to a notable discrepancy between Keats's supposed allegorical intention and the discursiveness and incoherence of his narrative, together with the strongly erotic character of much of the episode and imagery. These inconsistencies were, of course, evident to older critics, who explained them as the result of a gap between conception and execution understandable in a young poet distracted and at times misled by a powerfully sensuous nature. Such reasoning, however, is for Ford and Pettet mere rationalisation evolved by critics unwilling or unable to confront the frank expression of Keats's longing for an 'everlasting erotism',[3] or, more simply, the sexual fantasies of a maturing young man. With the possible exception of a few passages, the poem is for them an instance of romance in the simplest sense – a frank love poem powerfully energised by Keats's adolescent desires. It would be difficult to imagine two interpretations more at odds. Is the work a fable intended to convey certain settled conclusions as to the nature of beauty, truth, and poetic experience? Or is it rather a chain of daydreams and reveries, best interpreted as a psychiatrist interprets the free associations of a patient and useful primarily for what it reveals concerning the quality of Keats's unconscious life?

It would be wrong to imply that critics of the poem have necessarily embraced one view or the other, the traditional and allegorical or the erotic. Nevertheless the two approaches have to date proved most influential and have polarised debate around certain questions of crucial importance. In weighing the merits of such different arguments, one must begin by admitting that Keats never confided, even to friends with whom he was intimate, that he wrote the poem with any allegorical plan in mind. He wrote to George of having to 'make 4000 Lines of one bare circumstance and fill them with Poetry' [I, p. 170], and, divided equally between four books, the mark was one he approximated with extraordinary accuracy. Nor do his habits of composition suggest an allegorical scheme. Bailey, with whom Keats spent the month of September 1817 when he was at work on his third book, reported that Keats 'sat down to his task, – which was about 50 lines a day, – with his paper before him, & wrote with as much regularity, & apparently with as much ease, as he wrote his letters'.[4] If Keats intended his poem to be read as allegory in any strict sense, the key to its meaning was a well-kept secret among his friends throughout his lifetime and after his death.

Yet for all this it remains impossible to read the whole of Keats's narrative, regardless of how aimless and confusing much of it seems, as a mere play of erotic fantasy. Endymion's speech on happiness, the central argument of Book One, outlines an ascending order of imaginative values, beginning with a love of natural objects, leading on to sympathy and friendship, and culminating in human and divine love, a hierarchy of intensities that is both developed and put to trial in the books to come. Later in the poem Endymion's sympathy for Alpheus and Arethusa, Glaucus's pity for the drowned lovers and their joint service in restoring Circe's victims to life, and the ultimate revelation that Cynthia and the Indian Maiden are one are too clearly turning points within the narrative to be dismissed as random bits of episode. Even those critics most opposed to reading the poem as allegory are forced, in one way or another, to grant such episodes a calculated significance.[5] There was, moreover, the example set by Shelley, a fellow protégé of Hunt's whose progress Keats followed and measured himself against throughout his career and whose *Alastor or the Spirit of Solitude* had appeared only a year earlier.[6] The latter work, a poem of quest containing passages as erotic as any in *Endymion*, had taken as its theme both the ennobling heroism and the fatal self-absorption of visionary pursuit as set off by the contradictory dialectics of its preface. The dilemma Shelley depicted was one Keats found himself engrossed by: the plight of the artist who envisions to himself an image that 'unites all of wonderful, or wise, or beautiful, which the poet, the philosopher, or the lover could depicture'[7] but that can be pursued only at the expense of an enervating introspection that isolates and kills. What was particularly impressive was the combination of openness and subtlety with which Shelley developed various aspects of the paradox into a parable of complex thematic significance. More broadly, however, one cannot ignore the whole larger tradition on which Keats drew for the major handling of his narrative: the main line of Elizabethan pastoral-didactic verse that runs from Spenser to Milton and includes such writers as George Sandys, the translator and interpreter of Ovid.[8] It is a tradition of mythological verse in which one discovers, along with a prodigality and confusion of detail, and instinctive drift toward allegory, in Colvin's words an 'habitual wedding of allegory and romance'.[9]

It is, in fact, allegory in its broadest and most general sense that characterises *Endymion*. There is no reason for believing Keats began his poem with a plan for its development or its ultimate significance clearly in view. Quite the opposite is, in all likelihood, the case. Yet, at the same time, there is every reason to believe that he looked upon the composition as a necessary 'test, a trial', as he himself put it, not merely of his 'Powers of Imagination' [I, p. 169] but of his deepest instincts and beliefs. The poem must crystallise, if only for himself, the most important of his poetic convictions. Above all it must confront the whole question of visionary experience that had emerged throughout the early verse, concentrated in his fascination with the legend of Endymion. For the latter is obviously no simple love story. In its involvement with dreams and visions, its contrast between mortality and immortality, and its culmination in transcendence, the Endymion myth is unmistakably connected with the visionary concerns of the earlier poetry. As one who has 'burst our mortal bars' to ascend into 'some wond'rous region', Endymion offered an unmistakable analogue for the poet who gains 'Wings to find out an immortality' of poetic inspiration and fulfilment. The legend provided Keats a means for dramatising his fundamental conviction of 'the truth of imagination'. At the same time it possessed the flexibility to permit him to elaborate and test the reality of that belief as he proceeded.

Yet what form, more exactly, would the elaboration take? Beyond the necessity of treating the 'one bare circumstance' of his fable, Keats was bound only by the otherworldly bias of the legend – its ending in transcendence of mortality – and by the expectation of some joyous, triumphant conclusion like the marriage celebrations he had touched on briefly at the end of *I stood tip-toe*. Otherwise his plan for proceeding was pliable, even disconcertingly vague. Nevertheless his determination to adhere to his own methods of composition carried with it the necessity of trusting to his powers of invention, his ability to improvise the kind of episode that would keep his poem moving forward dramatically. As for its further significance, that would have to come organically, 'as naturally as the Leaves to a tree' [I, p. 238] or not at all. The poem must communicate knowledge and conviction but, in Arnold's phrase, 'insensibly, and in the second place, not the first', and through what would be essentially an act of self-discovery both for poet and reader. Much later, when his mind was 'pick'd up and sorted to a pip', he was to look back on the author of *Endymion* as one 'whose mind was like a pack of scattered cards' [II, p. 323]. Nevertheless the experience of writing the poem, however 'slip-shod' it might later seem to him, was one he could not entirely regret. As he wrote his publisher, James Hessey, in one of the most candid and noble paragraphs of self-criticism any poet has written:

I will write independantly.—I have written independently *without Judgment*—I may write independently & *with judgment* hereafter.—The Genius of Poetry must work out its own salvation in a man: It cannot be matured by law & precept, but by sensation & watchfulness in itself—That which is creative must create itself—In Endymion, I leaped headlong into the Sea, and thereby have become better acquainted with the Soundings, the quicksands, & the rocks, than if I had stayed upon the green shore, and piped a silly pipe, and took tea & comfortable advice.   [I, p. 374; Keats's italics][10]

As he instinctively realised, the poem represented a headlong plunge into the sea, into the reaches of his own unconsciousness and creativity, the region from which, as in his sonnet 'On the Sea', some voice or harmony would have in its own way to come. In working out the destiny of his hero he was in fact working out his own.

It was only natural that, faced with the necessity of making a beginning, he should start his poem with what was most fundamental: his commitment to his notion of the creative process. Following its initial declaration, the opening paragraph of *Endymion* proceeds to an enumeration of particular 'thing[s] of beauty' – the sun, moon, trees, sheep, flowers, rills and forest brakes. However its real concern is with the process by which these forms are converted, partly through the agency of sleep and dreams, into 'essences' that are well-nigh spiritual. The progression proceeds from the images of the natural world to their inclusion in works of imagination ('All lovely tales that we have heard or read') only to engross them all collectively within an image of supernal energy and delight – 'An endless fountain of immortal drink, / Pouring unto us from the heaven's brink.' The process is the now familiar one by which the images of nature are spiritualised in imagination and put into 'etherial existence' for man's enduring enjoyment. It is a process that both exalts and liberates man in imagination and at the same time 'binds' him ever more closely to the earth – the particular tension that Keats was to become steadily more preoccupied with as he proceeded.

The same progression dominates the poem's finest lyric, the 'Hymn to Pan', early in Book One. In the first four stanzas the god is celebrated as the presiding deity of the world of natural process, only to emerge in the final stanza as a symbol for something more:

> Be still the unimaginable lodge
> For solitary thinkings; such as dodge
> Conception to the very bourne of heaven,
> Then leave the naked brain: be still the leaven,
> That spreading in this dull and clodded earth
> Gives it a touch ethereal – a new birth:
> Be still a symbol of immensity;
> A firmament reflected in a sea;
> An element filling the space between;
> An unknown – but no more.   [*E.* I 293–302]

Ultimately Pan is something more than just a god of huntsmen, a god of the harvest. He is the symbol of a form of *thinking*. Yet he represents at most a tendency, a kind of thought that is only latent, as 'a touch ethereal', throughout the universe of natural life. He remains inscrutable, something 'unimaginable', precisely because he is too diverse and inexhaustible in his implications ever to be perfectly defined or brought to full 'conception'. He remains the symbol of a source of speculation that can have no limit, that can never be finally grasped or formulated. He endures as a symbol of the ultimate mystery of life but considered positively, as a source of endless investigation and discovery.

The principal argument of Book One, the lines Keats likened in effect to 'a kind of Pleasure Thermometer', has already been discussed at length within the context of his early notion of the creative process.[11] However, it is important to observe that within the dramatic structure of his poem Keats does not allow his hero's expression of faith in the validity of the imagination and its intensifying power to go unchallenged. Endymion may cling to his intimations of divinity as 'A hope beyond the shadow of a dream' [*E.* I 857], as something more than mere 'atomies / That buzz about our slumbers, like brain-flies, / Leaving us fancy-sick' [*E.* I 851–3]. Nevertheless from our first glimpse of him in the poem he seems pale and wan, alienated from the healthful pursuits of his fellow Latmians by his strange fits of abstraction. Indeed it is not long before Keats himself addresses him as 'Brain-sick shepherd-prince' [*E.* II 43]. More important, Endymion's affirmations of the truth of his visionary experiences are directly opposed by the counterarguments of his sister, Peona, who warns him against deceiving fantasies:

> The Morphean fount
> Of that fine element that visions, dreams,
> And fitful whims of sleep are made of, streams
> Into its airy channels with so subtle,
> So thin a breathing, not the spider's shuttle,
> Circled a million times within the space
> Of a swallow's nest-door, could delay a trace,
> A tinting of its quality: how light
> Must dreams themselves be; seeing they're more slight
> Than the mere nothing that engenders them!
> Then wherefore sully the entrusted gem
> Of high and noble life with thoughts so sick?
> Why pierce high-fronted honour to the quick
> For nothing but a dream?   [*E.* I 747–60]

Her argument is a plea for Endymion to return to the world of action from the life of solitary contemplation that has absorbed him. But more than this, her speech uses several of Keats's favorite metaphors for imaginative creation only to deny their validity. The whole process of associative interweaving and etherealisation is too subtle and attenuating to permit any genuine connection with reality to exist.

Thus from an early point in the poem Endymion's faith in the truth of his visionary pursuit is challenged by the warnings of his sister. Two attitudes toward his quest for happiness have emerged, one affirmative, the other sceptical. No doubt this complication was useful and even necessary to Keats for dramatic reasons, a part of the test his hero would have to undergo; but there is no reason to assume the conflict was entirely unconnected with important questions of his own. Keats was clearly committed to dramatizing his hero's struggles and ultimate reward by union with his goddess and the achievement of immortality: the conclusion was one largely determined by the fable he had chosen. Indeed we are reminded of this basic expectation from time to time along the way. At the beginning of Book Two, Endymion is informed that, like his namesake in *I stood tip-toe*, he

>   must wander far
> In other regions, past the scanty bar
> To mortal steps.   [*E.* II 123–5]

Again at the end of Book Three, after many disappointments, he is mysteriously reassured of his coming reward and of his love's intent to 'snatch' him 'into endless heaven' [*E.* III 1026–7]. Yet the deeper poetic elaboration of this intention is neither steady nor consistent. For one thing, as Endymion's dream-journeys toward his immortal love become more ecstatic, the end of the cycle – the fading of the dream, the return to earth, and the sense of loss and despondency – grows in intensity. The major action of the poem does not follow the pattern of gradual ascent but resembles more the parabolic structure we have seen emerge for the first time in the central vision of 'Sleep and Poetry', a pattern of longing, momentary fulfillment, then loss, despondency and doubt.

In dealing with the love interludes that provide the chief narrative involvement of the earlier books, it is necessary to examine the erotic character of the poem in closer detail. As I have indicated, it is for a number of reasons impossible to agree with critics who read *Endymion* as no more than a simple tale of sexual passion, the gratification of its author's suppressed desires. For time and again critics have failed to see that Keats's use of erotic imagery is integrally related to the visionary concerns of his poem, that it habitually calls into play instincts and feelings that, while connected with the sexual impulse, run deeper. Beginning with *I stood tip-toe*, he had been drawn to the Endymion legend as a search for 'endless bliss', an 'immortality of passion'. Yet in tracing the love-adventures of his hero, he was necessarily led to work out the implications of the quest at a deeper psychological level than any he had yet explored. At the height of his rapturous embrace with Cynthia in Book Two, Endymion exclaims:

> O known Unknown! from whom my being sips
> Such darling essence, wherefore may I not
> Be ever in these arms?   [*E.* II 739–41]

She is a 'second self', his 'breath of life', who promises him that

>   I will tell thee stories of the sky,
> And breathe thee whispers of its minstrelsy.
> My happy love will overwing all bounds!
> O let me melt into thee; let the sounds
> Of our close voices marry at their birth;
> Let us entwine hoveringly – O dearth   .
> Of human words! roughness of mortal speech!
> Lispings empyrean will I sometime teach
> Thine honied tongue – lute-breathings, which I gasp
> To have thee understand, now while I clasp
> Thee thus.   [*E.* II 812–22]

To read such passages as mere sexual description is to fail to see that something more than sensual passion is involved. The images of mouth and lips, of kissing, sipping, speech, possess a more than physical significance. Endymion draws emotional vitality and life from the unknown form he embraces who seems almost a part of his own unconscious being, the source of feelings that cannot be readily expressed in words. The imagery, that is to say, suggests not so much the physical passion of real lovers as the communion of the poet with the vital springs of his imaginative life. The larger context of the love-embrace suggests an ecstasy of imaginative fulfillment conveyed metaphorically through the details of bodily passion.

To interpet the love theme in *Endymion* as a part of Keats's broader visionary concern is not to explain away the erotic elements in the poem (or in Keats's nature) but to restore them to their proper perspective. For one thing, the sexual drive in any individual is never self-contained but overlaps with and is inseparable from a broad range of imaginative preoccupations. In the brief, awkwardly apologetic preface Keats published with the poem he wrote: 'The imagination of a boy is healthy, and the mature imagination of a man is healthy; but there is a space of life between, in which the soul is in a ferment, the character undecided, the way of life uncertain, the ambition thick-sighted.' The passage, in the kind of immaturity and indecisiveness it admits, possesses unmistakable sexual overtones; nevertheless, it is the imagination in its larger sense of which he writes.

In Book One Keats had boldly outlined the scale of various degrees of imaginative involvement leading to the 'chief intensity' of love. Yet it was primarily through the longing of Endymion for Cynthia and his pursuit of the goddess that he possessed the means of dramatising the psychological reality of visionary experience and thus of translating the terms of an abstract progression into action that is vital, fluid, and emotionally meaningful. In one sense Cynthia exists as a symbol, a mere abstraction. Yet she is a value that is variously defined and given significance by a powerful sensuality of imagination, a sensuality that itself develops and changes in implication as the poem proceeds. Even from the first our attention is not drawn to the love interludes for their own sake but for their part in the whole cycle of Endymion's visionary experience – of which the union with Cynthia is the culminating moment, but nevertheless only a part. As in the earlier poetry the process begins with a gradual withdrawal from the natural world; Endymion retreats through mossy caves and bowers until, feeling 'endued / With power to dream deliciously' [*E*. II 707–8], he falls asleep. Following the exclusion of the outer world, the dream begins through which a state of intense imaginative awareness is conveyed that underlies, at some far deeper level, the rational, conceptual functions of the mind:

> Yet it was but a dream: yet such a dream
> That never tongue, although it overteem
> With mellow utterance, like a cavern spring,
> Could figure out and to conception bring
> All I beheld and felt.   [*E*. I 574–8]

The dream is not characterised merely by images of sensual gratification but by synesthesia and effortless movement, by warmth and the sudden flowering of foliage, and by the vital, flowing quality that we associate with certain states of intense imaginative experience. It is a world of fluent harmony, the expression of a primitive experience and knowledge that forever seeks yet defies precise articulation or the power of human intelligence to arrest and define.

Endymion's love for Cynthia is the expression of Keats's romance with his muse. It represents the poet's need to explore, through the metaphor of carnal knowledge, his own relation to the hidden springs of inspiration on which the life of his art depends. Nevertheless it is necessary to see that, virtually from the outset of the poem, Endymion's desire for Cynthia is neither a simple nor an unqualified attraction. The emphasis on the goddess's inviolable chastity is evident, while the note of dire warning and taboo that extends even to the Indian Maiden in the final book [IV 751–8] is both explicit and implicit throughout the earlier love sections of the poem. Beyond the alluring warmth and security of Cynthia's embrace there extends a phantasmagoric world of meteors and falling stars, of chilling airs and awesome dens and caverns; and the 'dizzy sky', the hints of madness, and the threat of a precipitous fall [II 185ff.] reintroduce the theme of the

Daedalian overreacher Keats had touched on in 'Sleep and Poetry'. As the successful lover, Endymion is united with the source of all sweetness and joy; but he is also, like an infant, '*lapp'd* and *lull'd* along the *dangerous* sky' [I 646]. Moreover the pleasures he experiences are too intense to be long enjoyed. At or near their climax a counter-movement toward earth begins, the fabric of the dream collapses, and Endymion is left in mere slumber, in 'stupid sleep' [I 678]. The power of the dream destroys, by force of contrast, all the natural beauty of the Latmian glades and meadows, leaving Endymion with a waking vision that, in its surrealistic horror, Keats never surpassed:

> deepest shades
> Were deepest dungeons; heaths and sunny glades
> Were full of pestilent light; our taintless rills
> Seem'd sooty, and o'er-spread with upturn'd gills
> Of dying fish; the vermeil rose had blown
> In frightful scarlet, and its thorns out-grown
> Like spiked aloe. [*E.* I 692–8]

Despite the apparent logic of the 'Pleasure Thermometer', the destructive and inhibiting aspects of Endymion's passion do not diminish as the poem advances; they increase.

Such shifts and changes in the presentation of Endymion's quest reflect more than Keats's need to complicate and extend the interest of his narrative. They express, rather, genuine ambiguities and qualifications that came to mind only as he proceeded and as he grasped the deeper significance his treatment of the myth had begun to assume. No doubt he had from the first foreseen certain obstacles and difficulties in his hero's way. Endymion's isolation and neglect of his proper role as leader of his people are manifest. Similarly the fundamental message of the Alpheus and Arethusa episode and of that of Glaucus in Book Three seems unmistakable: in his pursuit of visionary beauty Endymion was not to be permitted to forget the need for sympathy and active service on behalf of fellow man. Yet in the implications they present such episodes resist reduction to any easy 'allegoric' reading. One can take as an example the Bower of Adonis in Book Two, which traditional critics of the poem have never been comfortable in discussing. With its accumulated store of cream and ripened fruit, the Bower represents a perfectly self-contained world of sensuous and imaginative luxury, idealised beyond all threat of interruption, where the sleeper dreams of his coming joys with Venus. Indeed the episode may directly prefigure, as proponents of the erotic interpretation have argued, the very apotheosis Keats intended for his hero.[12] Yet the Bower, in its dream-like isolation from the world of process and change, seems strangely etherised and shrouded in the quiet of a deathwatch. Although grown to a man, the sleeping Adonis resembles, as much as anything, the infant in the womb or cradle whose every need is gratified. The episode may portray an ideal of imaginative realisation; but it is at the same time enveloped in an air of sickliness and self-indulgence.

Such questions of nuance, and, more important, of interpretation, multiply throughout the second half of the poem. The story of Glaucus occupies almost the whole of Book Three and is the only sustained narrative interlude in *Endymion*; yet its relation to the thematic center of the poem is far from simple. On the most basic level its relevance to the themes of sympathy and humanitarian service is clear. However, the episode seems to bear upon the nature and the goal of Endymion's quest in a deeper way. More specifically, how is one to interpret Glaucus's misadventure in pursuit of his nymph Scylla? Does his failure merely serve to heighten the triumph and superior powers of his liberator, Endymion? Or does the episode possess a further significance? Does it serve as something of a warning to Keats's hero, a premonition that the search for fulfillment in imaginative experience can end in deception and enslavement rather than in happiness and truth? Does the episode stand in sharp contrast to, or does it subtly qualify, the ambition and significance of Endymion's own pursuit? The more one studies the episode, the more difficult it becomes to narrow its significance to any single implication in the thread of Keats's 'allegory'.

Like Endymion, Glaucus has longed for passionate joys

beyond his reach and taken the plunge 'for life or death' into a
denser element.

> Why was I not contented? Wherefore reach
> At things which, but for thee, O Latmian!
> Had been my dreary death? Fool! I began
> To feel distemper'd longings: to desire
> The utmost privilege that ocean's sire
> Could grant in benediction: to be free
> Of all his kingdom. Long in misery
> I wasted, ere in one extremest fit
> I plung'd for life or death. To interknit
> One's senses with so dense a breathing stuff
> Might seem a work of pain; so not enough
> Can I admire how crystal-smooth it felt,
> And buoyant round my limbs. At first I dwelt
> Whole days and days in sheer astonishment;
> Forgetful utterly of self-intent;
> Moving but with the mighty ebb and flow.
> Then, like a new fledg'd bird that first doth shew
> His spreaded feathers to the morrow chill,
> I tried in fear the pinions of my will.
> 'Twas freedom!   [*E.* III 372–91]

His plunge into the ocean brings to mind the way Keats
himself 'leaped headlong into the Sea' [I 374] in committing
himself to the act of self-discovery his poem represented. The
description also recalls, in its new-found liberation, the same
initial sense of release and exhilaration that animates the
dream voyages of Keats's hero. Like Endymion, Glaucus soon
becomes enamored of an otherworldly creature, the nymph
Scylla, who becomes the object of his desire and whom he
pursues, much as Alpheus pursues Arethusa, until, in a
moment of confusion, he falls prey to the charms of the
enchantress Circe. The division in his affections has no
counterpart in the earlier account of Endymion's quest,
although it prefigures the hero's dilemma when, at the outset
of Book Four, he suddenly finds himself in love with both the
Indian Maiden and his immortal goddess.

It is possible to regard Circe, like Acrasia (Keats's obvious
model), as an embodiment of false sensual attraction and

Glaucus's infatuation for her as a betrayal of his loyalty to Scylla that must not go unpunished. Yet once again such a pat rendering of Keats's allegory does little justice to our sense of the complexity the Glaucus episode introduces into the poem. The rose-canopied bower where Circe promises him the supreme enjoyment of 'a long love dream' [III 440] seems to reflect ironically on both the Bower of Adonis and certain aspects of the love-making between Endymion and Cynthia. Glaucus is enraptured:

> Who could resist? Who in this universe?
> She did so breathe ambrosia; so immerse
> My fine existence in a golden clime.
> She took me like a child of suckling time,
> And cradled me in roses.   [*E.* III 453–7]

We remember that only a little earlier Endymion, clasped in his goddess's embrace, had 'swoon'd / Drunken from pleasure's nipple' [II 868–9]. Glaucus, however, has confused Scylla with Circe, the Bower of Adonis with the Bower of Bliss, and one morning he awakes to find his 'specious heaven' transformed to 'real hell' [III 476]. Amid bursts of cruel, ironic laughter the enchantress, revealed in her true ugliness, proceeds to parody the whole conception of the love-nest and to mock the lassitude and self-indulgence of her victim:

> Ha! ha! Sir Dainty! there must be a nurse
> Made of rose leaves and thistledown, express,
> To cradle thee my sweet, and lull thee: yes,
> I am too flinty-hard for thy nice touch:
> My tenderest squeeze is but a giant's clutch.
> So, fairy-thing, it shall have lullabies
> Unheard of yet: and it shall still its cries
> Upon some breast more lily-feminine.   [*E.* III 570–7]

Glaucus has discovered not Cynthia but La Belle Dame. His infatuation and its end in powerlessness and withered age represents a caricature of the whole notion of the romantic quest which inevitably raises certain questions concerning

Endymion's own pursuit. One senses again that the larger meaning of the poem, the real 'allegory' of *Endymion*, lies in the way such episodes as those of Alpheus and Arethusa, Endymion's love-encounters with his goddess, the Bower of Adonis, and Glaucus's confusion between Scylla and Circe play off against and qualify each other. Together they reflect the gradual emergence of Keats's deeper attitude toward visionary experience rather than the elaboration of any settled plan.

Our suspicion that Endymion's dilemma has fully become Keats's own increases with Book Four. The induction to this book is the shortest and weakest of the four and introduces a note of despondency that virtually every commentator has in one way or another observed. Keats has now thoroughly tired of the poem and is already looking forward to *Hyperion* as a work that will accomplish what he knows *Endymion* cannot. More significant is the appearance of the Indian Maiden, an event that is sudden and altogether unprepared for. At the very time when he should be struggling upward on the final lap of his journey toward the 'chief intensity', Endymion is unexpectedly confronted with the choice between two quite different and opposing ideals of love – the one transcendent, ecstatic and immortal; the other warm, earthly and filled with the passion of the human heart. The dilemma, touched on by Shelley in *Alastor*, is one that from the first had fascinated Keats. Yet the struggle, crystallising ambiguities latent in the earlier part of the narrative, now begins to achieve the proportions of a crisis demanding a new and more profound kind of resolution than any he could have possibly foreseen. As Book Four progresses, the conflict between the two ideals for possession of Endymion's soul becomes steadily more intense and divisive, up until the abrupt conclusion. When, for example, Endymion and the Indian Maiden mount two winged steeds and soar into the region of the skies – the obvious dramatisation of Endymion's urge to reconcile his earthly and his heavenly loves – the moon appears from behind a cloud.

> While to his lady meek the Carian turn'd,
> To mark if her dark eyes had yet discern'd
> This beauty in its birth – Despair! despair!
> He saw her body fading gaunt and spare
> In the cold moonshine. Straight he seiz'd her wrist;
> It melted from his grasp: her hand he kiss'd,
> And, horror! kiss'd his own – he was alone.
> Her steed a little higher soar'd, and then
> Dropt hawkwise to the earth.   [*E.* IV 504–12]

Beautiful as it first appears, the moon assumes an openly destructive role, withering in its chill light the warm beauty by Endymion's side. The baleful part of Cynthia's influence is now fully evident. Attempting to kiss the Indian Maiden, Endymion kisses his own hand, an act of autoeroticism that clearly suggests the solipsistic dangers of the visionary ideal and its ability to dissolve the ties of real human love. From his lofty perch Endymion is plunged into the Cave of Quietude, a kind of Keatsian Center of Indifference. Here he regains his presence of mind but only to reassess, a few lines later, the significance of his quest in a new and startling way:

> I have clung
> To nothing, lov'd a nothing, nothing seen
> Or felt but a great dream! O I have been
> Presumptuous against love, against the sky,
> Against all elements, against the tie
> Of mortals each to each, against the blooms
> Of flowers, rush of rivers, and the tombs
> Of heroes gone!   [*E.* IV 636–43]

The very intensity of Endymion's otherworldly longing has fatally overtaxed the sustaining, elemental power of those bands of natural association and human affection that prompt man's higher intimations even while they bind him more securely to the earth. Gaining conviction, he proceeds to reject the whole reality and worth of his heavenly pursuit:

> Caverns lone, farewell!
> And air of visions, and the monstrous swell
> Of visionary seas! No, never more

Shall airy voices cheat me to the shore
Of tangled wonder, breathless and aghast.   [*E.* IV 651–5]

With such words he has, as it were, come round to agreeing
with his sister's judgement, and the whole value and meaning
of his pilgrimage is brought into question.

For critics of the older school such speeches are only the final
darkness before the onrushing dawn, Endymion's last moment
of doubt before the revelation that the conflicting attractions
that confront him are in fact but different aspects of a single
ideal. Such a reading, whatever its validity as an ex post facto
judgement, betrays the deeper meaning of the poem
considered as a process of creative self-discovery. For it ignores
the tone of real conviction and dramatic urgency that
characterises the struggle in Book Four and, by contrast, the
brief and remarkably spiritless conclusion. The final resolution
arrives in the last hundred lines with the bewildering speed of
anticlimax. Cynthia's light, once so hostile and destructive,
irradiates the features of the Indian Maiden with the force of a
maternal blessing. There is no time for rejoicing or acclaim or
the marriage festivities Keats had contemplated celebrating in
I stood tip-toe. The two lovers simply bless Peona, then flee
away into the night. Endymion's dilemma is thus disposed of,
but it is never really resolved. The point of the identification
Keats brings about in the closing lines is intellectually
unmistakable; but as Douglas Bush has written, it 'is only a bit
of "Platonic" algebra, not an equation felt on the pulses'.[13]

Reasons can be cited, virtually without end, to explain the
manifestly disappointing and unsatisfactory state of the
conclusion – Keats's boredom and fatigue with the ordeal the
completion of the poem had become, his eagerness to pass on to
other projects, his lack of concern for or want of experience in
creating an effective ending. Such explanations must,
however, be subordinated to the poem's underlying honesty,
an honesty that marks so much of Keats's writing and that
springs from genuine commitment to the act of composition
itself. The point can best be made by turning to a curious
passage not far from the end of Book Four. Momentarily
abandoning the turbulence and uncertainty of the action,

Keats intervenes as narrator to address some words of apology
to his hero which are, however, intended chiefly for the reader:

> Endymion! unhappy! it nigh grieves
> Me to behold thee thus in last extreme:
> Ensky'd ere this, but truly that I deem
> Truth the best music in a first-born song.   [*E.* IV 770–3]

Obviously it is Keats himself who is most of all unhappy,
embarrassed by the tangled involvements of his narrative and
aware that his poem should by now have achieved its
resolution. Yet the difficulty he faces is surely not that of
literally carrying out the conclusion required by his fable.
Endymion would have been 'Ensky'd ere this' were it not,
Keats tells us, that a kind of truth forbids, and the reason
deserves to be taken with full seriousness.

   The 'truth' seems to be not only that Keats had become
genuinely involved in the allegory of his poem but that, as
Glen O. Allen has argued, the emphasis of the allegory had
changed significantly in the course of composition and that the
'enskying' of his hero had lost much of its climactic
importance.[14] Endymion is not apotheosised in Cynthia's
visionary heaven. There is no ascension to the skies. The two
lovers merely slip quietly away together through the woods.
The conclusion his poem demanded, Keats realised, was not
his hero's elevation to the 'chief intensity' but rather some
balance between light and shade, desire and restraint,
mortality and immortality that he could only intimate in the
union of Cynthia and the Indian Maiden. Yet the need for
such a larger reconciliation was one he had only gradually
become aware of and did not lend itself to the old climactic
design and structure of his legend. Nor was it one that, for
deeper reasons, he could dramatise in any genuinely satisfying
or 'truthful' way. This is not to argue that toward the end of
his poem Keats suddenly lost faith in visionary experience. It is
to say, rather, that the obstacles to Endymion's success, as
Keats elaborated them, had so qualified the nature of his goal
as to become themselves part of a new and more complex
solution than any he had, however dimly, foreseen.

Such a hypothesis can be verified by examining within the course of the poem itself certain shifts of emphasis that reveal a remarkable change and maturing in Keats's aesthetic assumptions. The theoretical keystone of the structure of the work is the central passage in Book One, Endymion's speech on happiness which Keats likened to a 'Pleasure Thermometer'. Yet is is impossible to ignore the growing emphasis on disappointment and unhappiness as an integral part of human experience both as the poem proceeds and as a theme reflected increasingly in Keats's letters of the autumn of 1817, when he was at work on his last book.[15] As early as Book Two the lovers' ecstasy is broken by Cynthia's cry, 'Endymion: woe! woe! is grief contain'd / In the very deeps of pleasure, my sole life?' [II 823–4]. In the roundelay of the Indian Maiden in Book Four the perception of sorrow is for the first time admitted as an unavoidable and creative element in the experience of beauty. In his letter to Bailey of 22 November 1817, written when he was halfway through his final book, Keats cited *both* Book One and 'O Sorrow' as demonstrations of his 'favorite Speculation' as to the truth of the imagination. Yet he must himself have been aware of important differences between them, and if we return to look more carefully at the famous passage in his letter, we can see his concern to bring the two parts of his poem more fully into accord. 'I am certain of nothing', he wrote 'but of the holiness of the Heart's affections and the truth of Imagination—What the imagination seizes as Beauty must be truth–whether it existed before or not–for I have the *same* Idea of *all* our Passions *as of Love* they are *all* in their sublime, creative of essential Beauty' [I, p. 184; my italics]. Keats, in other words, had already begun to move toward that deeper conception of beauty springing from intense awareness of the whole of human life in all its mingled joy and sorrow that was to become a major theme of *Hyperion*. This is not to say that the '*Ode to Sorrow*' is much more than a weak and sentimental approximation to that ideal, but, in so far as it attempts to reconcile sorrow within a deeper apprehension of beauty, the shift it marks in the direction of Keats's allegory is clear. One might say, perhaps, that by the end of the poem the pleasure principle expounded in the first book had at least been qualified by a recognition of the need for a broader and deeper participation in the whole of human experience. In the same way the earlier idea of Endymion's quest as a search for 'oneness' or ecstatic self-annihilation in sympathetic feeling has in the end become partly modified (through the working out of Keats's fable) by an awareness much closer to a simultaneous apprehension of joy and sorrow, mortality and immortality, desire and human limitation.

Endymion, then, is a work whose scope and meaning to a large extent evolved during the months Keats worked on it and which is, therefore, not fully coherent as an allegory for the reason that it embodies new truths and insights Keats discovered only in the course of composition which could not be perfectly expressed within its old design. This is not to say, of course, that the poem is any less meaningful; it is to argue, rather, that its real significance lies as much in the questions it raises as in those it solves. Foremost among these was the whole problem for Keats of the adequacy of his habits and method of composition. In *Endymion* he had begun with a set of vague affirmations and a number of equally vague doubts and misgivings concerning the nature of visionary experience. His method for progressing had been to trust his own powers of improvisation, to let the poem find its own way, create its own involvements, and derive its own solutions. A clear, premeditated plan, even had he been able to conceive of one, was alien to the spirit and larger purpose of his undertaking. It was enough to 'send / My herald thought into a wilderness', as he wrote at the outset of Book One, 'and quickly dress / My uncertain path with green, that I may speed / Easily onward' [I 58–62]. His progress with the work had taken him from the long, increasingly complicated dream-involvements of the earlier books to the apparent digression of the Glaucus episode and to his innovation of the Indian Maiden as a necessary rival and counterpart of Cynthia is Book Four. But in the end he had finished with a work lacking real definition or coherence, having had to extricate himself through the patent device of a *dea ex machina* conclusion. Somewhat like his hero, he had become trapped in the convolutions of the poem without the ability to transcend it.

The irony was hardly lost on him. 'J.S. is perfectly right in regard to the slip-shod Endymion', he wrote Hessey. 'That it is so is no fault of mine.—No!–though it may sound a little paradoxical. It is as good as I had power to make it–*by myself*' [I, p. 374]. He would continue to write in the way he knew he must – 'independently'. He would continue faithful to the principles of 'sensation & watchfulness', to his belief that 'that which is creative must create itself'. He must, however, learn to write '*with judgment*', with greater deliberation and purpose. The realisation lies behind his first, somewhat puzzling, reference to *Hyperion* in a letter in which he declares a major contrast he intends between the two works. In *Hyperion*, he wrote Haydon several months before *Endymion* was published, 'the march of passion and endeavour will be undeviating–and one great contrast between them will be–that the Hero of the written tale being mortal *is led on*, like Buonaparte, *by circumstance*; whereas the Apollo in Hyperion *being a fore-seeing God will shape his actions like one*' [I, p. 207]. The comment reflects more light on his own poetic intentions than it does on the character of either hero. The question was, could he maintain his allegiance to Pan, his symbol for that generative mystery from which all that was truly valuable in poetry sprang, and at the same time cultivate the prescience and control of Apollo? He would continue to write in the only way he could, from within himself; but he must acquire the clearness and finality of utterance he knew he must achieve for greatness.

SOURCE: first published as an article in *Studies in Romanticism*, 2 (1962), pp. 38–53; reproduced as ch. 4 in *Keats the Poet* (Princeton, N.J. 1973), pp. 90–116 (the version used for this selection).

NOTES

[Revised and renumbered from the original – Ed.]

1. [Ed.] Letter-references are to *The Letters of John Keats, 1814–1821*, ed. Hyder E. Rollins, 2 vols (Cambridge, Mass. and Cambridge 1958).

2. See Sir Sidney Colvin, *John Keats* (London and New York, 1917), pp. 171–205; Ernest de Selincourt, *The Poems of John Keats*, 5th edn (London, 1926), pp. *xl–xli*, 428; and Robert Bridges, 'A Critical Introduction to Keats', reproduced in his *Collected Essays, Papers &c.* (London, 1929), IV, pp. 85–93. [Part of Colvin's discussion referred to here is excerpted in this selection – Ed.]

3. The phrase is used by Ford – in '*Endymion*: A Neo-Platonic Allegory?', *ELH*, XIV (1947), p. 69 – to describe the central theme of the poem. [Cf. also its use in Ford's later work, excerpted above – Ed.]

4. *The Keats Circle: Letters and Papers &c.*, ed. Hyder E. Rollins, 2 vols (Cambridge, Mass. and Oxford, 1948; 2nd edn 1965), II, p. 270.

5. Ford's account of the last two books as a development of the theme of infidelity in love – *The Prefigurative Imagination of John Keats* (Stanford, Cal., 1951), pp. 67, 74 & passim – is itself the makings of an allegorical interpretation, could it be fully worked out.

6. Leonard Brown argued persuasively that the poem evolved in Keats's mind partly in reaction to certain aspects of *Alastor*. In particular he suggested Shelley's Arab Maiden as a source for the Indian Maiden in Book Four of Endymion: see Brown's 'The Genesis, Growth and Meaning of *Endymion*', *Studies in Philology*, XXX (1933), pp. 618–53.

7. 'Preface' to *Alastor or the Spirit of Solitude*, in *The Complete Poetical Works of Percy Bysshe Shelley*, ed. Thomas Hutchinson (London and New York, 1904; repr. 1934), p. 14. Later citations of Shelley are to this edition.

8. See Joan Grundy, 'Keats and the Elizabethans', in *John Keats: A Reassessment*, ed. Kenneth Muir (Liverpool, 1958), pp. 1–19.

9. Colvin, op. cit., p. 171. [See the excerpt in this selection – Ed.]

10. [Ed.] See the fuller excerpt from this letter in Part One, above.

11. [Ed.] See Sperry's *Keats the Poet* (Princeton, N.J., 1973), pp. 48–9.

12. So Ford argues, op. cit., pp. 52–4 – as does E. C. Pettet, *On the Poetry of Keats* (Cambridge, 1957), p. 171.

13. Douglas Bush, *John Keats: Selected Poems and Letters* (Boston, Mass., 1959), p. 315.

14. Glen O. Allen, 'The Fall of Endymion: A Study in Keats's Intellectual Growth', *Keats-Shelley Journal*, IV (1957), pp. 37–57.

15. See Keats's remark to Bailey in late October: 'Health and Spirits can only be unalloyed to the Selfish Man–the Man who thinks much of his fellows can never be in Spirits' [I, p. 175]; his comment, again to Bailey, in early November on 'Griefs and Cares' [I, p. 182]; and, on 22 November, his remarks to Reynolds on 'Heart-vexations' [I, p. 188] and to Bailey on 'Worldy Happiness': 'I scarcely remember counting upon any Happiness–I look not for it if it not be in the present hour' [I, p. 186]. Keats's letters up to and including his early work on *Endymion* do not demonstrate a comparable maturity.

Louise Z. Smith   The Material Sublime: Keats and *Isabella*   (1974)

Isabella; or The Pot of Basil is the wallflower among Keats's narratives. While critics flatter its sisters, *The Eve of St Agnes* and *Lamia*, they recoil from the grotesque and sentimental in *Isabella* or, unable to account for these qualities, ignore this extended, complete poem in the short Keats canon. The most charitable commentator, Finney, sees Keats's reversion to sentimentality offset by growth in 'imaginative realism, . . . elegant diction and flexible but vigorous metre'. Rejecting Finney's view that Keats develops from naturalism to Platonism to humanism, Blackstone suggests instead a 'tidal movement' of good poems followed by poor ones; *Isabella* is the backwash from *Endymion*, 'a distillation of its weakness'. Similarly, Bush wonders how the convention of narrative romance could have led 'into sentimental pathos the maturing poet who had lately dismissed romance to welcome, in *King Lear*, "the fierce dispute / Betwixt damnation and impassioned clay" . . .'. For Bate, *Isabella* was Keats's way of 'marking time' between *Endymion* and *Hyperion*; Stillinger relegates it to oblivion as Keats's 'last poetic failure', and Evert dismisses the poem in less than a sentence: 'with all its felicities acknowledged, it is yet not a poem of which Keats or the majority of his readers have thought very highly'.[1] Assuredly, *Isabella* is a poem about which few readers have thought, but Keats thought about it more than critics suppose. His letters and his *Epistle to Reynolds* suggest that the problem of *Isabella* is not to be lightly dismissed, for the poem is a 'fierce dispute / Betwixt damnation and impassioned clay' ('On Sitting Down to Read *King Lear* Once Again' [5–6]),[2] rendered less fierce than *King Lear* by the double vision of Keats's narrative method. The *Epistle* defines the terms of the dispute, and *Isabella* develops it in narrative form.

The double vision of sympathy and detachment, of transcending imagination and jostling world, colors the short poems written between *Endymion* and *Isabella*. The balance of imaginative sensibility with detached objectivity is most obvious in the lighter poems. 'The mouldering arch / . . . Stands next door to Wilson the Hosier' ('On Oxford' [3–5]); the mundane world restrains Radcliffean sensibility to architecture. Keats rejects the 'palpable design' of Wordsworth's and Hunt's poetry in favor of the 'great and unobtrusive' poetry of 'the old Poets, and Robin Hood' (to Reynolds, 3 February 1818); he copies out in this letter 'Robin Hood' and 'Lines on the Mermaid Tavern', both juxtaposing old romance with modern commerce. If Robin and Marian could come back to life:

> He would swear, for all his oaks,
> Fall'n beneath the dockyard strokes,
> Have rotted on the briny seas;
> She would weep that her wild bees
> Sang not to her – strange! that honey
> Can't be got without hard money.   [43–8]

The past invigorates the present, but Keats has no more desire to flee the present than to exchange the comforts of Elysium for those of the Mermaid Tavern. One 'may love in spite of beaver hats' ('Modern Love' [17]), if he does not make love ridiculous by sentimentally mimicking the grand passions of the romantic past. In 'Welcome joy and welcome sorrow', incongruities enrich life; grotesque juxtapositions in imagination ('Infant playing with a skull' [12]), and picturesque contrasts in the jostling world ('Morning fair, and shipwrecked hull' [13]), combine in Keats's sensibility, affording him 'the sweetness of the pain' [23] without robbing him of the detachment to 'write / Of the day and of the night / Both together' [26–8]. Far from repudiating romance,[3] these poems show the complementary relation of romantic sensibility and realistic detachment.

The more serious poems clarify this relationship. Bush and Stillinger agree that 'On Sitting Down to Read *King Lear* Once Again' equates romance with a 'barren dream', dismissed by Keats as ineffectual and out of date. Romance, the 'Queen of

faraway', seems inappropriate 'on this wintry day', and Keats
bids her 'shut up thine olden pages, and be mute' [2–4]; 'once
again' he must read *King Lear*. Romance, in fact, is not
dismissed; it is only temporarily 'mute', as *King Lear* had been
to Keats before he decided to reopen its pages. There is no
reason to equate romance with the 'barren dream' Keats hopes
to avoid, once he has burned through 'the fierce dispute /
Betwixt damnation and impassioned clay' [5–6]; regardless of
genre, any literary work is a 'barren dream' if, instead of
giving refreshment, it leaves the reader weakened and
wandering. In burning through the 'fierce dispute' by means
of his compassion for King Lear, Keats hopes that the fire of
tragic catharsis will consume his own sorrows so that Phoenix-
like he will rise refreshed to 'fly at my desire' [14]. The nature
of his desire is undefined; although at the moment tragedy
appears more rewarding to him, it is quite possible that his
desire may prompt him to reopen the mute pages of romance.
In 'When I Have Fears', his first use of the Shakespearean
sonnet form, Keats expresses his desire to 'trace' [7] the
shadows of 'high romance' [6] and to 'have relish in the faery
power of unreflecting love' [11–12]. Although 'the most skyey
Knight-errantry is [incompetent] to heal' human suffering (to
Bailey, 23 January 1818), the realm of 'Flora and old Pan'
('Sleep and Poetry' [102]) must balance with 'the old oak
forest' ('On . . . *King Lear*' [11]) in the poetic sanctuary that
does heal and refresh by affording 'heart easing things' ('Sleep
and Poetry' [268]). Romance from which all 'disagreeables'
have been filtered cannot afford 'heart-easing things,' for one
recognises in such romance no relation to the 'disagreeables'
that oppress the heart (to George and Thomas Keats, 28
December 1817). Good romance, therefore, must contain
elements of human suffering in order to relate to the reader's
own afflictions; romance provides solace not by offering a
perfect world, but by revealing hope and beauty in an
imperfect world. Good romance, at least at this stage in
Keats's increasing artistic proficiency, must juxtapose
romantic sensibility and detached objectivity.
    Keats examines such juxtaposition in the *Epistle to John
Hamilton Reynolds*. The dreams with which Keats proposes to

entertain his ailing friend are surrealistic and paradoxical: 'Two Witch's eyes above a Cherub's mouth' [6], Voltaire in Knight's garb and Alexander in a nightcap [7-8], 'Mermaid's toes' [16], the Enchanted Castle, a magical conglomeration of pagan and Christian elements. 'Few are there who escape these visitings' [13], who perceive no paradoxical disagreeables and live simply in a harmonious world of 'flowers bursting out with lusty pride' [17] and of sacrifice serenely repeated. These fortunate few have no need of 'heart-easing things', and simple filtered romance would suffice for them. Keats does not share this harmonious vision. In the painting he finds the landscape 'alive to love and hate, / To smiles and frowns' [38-9]; 'some giant, pulsing underground' [40] seems to animate the scene. Keats's response to the painting resembles the herdsman's fear of the 'echo of sweet music' [62]; Keats's friends might be as sceptical of his dreams and his art criticism as the herdsman's friends are of his tale of the echo near the enchanted spring [61-6]. Even in the pastoral landscape sounds a note of mystery.

Keats's experience in the world of dreams brings him to consider philosophically the role of imagination as mediator between dream and reality [67-85]. The phrase 'material sublime' encapsulates the juxtaposition of romance and realism, or sensibility and detachment, expressed in the earlier poems. Which word is noun, which adjective? Stillinger paraphrases lines 67-71 thus: 'O that our dreamings would all their colours take from something sublime (= elevated, "uplifted from the world", ∴ unearthly, like the fantastic dreams of ll. 1-66) rather than from our own soul's daytime (the mind's or self's everyday experience).' Solving the problem by ignoring 'material' altogether, he misreads the passage and hence the poem. The sublime is not 'uplifted from the world' and 'unearthly'; it is firmly grounded in material phenomena, e.g. the sunset. Stillinger's reading makes no sense in terms of the earlier lines; why would Keats wish to return to the 'fantastic dreams' when he has already wished to be among the 'few are there who escape these visitings' [13]?

Stillinger's conclusion, that 'sublime dreamings are preferable to the mental repetition of daytime world jostling', is correct, but he defines 'sublime dreamings' incorrectly. Definition must cope with the 'material sublime'. 'Sublime' means either grandeur, magnitude and power, or the elevated emotions of awe, fear and rapture occasioned by perception of these phenomena. If the words mean 'material which is sublime', Keats probably refers to the mountains and sunset, landscape that is grand and elevating, as opposed both to the ordinary scene of the Mermaid Tavern and to the eerie scene of the Enchanted Castle. On the other hand, if 'material' is an adjective, it serves to emphasise that Keats's 'sublime' refers to material grandeur and power, not to sublime emotions of awe, fear and rapture; Keats's 'dreamings' [67] should arise from material, not from 'shapes, and shadows, and remembrances' [3] inhabiting his mind.

Keats is not so clumsy as to write 'material' merely as an unmeaning filler or to create unintentional syntactic ambiguity. 'Material sublime' should be read both as noun-adjective and as adjective-noun; the meanings are complementary, not mutually exclusive.[4] Our dreamings should arise from the sublime in the world rather than from the mundane or weird, and they should arise from external matter, not from subjective feeling. Dreaming is not an escape from the jostling world, but an intense perception of beauty and truth in that world. Imagination is not, *pace* Stillinger, an inadequate means to escape the jostling world; Evert more accurately sees it as an inadequate means of attaining truth.[5] Truth is balance of joy and suffering in the world, not escape to fantasy. The inadequacy of imagination is not its inability to lift us from the 'old oak forest' into the 'realms of Flora and old Pan'; imagination gives us a bittersweet glimpse 'beyond our bourne' [83], that is beyond the jostling world, into the 'material sublime' of sunsets and nightingales' songs, but unguided by 'any standard law / Of either earth or heaven' [81–2] it cannot assert the 'material sublime' strongly enough to balance the disagreeables of the jostling world. Imagination requires the aid of philosophy, but Keats is not yet expert enough in philosophical reasoning, 'my flag is not unfurl'd / On the Admiral staff' [72–3], and reasoning therefore cannot marshal his imagination.

Keats's imagination fails to reveal truth not only because it 'conceptualises',[6] but because without philosophical support it is too weak to produce poetry of high enough intensity to make 'disagreeables evaporate from their being in close relationship with Beauty and Truth' (to George and Thomas Keats, 28 December 1817). Instead of diffusing the destructive elements of Nature, 'The Shark at savage prey, – the Hawk at pounce' [103], so that they balance homogenously with the 'young spring leaves, and flowers gay' [100], Keats's imagination only glimpses the benign aspects of Nature and is immediately overwhelmed by the stronger force of destruction. The 'gentle Robin' is immediately replaced by the Robin 'ravening a worm' [104–5]. Imagination is 'Lost in a sort of Purgatory blind' [80], because it cannot see the harmonious balance of creation and destruction, joy and suffering, that constitutes the real world. Imagination cannot reach Keats's heaven, 'what we called happiness on Earth repeated in a finer tone' (to Bailey, 22 November 1817), because he now perceives earthly harmony too faintly to allow its repetition in a 'finer tone'. Keats's philosophy may in time grow strong enough to support such a harmonious perception of reality, but meanwhile he can only try to put off the 'horrid moods' [105] occasioned by the inability of imagination to assert the balanced truth of the real world.

Keats's resolve to take refuge 'from detested moods in new Romance' [111] cannot be interpreted as an effort to escape reality but rather to banish depression in a renewed examination of the problem of imagination. 'New romance' rejects escapist 'skyey Knight-errantry' and classical myth in favor of a story rooted firmly in the more real world of Shakespeare, Chaucer and Boccaccio; although poetry should come 'as naturally as Leaves to a tree', Keats cannot help 'looking into new countries with "O for a Muse of fire to ascend!"' (to Taylor, 27 February 1818). In seeking a new mode of writing, Keats tries to heed 'What the Thrush Said'. He writes to Reynolds on 19 February 1818: 'let us open our leaves like a flower and be passive and receptive – budding patiently under the eye of Apollo and taking hints from every noble insect that favours us with a visit.' The octave of the sonnet copied in this letter contains paradoxes: 'the spring will be a harvest time' [4], 'the light / Of supreme darkness' [5–6]; instead of struggling against paradox as Keats does a month later in the *Epistle*, the thrush counsels wise passiveness and acceptance of intuitive truth, 'and he's awake who thinks himself asleep' [14].

In the *Epistle*, Keats ignores the thrush's advice and in seeking after knowledge defines the limits of imagination. In *Isabella*, Keats presents a double view of imagination as wisely passive and vainly struggling. This double vision accounts for Keats's ambivalence toward the poem; he criticises its simplicity and stylistic inexperience, yet he values the poem. The public may ridicule *Isabella*, because 'very few would look to the reality'; it satisfies Keats and his intimates, but 'will not do to be public' (to Woodhouse, 25 April 1819). Perhaps Keats's disclaimer here, like his description of the *Epistle* as 'unconnected subject, and careless verse' (to Reynolds, 25 March 1818), is an attempt to ward off serious attention from a poem that concerns him deeply. The 'amusing sober-sadness' Keats finds in *Isabella* grows out of the balance of a realistic detachment and romantic sensibility in short poems following *Endymion*, the tragic balance achieved in the 'fierce dispute / Betwixt damnation and impassioned clay' resulting in catharsis and regeneration in the *Lear* sonnet, and the more philosophic struggle to balance the jostling world with the 'material sublime' in the *Epistle*.

Not perceiving Keats's balanced double vision, two critics call *Isabella* a failure. Blackstone traces the vegetative metaphors as negative movements from spring to winter, fruition to barrenness, health to decay, and 'frustration of biological destiny' in the frustration of Isabella's potential motherhood; he attributes this pessimism to Keats's despondency after the completion of *Endymion*. Blackstone sees the basil-pot as 'the locus of reversed metamorphosis' in which Lorenzo arises as a vegetable. Because he minimises the images of regeneration pervading the poem, his interpretation stresses the same sort of 'fierce destruction' which overwhelms Keats's imagination in the *Epistle*.[7]

Similarly, Stillinger sees the simple romance of the first half of *Isabella* gradually overwhelmed by increasing realism. Courtly love gives way to a psychological study of Isabella's deepening madness, lovesickness turns to real sickness, and simple romance is eroded by realistic 'wormy circumstance'.[8] As with the *Epistle*, Stillinger's interpretation has a certain amount of truth: there is indeed an element of anti-romance in *Isabella*. However, instead of a linear development from romance to realism, *Isabella* offers constant balance of sentiment and detachment; balance accounts for what Keats calls the 'amusing sober-sadness' of the poem.

Keats achieves this balance by means of two techniques: digression and juxtaposition. His digressions are the most striking modification of Boccaccio's story. F. E. L. Priestley argues that Hazlitt's lecture on Dryden and Pope suggested to Keats and Reynolds the translation of tales from Boccaccio and Chaucer; reading the manuscript of Hazlitt's lecture on Chaucer (having been too late to attend the lecture in person) prompted Keats to choose Chaucer as a model of stylistic strength and narrative intensity. Priestley's chronology, however, is wrong. He compares passages in *Endymion* and *Troilus and Criseyde* to illustrate Chaucerian invocations and digressions in Keats's work;[9] begun in late April and finished in November 1817, *Endymion* could hardly have been influenced by Hazlitt's lecture given in January 1818.[10] Hazlitt cannot therefore be wholly credited as beekeeper to Keats's passive flower awaiting the visitations of noble insects, and it is naive to suppose that Keats needed an authority for narrative digressions.

Keats's digressions from Boccaccio's tale balance romantic sympathy for the lovers with realistic detachment. Boccaccio begins his tale with information about Isabella's family, but Keats postpones these mundane details until stanza XIV and begins directly with the idyll of courtly love. In the first eleven stanzas, Isabella and Lorenzo apparently are among the fortunate 'few . . . who escape' [*Epistle*, 13] recognition of life's contradictions. Keats interrupts their idyll by reminding the reader not to waste his tears on lovers' sorrows [XII–XIII], for they have, after all, known happiness; Ariadne and Dido enjoyed love before separation from their lovers, and the same holds for Isabella: 'The little sweet doth kill much bitterness' [98]. Keats continues his digression from the romantic world of courtly love by indicting the brothers' capitalistic exploitation in the jostling world [XIV–XVIII]; their 'hungry pride and gainful cowardice' [130] are as fierce as 'The Shark at prey' [*Epistle*, 103], and their greed is immoral as well. Boccaccio's brothers are angered by Isabella and Lorenzo's 'Amorous League of Love', but Keats adds a mercenary motive; the brothers take a proprietary interest in wedding Isabella 'To some high noble and his olive-trees' [168]. Boccaccio's brothers show personal cruelty in threatening Isabella when she asks Lorenzo's whereabouts: 'If hereafter you make any more Demands for him we shall shape you such a Reply, as will be but little to your liking.'[11] In Keats the brothers are more devious with Isabella; instead of betraying their guilt through excessive harshness, they allow her to imagine many fates for Lorenzo. Their cruelty is larger in scope, affecting their mercantile relations all over the globe. However, indignation is interrupted by Keats's invocation to Boccaccio [XIX–XX], which draws away from involvement in the jostling world. These three digressions increasingly detach the reader from sympathetic involvement in the fate of Isabella and Lorenzo. In the first part of the poem, Keats balances romantic sympathy with realistic detachment.

Once these digressions achieve sufficient detachment, Keats plunges back into the tale, but in the second part [XXI–L], concerning the murder and visionary appearance of Lorenzo, there are no digressions until the end. Between stanza XLVIII in which Isabella 'felt the kernel of the grave' [383] and stanza L in which she decapitates Lorenzo's corpse, Keats enquires 'Ah! wherefore all this wormy circumstance?' [385] and yearns 'for the gentleness of old Romance, / The simple plaining of a minstrel's song!' [387–8]. Here Keats's critics unanimously throw up their hands, commenting only that the 'minstrel's song' excludes Boccaccio's romances from Keats's yearning. But Keats is speaking ironically in order to reiterate his assertions in earlier poems that good poetry offers no escape to a fantasy world where all the disagreeables have been filtered out. Prose or verse, the old romances Keats may have had in mind – *The Book of the Duchess, The Knight's Tale, Troilus,* and of course Boccaccio's tale – are anything but gentle. 'O turn thee to the very tale' [391] – if you can find one – 'And taste the music of that vision pale' [392]; synaesthesia here recommends an impossible task, just as impossible as finding a good poem that contains the 'realm of Flora and old Pan' without elements of the 'old oak forest'. In stanza XLIX Keats simultaneously draws back from the horror of Isabella's grisly task and makes the theoretical point that horror in some form must enter any good poem to balance with beauty so as to give an accurate account of the real world.

The two invocations of Melancholy [LV, LXI] in the third part [LI–LXIII] comment objectively on Isabella's situation. If one is inclined to weep with Isabella, Keats reminds him that her weeping provides solace in devotion; 'Spirits in grief, lift up your heads, and smile' [437]. But Melancholy is dismissed when the brothers destroy the basil pot, for Isabella is beyond comfort; 'Spirits of grief, sing not your "Well-a-way!" / For Isabel, sweet Isabel, will die' [485–6]. The reader sees Isabella's situation with both sympathy and detachment; he cannot yield to escapist sentimentality when objective digressions constantly restore him to the actual world.

Juxtaposition of horror and beauty is another device for achieving balance; considering such juxtapositions corrects Blackstone's onesided impression of pessimism and Stillinger's kindred over-emphasis on Isabella's 'anti-romantic' madness. Boccaccio briefly describes Lorenzo's murder, 'when they came to a solitary place, such as suited best their vile purpose: they ran suddenly upon *Lorenzo,* slew him, and afterward enterr'd his Body, where it hardly could be discover'd by any one'.[12] Boccaccio's brothers seize a fortunate opportunity for the murder, but Keats's brothers plan the crime carefully and lure their prey into the trap, cutting 'Mercy with a sharp knife to the bone' [174].[13] When they all ride away from Florence, after an ironically casual farewell to Isabella, Lorenzo is as good as dead, 'So the two brothers and their murder'd man / Rode past fair Florence . . .' [209–10]. The brothers' faces are 'sick and wan' [213] in anticipation of their deed, but Lorenzo's is 'flush with love' [215]. Such vitality is bound to resist attack, but Keats leaves the sacrifice to the imagination.

In Keats's other modifications of Boccaccio, this process is reversed. In Boccaccio, Lorenzo appears in Isabella's dream 'in torn and unbefitting Garments, his looks pale, meagre, and starving', and Isabella does not see his 'mangled body'. Keats describes at length the marring of Lorenzo's body [XXXV-XXXVII], but he perceives beauty in corruption; Lorenzo's 'eyes, though wild, were still all dewy bright / With love, and kept all phantom fear aloof / From the poor girl by magic of their light' [289–91]. The horror is not overwhelming, because beauty is juxtaposed; sentiment balances with detachment, and Lorenzo's farewell reinforces his own detachment from Isabella's world, 'thou art distant in Humanity' [312].

Keats likewise balances beauty and horror in the disinterment scene [XLVI-L]. Boccaccio says simply 'they digged not far, but they found the body of the murthered *Lorenzo*, as yet very little corrupted or impaired'. As in the vision, Keats does not deny the corruption of the grave, which to the nurse is a 'horrid thing' [381], but Isabella's love and beauty transform the horror: 'Clearly she saw as other eyes would know / Pale limbs at bottom of a crystal well; / Upon the murderous spot she seem'd to grow / Like to a native lily of the dell' [363–6]. The purity of the crystal well offsets the nurse's horror of the corrupt grave. Isabella's lily-like purity and grace, reinforced by her repeated gesture of throwing back her 'veiling hair' [376], offset her eager digging 'more fervently than misers' [368] like her greedy brothers. Following Ridley's suggestion,[14] Stillinger finds in Keats's substitution of 'duller steel than the Persean sword' [393] for Boccaccio's 'keen Razor' a suggestion of 'prolonged sawing or hacking' in order to decapitate the corpse; this argument of course supports the thesis of 'anti-romance', but the lines suggest a less imaginative interpretation. Perseus' sword was the sharpest in the world, so that steel could be 'duller' and still be very sharp; Keats could have said 'hacked' without damaging metre, and 'sawed' would have made for better alliteration, but in fact he does say simply 'cut'. Furthermore, Keats's final version of line 394 substitutes 'no formless monster's head' for the earlier 'no foul Medusa's head';[15] this change complements the 'duller steel' by emphasising that these are real people, not mythical fantasies. Keats must find truth in reality, not in escape. Stillinger sees a contradiction between the stated moral, 'Love never dies, but lives, immortal Lord' [397], and Lorenzo's love ceasing at death, 'There in that forest did his great love cease' [218], and 'If Love impersonate was ever dead' [398], which in an earlier version appears 'If ever any piece of love was dead.' Stillinger concludes that this earlier version 'makes it clear that no love was ever more dead than the love [Lorenzo's severed head] Isabella kissed.'[16] Just as he ignores 'material' in the *Epistle*, here he ignores 'impersonate' and 'piece', thereby seeing a contradiction in Keats where none in fact exists. Keats does not confuse the idea of love with its particular manifestations. Although an individual's love dies, Love itself 'lives immortal Lord', just as Isabella's love survives the death of its material object and as their love is celebrated 'through all the country' [502] long after her death. The horror of the disinterment scene Keats balances with Isabella's purifying love.

Throughout the poem, Keats offsets images of decay with images of regeneration. Before Isabella's grief begins, Keats warns that 'Even bees . . . know there is richest juice in poison-flowers' [103–4]. Her brothers, 'these men of cruel clay' [173], are impassioned by greed, but Isabella is impassioned by love to seek 'the clay, so dearly prized, / And sing to it one latest lullaby' [339–40]. Lorenzo's ghost and corpse are smeared with loam [279, 405]; 'fresh-thrown mould' [361] covers his grave, and Isabella fills the basil pot with mould [415]. 'Clay' often describes the body or material as opposed to spirit, but here the contrast of infertile clay with rich loam and mould balances barrenness with growth. Isabella's anxiety about Lorenzo's unexplained long absence 'bereaves' her beauty 'of some gold tinge' [251–2] until she seems to her brothers to be clad in a 'snowy shroud' [264], but her Seraph-like paleness fills Lorenzo with greater love [316–20]. At Lorenzo's grave the 'feverous hectic flame' [348] of love warms her, and she seems to grow 'like to a native lily of the dell' [366]. Lorenzo suggests that 'one tear upon my heather-bloom / . . . shall comfort me within the tomb' [303–4]: her spirit will greet his as any mourner's reaches 'through the clayey soil' [355], 'Pitying each form that hungry Death hath marr'd, / And filling it once more with human soul' [357–8].

This regenerative grief prevents Isabella from being destroyed; her tears of rapturous devotion are a balm for madness. To her, the head is the 'kernel of the grave, / And Isabella did not stamp and rave' [383–4]; instead the kernel grows to become 'all for Isabel' [402], both as her own private 'prize' and as her entire world, her all. Her cleansing of the head [LI] resembles artistic devotion, especially compared with the erotic necrophilia in Boccaccio: 'she washed the Head over and over with her tears, and bestowed infinite kisses thereon'.[17] Keats moderates this necrophilia, enabling Isabella to weep 'in peace' [422]; although grief hastens her death, 'She withers like a palm / Cut by an Indian for its juicy balm' [447–8]. The balm of her tears nourishes the basil plant so that it becomes 'thick, and green, and beautiful' [426], transformed into a 'jewel' [431]. Her regenerative devotion metamorphoses the mortal plant into an eternal gem in her eyes: 'it flourish'd, as by magic touch' [459]. Here again, however, Keats interrupts with the brothers' view the involvement of romantic sensibility. Their suspicions are aroused when attention to the plant weans Isabella from the jostling world of everyday concerns, 'pleasure gay, / And even remembrance of her love's delay' [463–4]. When they uproot the plant, horror untempered by love assails them, 'The thing was vile with green and livid spot' [475]; horror is the fitting 'guerdon of their murder' [477]. Ignorant of their destruction of the plant, Isabella continues to love although doubly deprived of her beloved, and her death is doubly hastened. She 'will die a death too lone and incomplete, / Now they have taken away her Basil sweet' [487–8]; the 'Now' implies that with the plant her death would have been to some purpose and in its own time, instead of hastened first by murder and then by destruction. Finally, Isabella and her plant are immortalised in legend [LXIII]. Images of regeneration through devotion balance images of death, although ultimately the latter overcome the former, just as in the *Epistle* 'fierce destruction' overwhelms glimpses of the 'material sublime'.

'The fierce dispute / Betwixt damnation and impassioned clay' is argued philosophically in the *Epistle* and exemplified in *Isabella*. Keats in the *Epistle* holds the 'material sublime' as an ideal, but in practice settles for the thrush's wise passiveness. In *Isabella* the heart-easing love of Isabella and Lorenzo contends with the jostling world. Ultimately, impassioned sensibility must yield to the damnation of the real world's fierce destruction, and the detachment Keats maintains by means of digression and juxtaposition affords the wisely passive acceptance of the tragically near-equal balance of love with destruction. The triumphs of Madeline and Porphyro's love and of Lamia's destruction offer more satisfying endings than Isabella's, yet recognising the truth of this balance, one can no longer ignore its beauty. *Isabella* may never be Keats's Cinderella, but surely it is at least his Sleeping Beauty.

SOURCE: article in *Studies in Romanticism*, 13 (1974), pp. 299–311.

NOTES

[Revised and renumbered from the original – Ed.]

1. Claude L. Finney, *The Evolution of Keats's Poetry* (Cambridge, Mass., 1936), I, p. 379; Bernard Blackstone, *The Consecrated Urn: An Interpretation of Keats in Terms of Growth and Form* (London, 1959), pp. 266–7; Douglas Bush, *John Keats* (New York, 1966), p. 77; Walter J. Bate, *John Keats* (Cambridge, Mass., 1963), p. 314; Jack Stillinger, 'Keats and Romance', in *Studies in English Literature*, 8 (1968), p. 593; Walter H. Evert, *Aesthetic and Myth in the Poetry of Keats* (Princeton, N.J., 1965), p. 225.

2. John Keats, *Complete Poems and Selected Letters*, ed. Clarence DeWitt Thorpe (New York, 1935), p. 203. All quotations from Keats's poetry and letters are from this edition.

3. Stillinger, op. cit. (note 1), p. 595.

4. The *Ode on a Grecian Urn* offers a comparable example of syntactic ambiguity in 'Thou still unravish'd bride of quietness'. 'Still' may be both adjective (modifying 'bride') and adverb (modifying 'unravish'd').

5. Evert, op. cit. (note 1), pp. 208–9.

6. Ibid., pp. 210–11.

7. Blackstone, op. cit. (note 1), pp. 269–70, 273.

8. Stillinger, op. cit., pp. 599–604.

9. The influence on *Isabella* of Chaucer through Hazlitt has been demonstrated. *The Book of the Duchess, The Nun's Priest's Tale* and *The Prioress's Tale* all exemplify the murder-will-out story, and in the former two the murder is revealed in a dream vision. *The Knight's Tale* shows the wasting of body and mind beneath the burden of great sorrow; and Keats's diction is demonstrably indebted to that tale. See F. E. L. Priestley, 'Keats and Chaucer', *MLQ* 5 (1944), pp. 439–41.

10. William Hazlitt, *Lectures on the English Poets*: in *The Spirit of the Age*, ed. Catherine MacD. MacLean (New York, 1964), p. *v*.

11. Maurice R. Ridley, *Keats's Craftsmanship: A Study in Poetic Development* (London, 1933; repr. 1963), pp. 23, 38.

12. Ibid., p. 32.

13. Priestley, op. cit. (note 9), p. 441, suggests this echoes Chaucer's 'My throot is kut unto the nekke bone' (*The Prioress's Tale*, B 1839; vii 649).

14. Ridley, op. cit., pp. 39, 43, 48.

15. Ibid., p. 48.

16. Stillinger, op. cit., p. 601.

17. Ridley, op. cit., p. 44.

Earl R. Wasserman 'A Series of Concentric Circles: *The Eve of St Agnes*' (1953)

. . . It is most convenient to examine first the central episode of the romance, the union of Madeline and Porphyro, and then to analyse the larger surrounding units until the entire poem is encompassed. The justification for proceeding in this manner is the fact that the structure of the poem is a series of concentric circles that expand and deepen each other's meaning.

The most striking feature about the climax is the peculiar confusion of wake and sleep that characterises Madeline's perception of Porphyro when she is being roused from her vision:

Her eyes were open, but she still beheld,
Now wide awake, the vision of her sleep. [298–9]

We have already seen that in Keats's mind dreams are synonymous with imagination, for both are powers whereby man may penetrate into heaven's bourne, where the intensities of mortal life are repeated in a finer tone and divested of their mutability. Keats had linked sleep and poetry in the title of one of his early poems and there asked 'what is higher beyond thought' than sleep. What, this is, brings us closer to heaven's bourne? Sleep comes

> . . . sometimes like a gentle whispering
> Of all the secrets of some wondr'ous thing
> That breathes about us in the vacant air;
> So that we look around with prying stare,
> Perhaps to see shapes of light, aerial lymning,
> And catch soft floatings from a faint-heard hymning;
> To see the laurel wreath, on high suspended,
> That is to crown our name when life is ended.
> Sometimes it gives a glory to the voice,
> And from the heart up-springs 'Rejoice! Rejoice!'
> Sounds which will reach the Framer of all things,
> And die away in ardent mutterings.   [*S. & P.* 29–40]

Moreover, Madeline's dream does not take place in the ordinary course of mortal events but is occasioned by the mystical power of St Agnes' Eve, when, by observing special rites, 'Young virgins might have visions of delight' [47]. It is a 'hallow'd hour' [66], an extraordinary condition that, being outside the normal framework of experience, permits the imagination to rise to supernatural heights and correspondingly to penetrate most deeply into the beauty-truth that is to come. If dreams are imaginative visions of a future reality, St Agnes' dreams are 'the sweetest of the year' [63].

The relation of dream-visions to the imagination, and the manner in which they both function, were most clearly stated by Keats in a famous letter to Bailey [of 22 November 1817]. 'I am certain of nothing', he wrote,

but of the holiness of the Heart's affections and the truth of Imagination—
What the imagination seizes as Beauty must be truth—whether it existed

before or not. . . . The Imagination may be compared to Adam's dream—he awoke and found it truth.

The reference is to that passage in *Paradise Lost* in which Adam tells of the creation of Eve. Overcome as with 'an object that excels the sense', 'Dazzl'd and spent' by the power of God's 'Colloquy sublime', Adam fell into a sleep:

> Mine eyes he clos'd, but op'n left the Cell
> Of Fancy my internal sight, by which
> Abstract as in a trance methought I saw,
> Though sleeping. . . .

In this divine trance Adam saw the creation of Eve,

>   so lovely fair,
> That what seem'd fair in all the World, seem'd now
> Mean, or in her summ'd up.

Awakening, he found his dream to be true, for before him was the corporeal beauty,

> Such as I saw her in my dream, adorn'd
> With what all Earth or Heaven could bestow
> To make her amiable.   [*P. Lost* VIII   452–89]

God had fulfilled his pledge to Adam to realise 'Thy wish, exactly to thy heart's desire'. Now, by making of Adam's dream in Eden a parable of the imagination Keats certainly did not mean that we shall know in our mortal careers that our imaginings are true; here we can know only a beauty that must die, but in awakening into the reality to come we shall discover that the extraordinary imaginative insights we experience here will hereafter be experienced under the conditions of immortality. Our earthly visions of an Eve, who is our heart's desire, the essence of all the beauty that earth or heaven can bestow or our imaginations fashion, will hereafter be enjoyed

as immutable realities. But Keats felt a conviction that this
heaven of immortal passion can be entered only through an
intensity of experience in this life, only by a mystic entrance
into the essence of that beauty which here fades; for we shall
each be allotted an immortality of that degree of passion that
our earthly careers have attained. Therefore,

O for a Life of Sensations rather than of Thoughts! It is 'a Vision in the form
of Youth' a Shadow of reality to come—and this consideration has further
convinced me for it has come as auxiliary to another favorite Speculation of
mine, that we shall enjoy ourselves here after by having what we called
happiness on Earth repeated in a finer tone and so repeated. And yet such a
fate can only befall those who delight in Sensation rather than hunger as you
do after Truth. Adam's dream will do here and seems to be a conviction that
Imagination and its empyreal reflection is the same as human Life and its
Spiritual repetition.

Briefly, a life of sensations provides us with experiences of
beauty that we shall later enjoy under those immortal
conditions that Keats called 'truth'; it foreshadows in the
transitory the 'reality' to come. Therefore, if we could, by a
supernal power, rise to perceive the empyreal reflection of
what our merely human imaginations create for us, we would
be perceiving the spiritual repetition of our human intensities,
and hence our future immortal existence.

    Such a supernal power is granted by the transcendent
occasion of St Agnes' Eve, and thus Madeline's dream-vision,
like Adam's, has carried her beyond the 'bar / That keeps us
from our homes ethereal'. So far has she been transported by
the empyreal reflection of her imagination, and therefore so
deep is she in the spiritual repetition of her earthly happiness,
that her bond with the mortal world is drawn thin and nearly
severed: hers was

            a midnight charm
    Impossible to melt as iced stream;   [282–3]

and it seemed that Porphyro

never, never could redeem
From such a stedfast spell his lady's eyes.   [286-7]

When, therefore, Madeline is awakened from her divine
vision, her capacity to perceive both human life and the
spiritual repetition of it that her transcendent dream has
divulged allows her to experience simultaneously both the mortal
and the immortal. Ideally, this sensory-visionary state should
correspond to the nature of heaven's bourne, where the human
and the ethereal, beauty and truth, are one. The mortal
Porphyro presented to her senses and the ideal Porphyro of her
vision should fuse mystically into an immortality of passionate
experience, as warmly human as the one and yet as immutable
as the other. The consummation of Madeline's equivocal
perceptions should be the experience of a love that is forever
panting and forever young.

But the poem is tending for the moment to follow the
downward course of the *Ode on a Grecian Urn* and *La Belle Dame
sans Merci*: in the mortal world beauty does not exist as truth,
and although human life is like its spiritual repetition in kind,
it is widely different in degree. Therefore the intrusion of
mortality is threatening to dispel the vision, exactly as the
recollection of the ravages of human passions dispelled the
beauty-truth of the urn's frieze, and exactly as the whisperings
of death-bound mortality called the knight out of the elfin grot.
The difference between the mortal Porphyro and the visionary
Porphyro – human life and its spiritual repetition – is too great
to allow the two to coalesce into a human-ethereal identity; and
consequently the sight of mortality was to Madeline 'a painful
change, that nigh expell'd / The blisses of her dream so pure
and deep' [300-1]. In her vision of immortality Porphyro's
eyes were 'spiritual and clear', but now she finds them 'sad',
sadness being inextricable from human existence. 'How
chang'd thou art! how pallid, chill, and drear!' she adds [311],
for Porphyro, like the knight-at-arms and his fellow mortals, is
death-pale with the pallor, chill and dreariness inherent in the
nature of mortality. And this perishing that man calls 'living'
has become especially vivid to her because she has seen it in the

light of the spiritual repetition of human happiness. Therefore Madeline pleads,

> Give me that voice again, my Porphyro,
> Those looks immortal, those complainings dear!
> Oh leave me not in this eternal woe,
> For if thou diest, my Love, I know not where to go.

The words 'immortal' and 'eternal' are diametrical opposites here and correspond to the difference we have encountered in the *Ode on a Grecian Urn* between the dimensionless essence of time and a plenitude of dimensional time. Immortality belongs to heaven's bourne and describes Porphyro's spiritual appearance; immortality has to do with a realm where existence is not merely endless, but where death and time are irrelevancies. Eternity, on the other hand, is an earthly measurement, and the two words underscore Madeline's precarious balance between these two conditions – the atemporality that belongs to her vision of Porphyro and the temporality in which the earthly Porphyro exists.

It is, however, entirely in the language of her ideal vision, and of her sensory perception, that she expresses a fear lest Porphyro die, for her extraordinary dream has revealed the immortal, or deathless Porphyro; although her awakened eyes are now looking at what man calls the 'living' Porphyro, from the perspective of her dream-vision, which coexists with her sensory perception, he is taking on the pallid, chill and drear form of mortality, i.e., deathliness. His dying, therefore, is a withdrawl from immortality, which is an everness of living, into a worldly existence, the active principle which is to die. Madeline's fear is that hers will be the fate of the knight-at-arms: the elfin grot will turn out to be merely the cold hill side; mortality will summon her back from her insight into the beauty-truth to come and leave her only a world in which man forever repeats his one mortal drama, a progress from town to sacrificial altar.

Madeline's dream, then, is Adam's – but her awakening is, for the moment, far different. By spiritual grace she has experienced in a finer tone what she has called happiness on earth. And yet, she has not awakened from her dream to find it truth, for in the mutable world into which she is awakening, beauty is not truth, passions are not immortal, eyes are not spiritual and clear. Only in heaven's bourne do men of sensations awaken to find that their empyreal imaginings are true. Hence Madeline is being called back to an existence that is necessarily sorrowful and to a world where every knight-at-arms is 'woe-begone'. The impending dissolution of her vision through the summons to mutability and decay causes her to

> weep,
> And moan forth witless words with many a sigh;
> While still her gaze on Porphyro would keep.   [302–4]

So, too, foreshadowing the imminent return of the knight to the mutable world because of the inability of mortals to remove the mutable from their visions, la belle dame 'wept and sigh'd full sore' when she and the knight arrived at the elfin grot.

In one sense, then, Madeline's double vision is an analogue of a heaven's bourne that for the moment refuses to come about because her ideal dream and her sensory perception refuse to coalesce. But in another sense Madeline is herself the ideal and coldly chaste steadfastness of the bright star which, when animated with an exquisite intensity of warm human passion, becomes the oxymoronic nature of life's spiritual repetition. For the magic of St Agnes' Eve has transformed her into a Cynthia, the completed form of all completeness. In her chastity, her visionary power, and the spiritual purity that St. Agnes' Eve has bestowed upon her, she is the immutability of the life to come, but not its human intensity. She is 'St Agnes' charmed maid' [192], 'a mission'd spirit' [193], 'all akin / To spirits of the air' [201–2], 'so pure a thing, so free from mortal taint' [225]; she seems a saint, 'a splendid angel, newly drest, / Save wings, for heaven' [222–4]. Caught up in her dream-vision, she is sheltered alike from joy and pain [240], those complementary passions that attend upon all man's experiences while he is on earth. In withdrawing into her own self in sleep she becomes the perfection of form, 'As though a rose should shut, and be a bud again' [243]; she is not the full-blown rose giving up its fragrance, just as living is an expenditure of life, but a self-contained and unexpended power with need of nothing beyond itself, an emblem of Becoming eternally captured, and therefore perfect and immutable. Consequently, the merely human Porphyro worships her as his 'heaven', while he sees himself as her 'eremite' [227]. She is, in short, the condition of immortality at heaven's bourne, its freedom from time, space and selfhood.

But at heaven's bourne love is not simply forever *to be* enjoyed; it is not immutable simply because it is never experienced. It is at the same time forever *being* enjoyed. And it is the human Porphyro, not graced by the supernal power of St Agnes' Eve, who is the human passion that Madeline will raise to an immortality. He must so 'delight in Sensation' that a 'Spiritual repetition' of his earthly happiness will be available to him.

In the two poems we have already examined, Keats allowed the intrusion of the mutable world to dispel his vision of heaven. But in *The Eve of St Agnes* he is concerned with pressing forward into the consequences of coalescing mortal experience and the condition of immortality, not with tracing the homeward journey of mortality to its habitual self, as he did in *La Belle Dame sans Merci* and the *Ode on a Grecian Urn*. Therefore the perception of the mortal Porphyro only '*nigh* expell'd / The blisses' of Madeline's dream. Having threatened to recall Madeline to mortality, Keats now reverses his strategy. Granted that in this world beauty is not truth, let us assume, he proposes, that mortality could rise to such heights that the difference between the two Porphyros would be blotted out because the intensity of his mortal passions would then correspond to the intensity of his spiritual repetition. Madeline would no longer be torn between truth and beauty, for the two would coincide; and the ideal Madeline and the human Porphyro could unite to experience the conditions of heaven. Granted this ideal situation, for which Keats himself yearned; granted what is beyond mortal capacity – into what transcendent wisdom could man then penetrate?

In the poem, therefore, a miracle is to be performed; and instead of being thrust back into humanity after the 'many hours of toil and quest' [338] which make up man's effort to become one with his ideal and to achieve an identity of truth and beauty, Porphyro will succeed in order that the mystery into which man would thereby penetrate may be revealed. For this purpose he is 'A famish'd pilgrim, – saved by miracle' [339]. Since only an intensity of passion can lead to a future repetition in a finer tone of what we call happiness on earth, and since such a repetition is permitted only to one who delights in sensations, Porphyro must first arise 'Beyond a mortal man impassion'd far' [316]. The ambiguous syntax (Keats first wrote, 'Impassioned far beyond a mortal man') implies that Porphyro's passion remains human in its nature and yet is raised to superhuman intensity. Only in this manner can the gap between mortal and immortal be bridged, for Porphyro thereby is raising human passion to the 'finer tone' in which it will be experienced hereafter. In this act Porphyro has become 'ethereal' [318]. The word, we have seen, is a favorite with Keats and usually describes the transfiguration of real things into values by means of ardor. By the straining of his passion Porphyro has become an 'ethereal thing', a value that is the ultimate significance of his mortal self and its experiences. Now, and only now, beauty may be united with truth, the mortal with the ethereal, to become the eternity of passion that exists only in heaven's bourne:

> Ethereal, flush'd, and like a throbbing star
> Seen mid the sapphire heaven's deep repose
> Into her dream he melted, as the rose
> Blendeth its odour with the violet, –
> Solution sweet.   [318–22]

The steadfastness of the bright star and the soft fall and swell of 'love's ripening breast' have coalesced; or rather, to use the images of the stanza, the throbbing of the star has been absorbed into the repose of the sky. The mortal Porphyro has risen to such a degree of passionate ardor that it may now blend with the chaste immutability that Madeline has become

by virtue of the grace of St Agnes' Eve. By the blending of
their powers Madeline and Porphyro are now experiencing the
spiritual repetition of human life and can therefore move into
its mystery, which is the pith of human life and with which
human life strives to nourish itself. For lack of this spiritual
nourishment the mortal Porphyro had been a 'famish'd
pilgrim' [339], just as for the same reason the death-pale
mortals of *La Belle Dame sans Merci* have starved lips.
Madeline's dream has turned out to be Adam's after all; by a
miracle she has awakened to find it truth.

While this immortality of passion is dramatically evolving in
the foreground through the overt actions which melt the
human ardor of Porphyro into the ideal constancy, the 'deep
repose', of Madeline's vision, a parallel development is also
taking place in the background which not only infuses into the
central drama a powerful tonal quality but also re-enacts
symbolically the union of Porphyro and Madeline so as to
expand the otherwise personal action to cosmic size and
significance. Waiting to be led to Madeline, Porphyro remains
in 'a little moonlight room, / Pale, lattic'd, chill, and silent as a
tomb' [112–13]. There Angela tells him of Madeline's
intention to observe the rites of St Agnes' Eve, and as a result

> Sudden a thought came like a full-blown rose,
> Flushing his brow, and in his pained heart
> Made purple riot.   [136–8]

These two symbols – cold and silvery pale moonlight, and the
warmly sensuous ruddiness of purple and rose – correspond to
the two conditions that are one in heaven's bourne. In the first
room Porphyro is in the presence of the moonlight, but it is
only lifeless and chill unless it is animated by the color of passion,
the roseate sensuousness that at length is born in Porphyro.
Silver and moonlight therefore hover about Madeline, the
Cynthia of the poem, the eternal form with which human
passion must blend. She carries 'a silver taper' [194] which
dies in the 'pallid moonshine' of her own chamber [200]; she
wears a silver cross [221]; and before Keats finally described

her as a 'splendid angel' [223] he tried 'immortal angel' and 'silvery angel'. She is Porphyro's 'silver shrine' [337], he her beauty's shield, 'heart-shap'd and vermeil dyed' [336].

The silveriness and moonlight belong to the realm of pure being, the rich blushes of color to the realm of passionate becoming. Consequently, when Madeline enters her chamber the two colors begin to run together, interpenetrating to prefigure the act which will coalesce human and spiritual into a love that is 'still to be enjoy'd'. The chaste moonlight shines through the stained-glass windows, whose gorgeous colors are 'Innumerable of stains and splendid dyes, / As are the tiger-moth's deep-damask'd wings' [212–13] so that the two colors partake of each other as though cosmic forces had shaped at an all-pervasive level the heaven's bourne that Madeline and Porphyro are to find at the human level. In this silver-red, or chaste-sensuous atmospheric fusion, the subsequent action of the spirit-sense union is bathed. The cold, virginal light of the 'wintry moon' throws a warm roseate stain on Madeline's white breast; it makes rose-bloom fall on her hands, which are clasped in holy prayer; it covers the silvery spirituality of her cross with the luxurious purple of amethyst [217–21].

The fusion continues to permeate the setting as Porphyro prepares for the union. In the 'dim, silver twilight' he places a cloth of 'woven crimson, gold, and jet' [253–6]; he fills with fruit golden dishes and baskets of 'wreathed silver' [271–3]; and lustrous salvers gleaming in the moonlight and golden-fringed carpets appear as adjacent images [284–5]. As the bloody dyes have become the sensuous vitality of the virginal moonlight, Porphyro now rises to ethereal passions to melt into Madeline's spiritual vision. The scents of the rose and the chaste violet dissolve into each other [320–2]. The union having been consummated and the conditions of heaven's bourne having been attained, the supernatural grace is no longer needed or pertinent. Porphyro and Madeline have fashioned their own heaven: 'St Agnes' moon hath set' [324].

. . .

Until now we have been examining mainly the actions of Porphyro and Madeline that take place in Madeline's chamber, and they constitute an ascent of the ladder of intensities and a formation of the mystic oxymoron which is the spiritual repetition of the 'happiness' of human life. Let us consider now Porphyro's other actions. Before he enters the chamber he has ridden across the moor to the castle; has stood outside the castle, where he was hidden by the buttress; has entered the castle and been led by Angela to a little room 'silent as a tomb', where he has learned of Madeline's plan and fashioned his own; and finally has been led to a closet of Madeline's chamber. This pattern of events, abstracted from the poem, appears to form some sort of progression as Porphyro moves from the outer darkness and cold to the warmth of the castle and then ascends in stages from the 'level chambers' [32] to the 'paradise' [244] of Madeline's room.

Doors, chambers and mansions seem to have possessed especially important symbolic values in Keats's mind. The mind has a 'cage-door'[1] or a casement 'To let the warm Love in';[2] it is made up of 'cerebral apartments' or is an 'enchanted palace'.[3] The imagination is a monastery, the poet its monk.[4] Pan is the 'Dread opener of the mysterious doors / Leading to universal knowledge'.[5] The doors of heaven 'appear'd to open' for Endymion's visionary flight to Cynthia;[6] and Apollo's chariot waits 'at the doors of heaven'.[7] The 'enchanted Portals' of heaven open wide for the poet.[8] The nightingale makes casements magic, and in the 'Enchanted Castle' the doors 'all look as if they oped themselves'.[9] These and other passages are suggestive enough to prompt the question of whether the apartments, doors and portals of *The Eve of St Agnes* embody a value beyond their narrative function.

Less than a year before he wrote his romance, Keats had been speculating on the significance of Wordsworth's poetry and attempting to determine the height that Wordsworth had attained in the range of values. By using as his scale the pattern of life that Wordsworth had outlined in *Tintern Abbey*, Keats was also hoping to see more vividly the stage of human values that he himself had grown to make central in his art. In May 1818, approximately eight months before he began to compose *The Eve of St Agnes*, he wrote to John Hamilton Reynolds that he had been turning over in his mind whether Wordsworth 'has an extended vision or a circumscribed grandeur'.

And to be more explicit and to show you how tall I stand by the giant, I will put down a simile of human life as far as I now perceive it; that is, to the point to which I say we both have arrived at—Well—I compare human life to a large Mansion of Many Apartments, two of which I can only describe, the doors of the rest being as yet shut upon me. The first we step into we call the infant or thoughtless Chamber, in which we remain as long as we do not think—We remain there a long while, and notwithstanding the doors of the second Chamber remain wide open, showing a bright appearance, we care not to hasten to it; but are at length imperceptibly impelled by the awakening of this thinking principle within us—we no sooner get into the second Chamber, which I shall call the Chamber of Maiden-Thought, than we become intoxicated with the light and the atmosphere, we see nothing but pleasant wonders, and think of delaying there for ever in delight: However among the effects this breathing is father of is that tremendous one of sharpening one's vision into the heart and nature of Man—of convincing one's nerves that the world is full of Misery and Heartbreak, Pain, Sickness and oppression—whereby this Chamber of Maiden Thought becomes gradually darken'd and at the same time on all sides of it many doors are set open—but all dark—all leading to dark passages—We see not the ballance of good and evil. We are in a Mist. *We* are now in that state—We feel the 'burden of the Mystery', To this Point was Wordsworth come, as far as I can conceive when he wrote 'Tintern Abbey' and it seems to me that his Genius is explorative of those dark Passages. Now if we live, and go on thinking, we too shall explore them.[10]

The stages outlined here correspond roughly to the three implicit in *Tintern Abbey*: a period of thoughtless animal pleasure without even awareness of the pleasure, one of consciousness of emotional power, and at last a perception of the 'still, sad music of humanity' which brings a sense of 'something far more deeply interfused' and consequently lightens 'the burden of the mystery'. The relation Keats's letter has to Wordsworth's pattern of life and of the growth of the poetic mind reveals how deeply indebted Keats was to the older poet for his own most profound inquiry into the meaning of human existence.

In the career of Porphyro, then, Keats has incorporated his semi-Wordsworthian vision of life as a progress from mere animal existence to an understanding of the mystery that permeates life; and the castle is that Mansion of Many Apartments in which human existence plays out its part. When Porphyro arrives at the castle he stands beside the portal doors, 'Buttress'd from moonlight' [77], merely hoping that he may gaze on Madeline, the beauty for which he longs. In this infant existence of his spirit, he is shut off from the light of the ideal moon which shines on mortal things to reveal them in their immortal aspects; and consequently in the 'tedious hours' [79] which make up life he can do no more than yearn for an entrance into existence so as to experience its riches: 'Perchance speak, kneel, touch, kiss' [80–1]. Shaded from the visionary splendor by the buttress of human life, he can have only a sensory impulse towards the perfect mortal beauty and can expect little more than that he might gaze upon it and worship it 'But for one moment in the tedious hours' of his mortal days.

But this worldly beauty towards which he is impelled before he enters the castle is not transfigured by the spiritual light of the moon-goddess, and hence he has no understanding of the meaning of his impulse. However, having entered the castle of human life, he quickly circumvents the level chambers of the 'mansion foul' [89] in which life is a distracting game played for its own sake and where the 'barbarian hordes' resent all that he represents. Led by Angela to the first chamber, he is there bathed in the light of ideality, but, since the intensity of human passion is lacking, the room is only 'Pale, lattic'd, chill, and silent as a tomb' [113]. In this 'thoughtless Chamber, in which we remain as long as we do not think', Porphyro merely exists, resting in childlike innocence and awe, 'Like puzzled urchin', while Angela tells of Madeline's plan. In this spiritual adolescence he is driven by an impulse of his senses, but not by a consciousness of his sensuous desires. Angela's revelation, however, arouses him from the thoughtlessness which allows him to remain in the first chamber, and knowledge of Madeline's intention to experience the spiritual repetition of earthly happiness awakens the thinking principle within him and impels him to seek out Madeline's chamber: 'Sudden a thought came like a full-blown rose, . . . then doth he propose / A stratagem' [136–

9]. The consciousness of his sensuous powers drives him then to Madeline's chamber – the 'Chamber of Maiden-Thought'.

The spiritual ascent that is implicit in Porphyro's progress from chamber to chamber becomes clear by the fact that he remains in a closet adjacent to Madeline's chamber, for Keats originally called this closet a 'Purgatory sweet' and retained his description of the chamber itself as a 'paradise'. In other words, Porphyro has transcended the merely human life of the 'level chambers' and is now in the purgatory to which he must move before he can attain the heavenly repetition of earthly happiness. From this purgatory he can look upon 'all that he may attain', 'love's own domain'.[11] In the Chamber of Maiden-Thought we are intoxicated with the light and atmosphere and see nothing but pleasant wonders; and thus Porphyro looks upon the disrobing Madeline, the ideal revealing its naked perfection. Entranced, breathless, he is wholly engaged in the splendor of the revelation, just as the knight-at-arms sees nothing but the fairy's child because his self is being absorbed; and because each man reaches this stage only within himself as an inward experience of his total self, Porphyro is seeing the 'beauty unespied', 'in close secrecy' [163, 166]. Here in the Chamber of Maiden-Thought the ascent of the scale of intensities is acted out, and Porphyro and Madeline unite in a mystic blending of mortality and immortality, chastity and passion, the moonlight of perfect form and the ruddiness of intense experience. They have attained the stage where life's self is nourished by its own pith, and they can now progress into the mystery that is the core of life.

In the *Ode on a Grecian Urn* and in *La Belle Dame sans Merci*, Keats had found that merely human life cannot continue to experience the life that our imaginations tell us is to come. However, the points on which he tipped the web of *The Eve of St Agnes* are an hypothesis. Suppose we could penetrate into heaven's bourne by elevating our human passions to an intensity that would allow them to blend with a changeless immortality and thus be spiritually transfigured – suppose we could experience our heaven on earth – to what sphery sessions would we be admitted? One of the effects of the splendid vision we perceive in the Chamber of Maiden-Thought is 'that tremendous one of sharpening one's vision into the heart and nature of Man—of convincing one's nerves that the world is full of Misery and Heartbreak, Pain, Sickness and oppression'. Hence, when the union has been consummated and the lovers are experiencing the spiritual repetition of life, the supernal power that has granted them the vision is now no longer relevant. The moon has set and the chamber has grown dark because the mystery to which they are now admitted can be known to man only as a darkness. This is not the darkness of ignorance that surrounded Porphyro before his entrance into the castle, but the darkness that Keats invoked in his sonnet 'Why did I laugh to-night?' It is the mist in which man's knowledge of heaven, hell, and his own self are wrapped.[12] It is the darkness which God made 'his secret place' so that 'his pavilion round about him were dark waters and thick clouds of the skies'.[13] The moon has made possible a transcendence of human life in order that the lovers may progress, not to light, but to the dark secret beyond the castle which confines them to the activities of mortal life. Hence they find 'a darkling way' [355], the 'dark passages' to which the Chamber of Maiden-Thought leads. Hearing no human sound, they escape into the mysterious elfin storm which is 'Of haggard seeming, but a boon indeed' [343–4], the dark secret of life, the 'vision into the heart and nature of Man', which terrifies sublunary mortals, but which guards one from the savagery of the world and allows him to 'see into the life of things'. Only to this point is Keats willing to go; he feels the burden of the mystery, but he is not yet ready to explore the dark passages through which Porphyro and Madeline are now travelling.

Having experienced the spiritual repetition of human happiness, Porphyro and Madeline are no longer active powers. Of his friend Dilke, Keats wrote that he will never arrive at a truth because he is always striving after it;[14] and Coleridge, he complained, will 'let go by a fine isolated verisimilitude caught from the Penetralium of mystery, from being incapable of remaining Content with half knowledge'.[15] One enters the mystery, not by wilfull probing, but by allowing himself to be absorbed into it. Once man has experienced the wonders of the Chamber of Maiden-Thought and gained insight into the agony of human life, the mystery unfolds itself; and an effort to pry open its doors would only shut them more tightly. Therefore, in the poem the light grows dark, and the mystery opens its own doors upon itself: 'on all sides of it', as the letter to Reynolds says, 'many doors are set open'. So, too, Pan, being a knowable 'unknown', the link between heaven and earth, the spirit that makes earth ethereal, is himself the 'Dread opener of the mysterious doors / Leading to universal knowledge'; for he is a symbol of the mystic sense-spirit union the lovers have fashioned.

With the enactment of this theme of passive absorption Keats now rounds out the conclusion of his romance. In one of the most dramatically controlled passages in English poetry he melts the lovers into a spaceless, timeless, selfless realm of mystery, exactly as the poet of the *Ode on a Grecian Urn* and the knight-at-arms were selflessly assimiliated into a visionary heaven. At first we perceive the lovers preparing to escape into the storm that lies beyond human existence; they themselves are the object of our attention as we see them moving down the wide stairs. They act directly before us in the historical past. Then, almost imperceptibly they are gradually released from dimensions. First they tend to fade as active powers. After having been vividly active before us and the center of our attention, they govern little directly in the last three stanzas; in the main the action passes from them into the control of the things that surround them – the lamp, arras, carpets, bloodhound, chains, key and door; and the sense of their active presence is further dimmed by the introduction of the passive verb: 'In all the house was heard no human sound' [356].

They further lose selfhood and palpable existence as the reader becomes identified with them, moving in them through the passageways and seeing, no longer the lovers, but what could be seen by them in the progress – the flickering of the lamp, the fluttering of the arras, the rising of the carpets with the wind. The camera is no longer focused on the lovers, but has become their eyes so that as we watch what the lovers see, they themselves may steal away from our mode of existence. When next we glance at them they have become indistinct and have blurred into insubstantial things; their movement is the insubstantial essence of movement, not a human act, and they themselves have become visionary:

> They glide, like phantoms, into the wide hall;
> Like phantoms, to the iron porch, they glide.   [361–2]

Meanwhile, the narrative becomes not merely one of the historical past, an action completed at some specific date in the past, but also one that is both immediate and universal; and this effect is controlled by the subtle manipulation of the past tense and the historical present. At first all the action is expressed by the past tense: the lovers 'found' their way, the lamp 'was flickering', the arras 'flutter'd'. At this point Keats mingles past and present: the lovers 'glide', the porter 'lay', the bloodhound 'rose' and 'shook' his hide, and his eye 'owns' an inmate. The intermingling of tenses is not careless, but nicely shapes a confusion of the sense of time by making the reader teeter between past and present. Both tenses are appropriate to a description of past events, for the historical present ('glide' and 'owns') gives a sense of presentness to past events; but the effect of the intermingling of the tenses is to bring the action out of a fixed position in time and dim all impression of temporality: the lovers seem to glide this very moment before us, and yet they have left the castle in the remote past. However, the introduction of the present tense blurs the sense of time through even greater ambiguity, for it may be the historical present, the immediate present, or the universal present; and indeed in the poem it is all these, and all at the same time. Hence it is this multivalent present tense that emerges from the intermingling of the past and present, and governs the account of all the final action: the bolts 'slide', the chains 'lie' silent, the key 'turns', and the door 'groans'; and the previous confusion of the temporal reference now causes these present tenses to place the actions outside the context of time: the chains lay silent in the past, lie silent now, and indeed always lie silent.

With this evaporation of time, all human agency also

vanishes as the lovers fade entirely from the scene. We do not see them as they make the bolts of the castle door slide open, nor are we the lovers seeing their own action of moving the bolts; for the effect of one's arrival at the border of the mystery is that 'many doors *are set* open'. No agency at all slides the bolts and chains, and yet the bolts and chains slide, and the door groans on its hinges – and Porphyro and Madeline are outside the human order, beyond the 'mysterious doors' that lead to 'universal knowledge'. The lovers are wholly caught up in timelessness and no longer exist as human actors. 'And they are gone': the action of the participle ('gone') belongs to the past, but the adjectival use of the participle here divests it of its verbal quality; it is a description, a quality of being, not an act, and therefore it implies no agency. The lovers' being gone is outside time and activity. The poet now catches up this sense of timelessness and swells it by having endless ages spin away before our time-bound minds:

> And they are gone: ay, ages long ago
> These lovers fled away into the storm.   [370–1]

No longer are Porphyro and Madeline human actors, or even phantoms, but the selfless spirit of man forever captured in the dimensionless mystery beyond our mortal vision.

The symbolising act that takes place in the first three stanzas of *La Belle Dame sans Merci* is performed at the conclusion of the romance. In the ballad Keats began by shaping image and value until he had dramatised the fact that the poem is symbolic. Here, at the conclusion of the romance, the vital current of the actors flows beyond them while they are being refined out of existence. The vitality has impersonalised itself to become vital values beyond and independent of the actors who gave them their impetus.

In the background of the narrative we have been tracing there are three other sets of characters who, by their contrast with the warmth, passion and ardor of the youthful lovers, not only give the central narrative an artistic depth, but also act out their various roles in the Mansion of Many Apartments to reveal other ways in which life may be lived. The beadsman, who surrounds the entire poem with a framework of chill, plays his part in the outer passages of the castle. His movement takes him along the chapel aisles and to his place of penance; he only skirts the chambers in which the revelry takes place. Hearing the music of the gay dance, he is tempted to move towards the joys of life; but 'already had his deathbell rung' [22], and he continues his way outside the central chambers, avoiding the sensuous intensities of life, despite the temptation. The beadsman, then, is eschewing the vigors of human experience and has dedicated himself to heaven alone. He is the chill of that life which avoids sensuous warmth: his breath is 'frosted' [6], and he tells his rosary with numb fingers [5]. He leads his mortal life only that he may put it aside; by praying for his soul's reprieve and grieving for sinners' sake he hopes to stifle his physical existence and thereby exalt and assure his spiritual salvation.

But the enjoyment in a finer tone hereafter of what we have called happiness on earth is a fate that 'can only befall those who delight in Sensation rather than hunger as you do after Truth', Keats wrote to his clerical friend Benjamin Bailey.[16] Adam's dream does not apply to those who, like the beadsman, hunger after 'truth'. Even the beadsman's breath symbolises the misdirection of his life: his breath (spirit) 'Seem'd taking flight for heaven, without a death' [8]. But death, Keats tells us elsewhere, is 'Life's high meed'[17] – the final intensity that climaxes the intensities of human existence and unites life with its proper pith. For the man of sensations, human experiences are a progress to heaven's bourne, and death is the last and most vigorous of these experiences.

The beadsman's, however, is 'Another way' [25]; he hopes, not to make sensuous earthly existence an ascent to a spiritual repetition but to dodge life and its high meed, death, and to be as oblivious to the senses as his fingers are numb with the cold. He would grasp 'truth' alone, without beauty, in one leap. For such a life which avoids sensations there is no spiritual repetition in a finer tone; and the beadsman, after thousand futile aves, becomes only the mutable physical substance that belongs to this world: 'For aye unsought for slept among his ashes cold' [378]. The irony is that on the very night that the lovers are caught up in the mystery through the fixing of exquisite passion in an immortality, the beadsman, seeking to subdue the flesh to the spirit, becomes only meaningless, lifeless matter among the very ashes that symbolise the meaninglessness of the mortal body. In this light we can understand somewhat better why Keats felt an impulse – not dictated by a sense of poetic effect – to make even more grotesque and gruesome the beadsman's fate, and at one point in the composition of the poem made the last few lines read:

> *and with face deform*
> *The beadsman stiffen'd, 'twixt a sigh and laugh*
> *Ta'en sudden from his beads by one weak little cough.*

Originally Keats included between stanzas three and four another stanza that reveals the progression he intended in passing from the beadsman to the revelers and then to the lovers. After describing the beadsman's avoidance of the life of sensations he added:

> *But there are ears may hear sweet melodies,*
> *And there are eyes to brighten festivals,*
> *And there are feet for nimble minstrelsies,*
> *And many a lip that for the red wine calls. –*
> *Follow, then follow to the illumined halls,*
> *Follow me youth – and leave the eremite –*
> *Give him a tear – then trophied banneral*
> *And many a brilliant tasseling of light*
> *Shall droop from arched ways this high baronial night.*

Clearly the meagre and wan beadsman is to be thrust aside as one who considers the world '"a vale of tears" from which we are to be redeemed by a certain arbitrary interposition of God and taken to Heaven—What a little circumscribed straightened notion!'[18] For such a misguided view we may feel a touch of sadness – 'Give him a tear' – but we are to move instead to a somewhat higher view of life by an entrance into its strenuosity and riches.

And yet, the revelers in the hall, the converse of the beadsman, cannot perceive beyond the limits of their momentary excitement. In the 'level chambers' they seek pleasure and agitation merely as an end in itself and hope to find happiness on earth so that 'the whole troubles of life which are now frittered away in a series of years, would then be accumulated for the last days of a being who instead of hailing [Death's] approach, would leave this world as Eve left Paradise'.[19] Therefore these, too,

> let us wish away,
> And turn, sole-thoughted, to one Lady there.   [41–2]

Originally, Keats made even more vivid his rejection of the revelers as he leads the reader through the increasing stages from beadsman, to revelers, to the lovers. Of the revelers he wrote:

> *Ah what are they? the idle pulse scarce stirs[.]*
> *The Muse should never make the spirit gay;*
> *Away, bright dulness, laughing fools away, –*
> *And let me tell of one sweet lady there.*

Thus the beadsman and the baron's guests are antitheses: the first avoids life for soul; the latter neglect soul for life alone. For this very reason the beadsman is irrelevant to the lovers and moves about the periphery of the castle; but the baron and his guests are hostile to them. By being unable to rise above the confines of mortality and by remaining in the glowing 'level' chambers sheltered from the gleam of the ideal moon, they are the death-pale kings and princes who warn that 'La Belle Dame sans Merci / Hath thee in thrall!'; and thus they conduct a feud against all that Porphyro represents:

> For him, those chambers held barbarian hordes,
> Hyena foemen, and hot-blooded lords,

Whose very dogs would execrations howl
Against his lineage.   [85–8]

The revelers engage in only the petty passions of the world:
'whisperers in anger, or in sport; / 'Mid looks of love, defiance,
hate, and scorn' [68–9]; and only because 'her heart was
otherwhere' [62] could Madeline fulfill the rites of St Agnes'
Eve and experience the spiritual repetition of life. It is this
world of the revelers that is always threatening to obtrude itself
upon visions of a love that is still to be enjoyed, and thereby to
withdraw man to the cold hill side. Even in the midst of
Madeline's dream-vision in the paradise of her chamber and in
the midst of Porphyro's preparations for the union, the
noisiness of the mortal world promises to reduce all to mere
flesh-and-blood mutability:

O for some drowsy Morphean amulet!
The boisterous, midnight, festive clarion,
The kettle-drum, and far-heard clarionet,
Affray his [Porphyro's] ears, though but in dying tone: –
The hall door shuts again, and all the noise is gone.   [257–61]

For this life of the senses alone, Keats cannot restrain his
contempt. The 'barbarian hordes' are 'bloated wassaillers'
[346] who, being 'Drown'd all in Rhenish and the sleepy
mead', do not have 'ears to hear, or eyes to see' the passage of
the lovers from the castle of mortality into the mystery of the
elfin storm [348–9]. Consequently, the dreams of the baron
and his guests – 'the whole blood-thirsty race' [99] – unlike
Madeline's dream, are only of the world in which all things
decay. Instead of rising by dream-vision to the spiritual
repetition of human life, they can dream only of human life,
whose central principle is its deathliness:

That night the Baron dreamt of many a woe,
And all his warrior-guests, with shade and form
Of witch, and demon, and large coffin-worm,
Were long be-nightmar'd.   [372–5]

Similarly, the inability of the knight-at-arms to remain at the spiritual level of the elfin grot caused him to dream of 'pale kings and princes too, / Pale warriors, death-pale were they all'.

Finally, both the drama and the theme of the poem are completed by Angela, who is a kind of norm of humanity. Like the beadsman, she is careful of her soul; and yet she belongs to the halls of revelry rather than the higher chambers, although she alone is able to wander at will in both, unaffected by either. She will never experience a love that is forever warm and still to be enjoyed because she is devoid of both sensuous and spiritual intensity: she is an 'old beldame, weak in body and in soul' [90], a 'poor, weak, palsy-stricken, churchyard thing' [155]. Madeline's desire for a vision of her love is to Angela only a child's wish for an unreal, deceptive dream-world; and consequently, failing to recognise it as an ascent to the sensuous-spiritual life of heaven, she laughs 'in the languid moon' [127], the light of the ideal, while she tells Porphyro of the plan. Despite her interest in her own soul, she can think of love only as the 'mere commingling of passionate breath', not knowing that it can produce 'more than our searching witnesseth';[20] and thus she understands Porphyro's plan to result only from an evil sensual desire which must be purified by marriage.

Although she aids in Porphyro's enactment of the vision, the part she plays is almost too exacting for her feeble spirit and senses. She rises to a height beyond her strength, and so Madeline must lead her from the upper chambers down 'To a safe level matting' [196], the level at which merely human existence is carried on and at which the baron and his guests seek worldly happiness. Since such weakness can never penetrate into the mystery, Angela, whose 'passing-bell may ere the midnight toll' [156], on the very same night (we are left to assume) died 'palsy-twitch'd, with meagre face deform' [375–6]. Certainly a set of values that embrace more than esthetics drove Keats, as Richard Woodhouse reports, to alter 'the last 3 lines to leave on the reader a sense of pettish disgust, by bringing Old Angela in (only) dead stiff & ugly.—He says he likes that the poem should leave off with this Change of

Sentiment–it was what he aimed at, & was glad to find from my objections to it that he had succeeded.'[21] . . .

SOURCE: excerpted from *The Finer Tone: Keats's Major Poems* (Baltimore, Md., 1953; repr. 1967), pp. 101–12, 116–31.

NOTES

[Reorganised and renumbered from the original – Ed.]

1. 'Fancy', 7.
2. *Ode to Psyche*, 66–7.
3. Letter to George and Georgiana Keats, 14 February – 3 May 1819.
4. Letter to Shelley, 16 August 1820.
5. *Endymion*, I 288–9.
6. Ibid., 581–2.
7. Ibid., III 959.
8. *To My Brother George*, 30.
9. 'To J. H. Reynolds, Esq.', 49.
10. Letter to Reynolds, 3 May 1818.
11. Stanza 21, variant.
12. 'Written upon the Top of Ben Nevis'.
13. Psalms, XVIII 11.
14. Letter to George and Georgiana Keats, 17–27 September 1819.
15. Letter to George and Thomas Keats, 21 December 1817.
16. Letter to Bailey, 22 November 1817.
17. 'Why did I laugh to-night?'
18. Letter to George and Georgiana Keats, 14 February – 3 May 1819.
19. Ibid.
20. *Endymion*, I 833–44.
21. Richard Woodhouse's letter to Taylor, 19–20 September 1819; in *The Keats Circle*, ed. Hyder E. Rollins (Cambridge, Mass. and Oxford, 1948), I, p. 91.

Jack Stillinger   The Hoodwinking of
Madeline: Scepticism in
The Eve of St Agnes   (1961)

I

The commonest response to *The Eve of St Agnes* has been the
celebration of its 'heady and perfumed loveliness'. The poem
has been called 'a monody of dreamy richness', 'one long
sensuous utterance', 'an expression of lyrical emotion', 'a
great affirmation of love', 'a great choral hymn', an expression
of 'unquestioning rapture' – and many other things else. Remarks like these tend to confirm one's uneasy feelings that what
is sometimes called 'the most perfect' of Keats's longer poems is
a mere fairy-tale romance, unhappily short on meaning. For
many readers, as for Douglas Bush, the poem is 'no more than
a romantic tapestry of unique richness of color'; one is 'moved
less by the experience of the characters than . . . by the
incidental and innumerable beauties of descriptive phrase
and rhythm'.[1]

To be sure, not all critics have merely praised Keats's
pictures. After all, the poem opens on a note of 'bitter chill',
and progresses through images of cold and death before the
action gets under way. When young Porphyro comes from
across the moors to claim his bride, he enters a hostile castle,
where Madeline's kinsmen will murder even upon holy days;
and in the face of this danger he proceeds to Madeline's
bedchamber. With the sexual consummation of their love, a
storm comes up, and they must escape the castle, past
'sleeping dragons', porter, and bloodhound, out into the
night. The ending reverts to the opening notes of bitter chill
and death: Madeline's kinsmen are benightmared, the old
Beadsman and Madeline's nurse Angela are grotesquely
dispatched into the next world. Some obvious contrasts are
made in the poem: the lovers' youth and vitality are set against

the old age and death associated with Angela and the Beadsman; the warmth and security of Madeline's chamber are contrasted with the coldness and hostility of the rest of the castle and the icy storm outside; the innocence and purity of young love are played off against the sensuousness of the revelers elsewhere in the castle; and so on. Through these contrasts, says one critic, Keats created a tale of young love 'not by forgetting what everyday existence is like, but by using the mean, sordid and commonplace as a foundation upon which to build a high romance'; the result is no mere fairy tale, but a poem that 'has a rounded fulness, a complexity and seriousness, a balance which remove it from the realm of mere magnificent tour de force'.[2]

But still something is wanting. The realistic notes all seem to occur in the framework, and the main action is all romance. There is no interaction between the contrasting elements, and hence no conflict. Porphyro is never really felt to be in danger; through much of the poem the lovers are secluded from the rest of the world; and at the end, when they escape, they meet no obstacle, but rather 'glide, like phantoms, into the wide hall; / Like phantoms, to the iron porch, they glide. . . . By one, and one, the bolts full easy slide:– / The chains lie silent . . . The key turns . . . the door upon its hinges groans. / And they are gone' [361–70]. It is all too easy. Though the poem ends with the nightmares of the warriors, and the deaths of Angela and the Beadsman, the lovers seem untouched, for they have already fled the castle. And besides, this all happened 'ages long ago' [370]. We are back where we started, with a fairy-tale romance, unhappily short on meaning.

The only serious attempt to make something of the poem has come from a small group of critics whom I shall call 'metaphysical critics' because they think Keats was a metaphysician.[3] To them the poem seems to dramatise certain ideas that Keats held a year or two earlier about the nature of the imagination, the relationship between this world and the next, and the progress of an individual's ascent toward spiritualisation.

According to the popular superstition connected with St Agnes' Eve, a young maiden who fasts and neither speaks nor looks about before she goes to bed may get sight of her future husband in a dream. Madeline follows this prescription, dreams of her lover, then seems to awaken out of her dream to find him present in her chamber, an actual, physical fact. Her dream in a sense comes true. The events are thought to relate to a passage in the well-known letter to Benjamin Bailey, 22 November 1817, in which Keats expressed his faith in 'the truth of Imagination': 'What the imagination seizes as Beauty must be truth–whether it existed before or not. . . . The Imagination may be compared to Adam's dream–he awoke and found it truth.' For the metaphysical critics, just as Adam dreamed of the creation of Eve, then awoke to find his dream a truth – Eve before him a beautiful reality – so Madeline dreams of Porphyro and awakens to find him present and palpably real.

But the imagination is not merely prophetic: it is 'a Shadow of reality to come' hereafter; and in the same letter Keats is led on to 'another favorite Speculation' – 'that we shall enjoy ourselves here after by having what we called happiness on Earth repeated in a finer tone and so repeated. . . . Adam's dream will do here and seems to be a conviction that Imagination and its empyreal reflection is the same as human Life and its spiritual repetition'.[4] The idea is that a trust in the visionary imagination will allow us to 'burst our mortal bars', to 'dodge / Conception to the very bourne of heaven',[5] to transcend our earthly confines, guess at heaven, and arrive at some view of the reality to come. If the visionary imagination is valid, the earthly pleasures portrayed in our visions will make up our immortal existence – will be spiritually 'repeated in a finer tone and so repeated'.

In this sense, Madeline's dream of Porphyro is a case history in the visionary imagination. According to the metaphysical critics, she is, in her dream, at heaven's bourne, already enjoying a kind of spiritual repetition of earthly happiness. On being roused by Porphyro, she finds in him 'a painful change' [300]: 'How chang'd thou art! how pallid, chill, and drear!' she says to him; 'Give me that voice again . . . Those looks immortal' [311–13]. Porphyro's reply takes the form of action: 'Beyond a mortal man impassion'd far / At these voluptuous accents, he arose' [316–17]. He transcends his mortal existence, joins Madeline at heaven's bourne by melting into her dream, and together they store up pleasures to be immortally repeated in a finer tone.

The other main strand of the critics' thinking concerns the apotheosis of Porphyro. By relating the poem to Keats's simile of human life as a 'Mansion of Many Apartments', the critics would persuade us that the castle of Madeline's kinsmen allegorically represents human life, and that Porphyro, passing upward to a closet adjoining Madeline's bedchamber, and thence into the chamber itself, progresses from apartment to apartment in the mansion of life, executing a spiritual ascent to heaven's bourne. For a number of reasons, Keats's simile confuses rather than clarifies the poem.[6] But the idea of spiritual pilgrimage is not entirely to be denied. Porphyro says to the sleeping Madeline, 'Thou art my heaven, and I thine eremite' [277], and when she awakens, after the consummation, he exclaims to her: 'Ah, silver shrine, here will I take my rest / After so many hours of toil and quest, / A famish'd pilgrim, – saved by miracle' [337–9].

In brief summary, the main points of the metaphysical critics' interpretation are that Madeline's awakening to find Porphyro in her bedroom is a document in the validity of the visionary imagination; that Porphyro in the course of the poem makes a spiritual pilgrimage, ascending higher by stages until he arrives at transcendent reality in Madeline's bed; and that there the lovers reenact earthly pleasures that will be stored up for further, still more elevated repetition in a finer tone. If these ideas seem far-fetched and confused, the fact should be attributed in part to the brevity of my exposition, and to the shortcomings of any attempt to abstract ideas from a complicated poem, even when it is treated as allegory. Yet one may suggest reasons for hesitating to accept them.

For one thing, when the imaginative vision of beauty turns out to be a truth – when Madeline awakens to find Porphyro in her bed – she is not nearly so pleased as Adam was when he awoke and discovered Eve. In fact, truth here is seemingly undesirable: Madeline is frightened out of her wits, and she laments, 'No dream alas! alas! and woe is mine! / Porphyro will leave me here to fade and pine' [328–9]. For another, it is a reversal of Keats's own sequence to find in the poem the spiritual repetition of earthly pleasures. In Madeline's dream the imaginative enactment of pleasure comes first; it is an earthly repetition of spiritual pleasure that follows, and perhaps in a grosser, rather than a finer, tone. That the lovers are consciously intent on experiencing the conditions of immortality – consciously practising for the spiritual repetition of pleasure at an even higher level of intensity – implies, if one reads the critics correctly, that both Madeline and Porphyro had read *Endymion*, Keats's letters, and the explications of the metaphysical critics.[7]

Much of the critics' interpretation rests on the religious language of the poem. Madeline is 'St Agnes' charmed maid', 'a mission'd spirit' [192–3], 'all akin / To spirits of the air' [201–2], 'a saint', 'a splendid angel, newly drest, / Save wings, for heaven', 'so pure a thing, so free from mortal taint' [222–5]. To Porphyro, her 'eremite', she is 'heaven' [277], and from closet to bedchamber he progresses from purgatory to paradise. Finally, Porphyro is 'A famish'd pilgrim, – saved by miracle' [339]. But the significance of such language is questionable. In *Romeo and Juliet*, with which *The Eve of St Agnes* has much in common, Juliet's hand at the first meeting of the lovers is a 'holy shrine', and Romeo's lips are 'two blushing pilgrims'; subsequently Juliet is a 'dear saint', a 'bright angel', a 'fair saint'; 'heaven is . . . Where Juliet lives', and outside Verona is 'purgatory, torture, hell itself'; she is compared to a 'winged messenger of heaven', and her lips carry 'immortal blessing'. At the same time Romeo is 'the god of [Juliet's] idolatry', and a 'mortal paradise of . . . sweet flesh'.[8] In other poems Keats himself, in the manner of hundreds of poets before him, uses religious terms in hyperbolic love language: for example, Isabella's lover Lorenzo is called 'a young palmer in Love's eye', he is said to 'shrive' his passion, and (in a stanza ultimately rejected from the poem) he declares that he would be 'full deified' by the gift of a love token.[9]

What is perhaps most telling against the critics, in connection with the religious language of *The Eve of St Agnes*, is that when Porphyro calls himself 'A famish'd pilgrim, – saved by miracle', his words must be taken ironically, unless Keats has forgotten, or hopes the reader has forgotten, all the action leading to the consummation. The miracle on which Porphyro congratulates himself is in fact a *stratagem* that he has planned and carried out to perfection. Early in the poem, when he first encounters Angela, she is amazed to see him, and says that he 'must hold water in a witch's sieve, / And be liege-lord of all the Elves and Fays, / To venture' into a castle of enemies [120–2]. Although Porphyro later assures Madeline that he is 'no rude infidel' [342], the images in Angela's speech tend to link him with witches and fairies rather than with the Christian pilgrim. By taking a closer look at the poem, we may see that Keats had misgivings about Porphyro's fitness to perform a spiritual pilgrimage and arrive at heaven.

II

Porphyro's first request of Angela, 'Now tell me where is Madeline' [114], is followed by an oath upon the holy loom used to weave St Agnes' wool, and it is implied that he is well aware what night it is. 'St Agnes' Eve', says Angela, 'God's help! my lady fair the conjuror plays / This very night: good angels her deceive!' [123–5]. While she laughs at Madeline's folly, Porphyro gazes on her, until 'Sudden a thought came like a full blown rose . . . . then doth he propose / A stratagem' [136–9]. The full force of 'stratagem' comes to be felt in the poem – a ruse, an artifice, a trick for deceiving. For Angela, the deception of Madeline by good angels is funny; but Porphyro's is another kind of deception, and no laughing matter. She is startled, and calls him 'cruel', 'impious', 'wicked' [140, 143]; the harshness of the last line of her speech emphasises her reaction: 'Thou canst not surely be the same that thou didst seem' [144].

Porphyro swears 'by all saints' not to harm Madeline: 'O may I ne'er find grace / When my weak voice shall whisper its last prayer, / If one of her soft ringlets I displace' [145–8]. He next enforces his promise with a suicidal threat: Angela must believe him, or he 'will . . . Awake, with horrid shout' his foemen, 'And beard them' [151–3]. Because Angela is 'A poor, weak, palsy-striken, churchyard thing' [155], she presently accedes, promising to do whatever Porphyro wishes –

> Which was, to lead him, in close secrecy,
> Even to Madeline's chamber, and there hide
> Him in a closet, of such privacy
> That he might see her beauty unespied,
> And win perhaps that night a peerless bride,
> While legion'd fairies pac'd the coverlet,
> And pale enchantment held her sleepy-eyed.   [163–9]

At this point our disbelief must be suspended if we are to read the poem as an affirmation of romantic love. We must leave our world behind, where stratagems like Porphyro's are frowned on, sometimes punished in the criminal courts, and enter an imaginary world where 'in sooth such things have been' [81]. But the narrator's summary comment on the stratagem is that 'Never on such a night have lovers met, / Since Merlin paid his Demon all the monstrous debt' [170–1]. The allusion is puzzling. Commentators feel that the 'monstrous debt' is Merlin's debt to his demon-father for his own life, and that he paid it by committing evil deeds, or perhaps specifically by effecting his own imprisonment and death through the misworking of a spell.[10] However it is explained, it strengthens rather than dispels our suspicion, like Angela's, that Porphyro is up to no good; and, with the earlier images of 'legion'd fairies' and 'pale enchantment', it brings further associations of fairy lore and sorcery to bear on his actions. Then Angela asserts a kind of orthodox middle-class morality: 'Ah! thou must needs the lady wed' [179].

She now leads Porphyro to Madeline's chamber, 'silken, hush'd, and chaste', where he takes 'covert' [187–8]. In the first draft stanza XXI is incomplete, but two versions that can be pieced together call Porphyro's hiding place '*A purgatory sweet to view loves own domain*' and '*A purgatory sweet to what may he attain*'.[11] The rejected lines, mentioning '*purgatory sweet*' as a stage toward the 'paradise' [244] of Madeline's chamber, are documents in Porphyro's spiritual pilgrimage, perhaps. The ideas of viewing love's own domain, or what he may attain, are documents in the peeping-Tomism that occupies the next few stanzas. As Angela is feeling her way towards the stair, she is met by Madeline, who turns back to help her down to 'a safe level matting' [196]. If the action is significant, its meaning lies in the juxtaposition of Madeline's unselfish act of 'pious care' [194] with the leering overtones just before of Porphyro's having hidden himself in her closet, 'pleas'd amain' [188] by the success of his stratagem, and with the tone of the narrator's words immediately following: 'Now prepare, / Young Porphyro, for gazing on that bed; / She comes, she comes again, like ring-dove fray'd and fled' [196–8].

The mention of 'ring-dove' is interesting. Porphyro has taken 'covert' – the position of the hunter (or perhaps merely the bird-watcher). There follows a series of bird images that perhaps may be thought of in terms of the hunter's game. In a variant to the stanza Madeline is '*an affrighted Swan*'; here she is a 'ring-dove'; in the next stanza her heart is 'a tongueless nightingale' [206]; later in the poem she is 'A dove forlorn' [333]; still later Porphyro speaks of robbing her nest [340], and in a variant says, '*Soft Nightingale, I'll keep thee in a cage /*
To sing to me.'[12] It is unlikely that all these images carry connotations of hunting, nest-robbing, and caging; Romeo will 'climb a bird's nest' when he ascends the ladder to Juliet's room [*R. & J.* II v 76]. But the single comparison of Madeline's heart to a 'tongueless nightingale' seems significant. Leigh Hunt naturally missed the point: 'The nightingale! how touching the simile! the heart a "tongueless nightingale", dying in that dell of the bosom. What thorough sweetness, and perfection of lovely imagery!'[13] Critics pointing to Sotheby's translation of Wieland's *Oberon* [VI 17], or to *Troilus and Criseyde* [III 1233–9], may also have missed the significance.[14] For Keats's image embraces the entire story of the rape of Philomel, and with it he introduces a further note of evil that prevents us from losing ourselves in the special morality of fairy romance. Madeline has the status of one of St Agnes' 'lambs unshorn' [71]; she is a maiden innocent and pure, but also is about to lose that status through what is in some ways a cruel deception. The comparison with Philomel is not inappropriate.

In stanza XXV, as Madeline is described kneeling, we are told that 'Porphyro grew faint: / She knelt, so pure a thing, so free from mortal taint' [224–5]. Though many reasons will suggest themselves why Porphyro grows faint, a novel one may be offered here. In his copy of *The Anatomy of Melancholy*, after a passage in which Burton tells how 'The Barbarians stand in awe of a fair woman, and at a beautiful aspect, a fierce spirit is pacified', Keats wrote: 'abash'd the devil stood'.[15] He quotes from Book IV of *Paradise Lost*, where Satan is confronted by the beautiful angel Zephon: 'Abasht the Devil stood, / And felt how awful goodness is, and saw / Virtue in her shape how lovely, saw, and pin'd / His loss' [846–9]. But since Burton speaks of standing 'in awe of a fair woman', Keats must also have recalled Book IX, in which Satan's malice is momentarily overawed by Eve's graceful innocence: 'That space the Evil one abstracted stood / From his own evil, and for the time remain'd / Stupidly good' [463–5]. Porphyro's faintness may in some way parallel Satan's moment of stupid goodness. 'But the hot Hell that always in him burns' soon ends Satan's relapse from evil intent, as he goes about Eve's ruin. So with Porphyro; for 'Anon his heart revives' [226], as he pursues the working-out of his stratagem.

Madeline undresses, then falls fast asleep. Porphyro creeps to the bed, 'Noiseless as fear in a wide wilderness' [250], and ''tween the curtains peep'd, where, lo! – how fast she slept' [252]. At the bedside he sets a table, when, in the midst of his preparations, a hall door opens in the castle, and the revelers' music shatters the silence of the room. Porphyro calls for a 'drowsy Morphean amulet' [257] – and then 'The hall door shuts . . . and all the noise is gone' [261]. Madeline continues sleeping, while he brings from the closet the feast of candied apple, quince, plum, and all the rest.

Aside from the unheroic implications of 'Noiseless as fear in a wide wilderness' and of the word 'peep'd', there are three things worth noting in the stanzas just summarised. One is the relationship the poem has here with *Cymbeline* [II ii 11–50], in which the villainous Iachimo emerges from the trunk, where he has hidden himself, to gaze on the sleeping Imogen. Readers since Swinburne have noted resemblances.[16] Imogen is 'a heavenly angel', and like Madeline a 'fresh lily', 'whiter than the sheets', as she lies in bed, sleeping, in effect, an 'azure-lidded sleep' [262] – and so on. But no critic has been willing to include among the resemblances that Porphyro's counterpart in the scene is a villain. In the speech from which these details have been drawn, Iachimo compares himself with Tarquin, who raped Lucrece, and he notes that Imogen 'hath been reading late / The tale of Tereus; here the leaf's turn'd down / Where Philomel gave up'.

The second point concerns Porphyro's call for a 'drowsy Morphean amulet' – a sleep-inducing charm to prevent Madeline's awakening when the music bursts forth into the room. Earlier he has wished to win Madeline while 'pale enchantment held her sleepy-eyed' [169]. Here he would assist 'pale enchantment' with a 'Morphean amulet'. It may not be amiss to recall Lovelace, and the stratagem by which he robbed Clarissa of her maidenhood. 'I know thou wilt blame me for having had recourse to *Art*', writes Lovelace to John Belford, in Richardson's novel. 'But do not physicians prescribe opiates in acute cases.' Besides, 'a Rape, thou knowest, to us Rakes, is far from being an undesirable thing'.[17]

The third point has to do with the feast that Porphyro sets out. In his copy of *The Anatomy of Melancholy*, opposite a passage in which Burton commends fasting as an excellent means of preparation for devotion, 'by which chast thoughts are ingendred . . . concupiscence is restrained, vicious . . . lusts and humours are expelled', Keats recorded his approval in the marginal comment 'good'.[18] It is for some reason of this sort that Madeline fasts, going 'supperless to bed' [51]. Porphyro's feast seems intended to produce the opposite results, and there is more than a suggestion of pagan sensuality in the strange affair of eastern luxuries that he heaps as if by magic – 'with glowing hand' [271] – on the table by the bed.[19]

Next Porphyro tries to awaken Madeline, or so it seems: 'And now, my love, my seraph fair, awake! / Thou art my heaven, and I thine eremite' [276–7]. The last line carries the suggestion that Porphyro has been reading of the martyrdom, not of St Agnes, but of Donne's lovers in *The Canonization*, whose bodies are by 'reverend love' made 'one anothers hermitage'. It is curious that in the proposition that follows, 'Open thine eyes . . . Or I shall drowse beside thee' [278–9], Porphyro does not wait for an answer: 'Thus whispering, his warm, unnerved arm / Sank in her pillow' [280–1]. 'Awakening up' [289], he takes Madeline's lute and plays an ancient ditty, which causes her to utter a soft moan. It would seem that she does at this point wake up: 'Suddenly / Her blue affrayed eyes wide open shone. . . . Her eyes were open, but she still beheld, / Now wide awake, the vision of her sleep' [295–9]. Not unreasonably, we might think, she weeps, sighs, and 'moan[s] forth witless words' [303].

We shall see in a moment, however, that she has not after all awakened from her trance. The 'painful change' she witnesses – the substitution of the genuine Porphyro for the immortal looks and voice of her vision – '*nigh* expell'd / The blisses of her dream' [300–1], came near expelling them, but did not in fact do so. Apparently she is to be thought of as still in her trance, but capable of speaking to the Porphyro before her, when she says, 'Ah, Porphyro! . . . but even now / Thy voice was at sweet tremble in mine ear' [307–8]. To her request for 'that voice again . . . Those looks immortal' [312–13], Porphyro offers neither, but rather impassioned action of god-like intensity. At the end of stanza XXXVI, the image of 'St Agnes' moon' combines the notions of St Agnes, the patron saint of maidenhood, and Cynthia, the goddess of chastity, and the symbolic combination has 'set', gone out of the picture to be replaced by a storm: 'meantime the frost-wind blows / Like Love's alarum pattering the sharp sleet / Against window-panes; St Agnes' moon hath set' [322–4].

Keats's final manuscript version of the consummation, rejected by his publishers on moral grounds, as making the poem unfit to be read by young ladies, is more graphic. For a rather lame conclusion to Madeline's speech [314–15], he substituted the lines, '*See, while she speaks his arms encroaching slow, / Have zoned her, heart to heart, – loud, loud the dark winds blow!*' Then he rewrote stanza XXXVI:

For on the midnight came a tempest fell;
More sooth, for that his quick rejoinder flows

Into her burning ear: and still the spell
Unbroken guards her in serene repose.
With her wild dream he mingled, as a rose
Marrieth its odour to a violet.
Still, still she dreams, louder the frost wind blows,
Like Love's alarum pattering the sharp sleet
Against the window panes: – St Agnes' Moon hath set.[20]

The revised version makes clearer that Madeline is still
dreaming: '*still the spell / Unbroken guards her in serene repose*'. And
it makes clearer the connection between the sexual
consummation, the setting of St Agnes' moon, and the rising
of the storm. When Porphyro's '*quick rejoinder flows / Into her
burning ear*' ('*close rejoinder*' in the *E* transcript), we may or may
not recall Satan 'Squat like a Toad, close at the ear of *Eve*';[21]
but one would go out of his way to avoid a parallel between the
advent of the storm in Keats's poem and the change in Nature
that comes about when our first mother in an evil hour reached
forth and ate the fruit: 'Earth felt the wound, and Nature from
her seat / Sighing through all her Works gave signs of woe, /
That all was lost'.[22] Unlike Eve, however, rather more like
Clarissa, Madeline by this time has no choice; the revision
heightens the contrast between her innocent unconsciousness
and the storm raging outside: '*Still, still she dreams, louder the frost
wind blows.*'

As printed, the poem continues: ' 'Tis dark: quick pattereth
the flaw-blown sleet.' Then Porphyro: 'This is no dream, my
bride, my Madeline!' Another line describes the storm: ' 'Tis
dark: the iced gusts still rave and beat' [325–7]. And now
Madeline finally does wake up, if she ever does. Her speech
shows a mixed attitude toward what has happened, but above
all it is the lament of the seduced maiden: 'No dream, alas!
alas! and woe is mine! / Porphyro will leave me here to fade
and pine. – / Cruel! what traitor could thee hither bring?' [328–
30]. She will curse not, for her heart is lost in his, or, perhaps
more accurately, still lost in her romantic idealisation of him.
But she is aware that her condition is woeful: Porphyro is
cruel; Angela is a traitor; and Madeline is a 'deceived thing; –
/ A dove forlorn and lost' [333]. In subsequent stanzas
Porphyro soothes her fears, again calls her his bride, and

seems to make all wrongs right. He tells her that the storm outside is really only 'an elfin-storm from faery land' [343], and that she should 'Awake! arise! . . . and fearless be, / For o'er the southern moors I have a home for thee' [350–1]. They hurry out of the chamber, down the wide stairs, through the castle door – 'And they are gone . . . fled away into the storm' [370–1].

III

After giving so much space to Porphyro, in admittedly exaggerated fashion, portraying him as peeping Tom and villainous seducer, I must now confess that I do not think his stratagem is the main concern of the poem. I have presented him as a villain in order to suggest, in the first place, that he is not, after all, making a spiritual pilgrimage, unless the poem is to be read as a satire on spiritual pilgrimages; in the second place, that the lovers, far from being a single element in the poem, are as much protagonist and antagonist as Belinda and the Baron, or Clarissa and Lovelace; and in the third place, that no matter how much Keats entered into the feelings of his characters, he could not lose touch with the claims and responsibilities of the world he lived in.

Certainly he partially identified himself with Porphyro. When Woodhouse found his revisions objectionable, Keats replied that he should 'despise a man who would be such an eunuch in sentiment as to leave a maid, with that Character about her, in such a situation: & sho^d despise himself to write about it'.[23] One may cite the narrator's obvious relish in Porphyro's situation as Madeline is about to undress – 'Now prepare, / Young Porphyro, for gazing on that bed' [196–7] – and Keats's later objection to the poem that 'in my dramatic capacity I enter fully into the feeling: but in Propria Persona I should be apt to quiz it myself'.[24] But sexual passion worried him: to Bailey he confessed in July 1818, 'When I am among Women I have evil thoughts',[25] and he wrote in his copy of *The Anatomy of Melancholy*, 'there is nothing disgraces me in my own eyes so much as being one of a race of eyes nose and mouth beings in a planet call'd the earth who . . . have always mingled goatish winnyish lustful love with the abstract adoration of the deity.'[26] Though it has touches of humor,[27] *The Eve of St Agnes* is a serious poem; regardless of the extent to which Keats identified with his hero, he introduced enough overtones of evil to make Porphyro's actions wrong within the structure of the poem.

From now on, however, it may be best to think of Porphyro as representing, like the storm that comes up simultaneously with his conquest, the ordinary cruelties of life in the world. Like Melville, Keats saw

> Too far into the sea; where every maw
> The greater on the less feeds evermore.
> . . .
> Still do I that most fierce destruction see,
> The shark at savage prey – the hawk at pounce,
> The gentle Robin, like a pard or ounce,
> Ravening a worm.   [*Letters*, I, p. 262]

Let Porphyro represent one of the sharks under the surface. And to borrow another figure from Melville, let the main concern of the poem be the young Platonist dreaming at the masthead: one false step, his identity comes back in horror, and with a half-throttled shriek he drops through transparent air into the sea, no more to rise for ever. There are reasons why we ought not entirely to sympathise with Madeline. She is a victim of deception, to be sure, but of deception not so much by Porphyro as by herself and the superstition she trusts in. Madeline the self-hoodwinked dreamer is, I think, the main concern of the poem, and I shall spend some time documenting this notion and relating it to Keats's other important poems – all of which, in a sense, are about dreaming.

If we recall Keats's agnosticism, his sonnet 'Written in Disgust of Vulgar Superstition' (Christianity), and his abuse in a spring 1819 journal letter of 'the pious frauds of Religion',[28] we may be prepared to see a hoodwinked dreamer in the poem even before we meet Madeline. He is the old Beadsman, so engrossed in an ascetic ritual that he is sealed off from the joys of life. After saying his prayers, he turns first through a door leading to the noisy revelry upstairs. 'But no. . . . The joys of all his life were said and sung: / His was a harsh penance on St Agnes' Eve' [22–4]. And so he goes another way, to sit among rough ashes, while the focus of the narrative proceeds through the door he first opened, and on into the assembly of revelers, where we are introduced to Madeline and the ritual she is intent on following. In the final manuscript version, between stanzas VI and VII, Keats inserted an additional stanza on the ritual, in part to explain the feast that Porphyro sets out:

> 'Twas said her future lord would there appear
> Offering, as sacrifice – all in the dream --
> Delicious food, even to her lips brought near,
> Viands, and wine, and fruit, and sugar'd cream,
> To touch her palate with the fine extreme
> Of relish: then soft music heard, and then
> More pleasures follow'd in a dizzy stream
> Palpable almost: then to wake again
> Warm in the virgin morn, no weeping Magdalen.[29]

Then the poem, as it was printed, continues describing Madeline, who scarcely hears the music, and, with eyes fixed on the floor, pays no attention to anyone around her.

Several things deserve notice. By brooding 'all that wintry day, / On love, and wing'd St Agnes' saintly care' [43–4], and by setting herself apart from the revelers, Madeline presents an obvious parallel with the Beadsman. Both are concerned with prayer and an ascetic ritual; both are isolated from the crowd and from actuality. A second point is that the superstition is clearly an old wive's tale: Madeline follows the prescription that 'she had heard old dames fully many times declare' [45]. It is called by the narrator a 'whim': 'Full of this whim was thoughtful Madeline' [55]. The irony of the added stanza enforces the point. Madeline's pleasures turn out to be palpable in fact. When she awakens to find herself with Porphyro, she is anything but warm: rather, she wakes up to 'flaw-blown sleet' and 'iced gusts' [325, 327]; it is no virgin morn for her; and she is a '*weeping Magdalen*', who cries, 'alas! alas! and woe is mine!' [328]. But here, early in the poem, 'she saw not: her heart was otherwhere: / She sigh'd for Agnes' dreams, the sweetest of the year' [62–3]. Perfunctorily dancing along, she is said to be 'Hoodwink'd with faery fancy; all amort, / Save to St Agnes and her lambs unshorn' [70–1].

The superstition is next mentioned when Angela tells that Madeline 'the conjuror plays / This very night: good angels her deceive!' [124–5]. Porphyro thinks of the ritual in terms of 'enchantments cold' and 'legends old' [134–5]. Proceeding to her chamber, Madeline is called 'St Agnes' charmed maid', 'a mission'd spirit, unaware' [192–3]. When she undresses, 'Half-hidden, like a mermaid in sea-weed' [231], she is perhaps linked briefly with the drowning Ophelia, whose spreading clothes momentarily support her 'mermaid-like' upon the water; like Ophelia, she is engrossed in a fanciful dream-world.[30] 'Pensive awhile she dreams awake, and sees, / In fancy, fair St Agnes in her bed, / But dares not look behind, or all the charm is fled' [232–4]. This last line carries a double meaning: in following her ritual, Madeline must look neither 'behind, nor sideways' [53]; but the real point is that if she did look behind, she would discover Porphyro, and then 'the charm' would be 'fled' for a more immediate reason.

Asleep in bed, Madeline is said to be 'Blissfully haven'd both from joy and pain . . . Blinded alike from sunshine and from rain, / As though a rose should shut, and be a bud again' [240–3]. Her dream is 'a midnight charm / Impossible to melt as iced stream', 'a stedfast spell' [282–3, 287]. It is while she is in this state of stuporous insensibility – while '*still the spell / Unbroken guards her in serene repose*', '*Still, still she dreams, louder the frost wind blows*' – that Porphyro makes love to her. On awakening to learn, 'No dream, alas! alas! and woe is mine', she calls herself 'a deceived thing', echoing Angela's words earlier, 'good angels her deceive!' Her condition is pitiful, yet at the same time reprehensible. Her conjuring (perhaps like Merlin's) has backfired upon her, and as hoodwinked dreamer she now gets her reward in coming to face reality a little too late. The rose cannot shut, and be a bud again.

IV

Whether *The Eve of St Agnes* is a good poem depends in large part on the reader's willingness to find in it a consistency and unity that may not in fact be there.[31] But however it is evaluated, it stands significantly at the beginning of Keats's single great creative year, 1819, and it introduces a preoccupation of all the major poems of this year: that an individual ought not to lose touch with the realities of this world.

In the poems of 1819, Keats's most explicit, unequivocal pronouncement on the conditions of human life comes in the *Ode on Melancholy*. Life in the world, we are told five or six times in the statements and images of the third stanza, is an affair in which pleasure and pain are inseparably mixed. There is no pleasure without pain, and, conversely, if pain is sealed off, so also is pleasure. One accepts life on these terms, or else suffers a kind of moral and spiritual emptiness amounting to death. The former is the better choice: he lives most fully 'whose strenuous tongue / Can burst Joy's grape against his palate fine'. The images of the first stanza – forgetfulness, narcotics, poisons, death – represent various ways of avoiding pain in life. But they are rejected (the whole stanza is a series of negatives) because they also exclude pleasure and reduce life to nothing ('For shade to shade will come too drowsily, / And drown the wakeful anguish of the soul'). The equivalent of these anodynes elsewhere in Keats's poems is dreaming, trusting in the visionary imagination; and, to cut short further explanation, the dreamer in the works of 1819 is always one who would escape pain, but hopes, wrongly, to achieve pleasure.

Take Madeline as the first instance. In bed, under the delusion that she can achieve bliss in her dream, yet wake up in the virgin morn no weeping Magdalen, she is 'Blissfully haven'd both from joy and pain' [240] – for all practical purposes in the narcotic state rejected by the *Ode on Melancholy*, experiencing nothing. Keats reiterates the idea two lines later, 'Blinded alike from sunshine and from rain', and the folly of her delusion is represented by the reversal of natural process,

'As though a rose should shut, and be a bud again' [242–3]. As generally in Keats's poems, dreaming is attended by fairy-tale imagery: under the spell of 'faery fancy', Madeline plays the conjuror, and Porphyro is linked in several ways with fairy lore, witchcraft and sorcery, as well as pagan sensuality. It is possible that Madeline never completely awakens from her fanciful dream; for she believes Porphyro when he tells her that the storm is 'an elfin-storm from faery land' [343], and she imagines 'sleeping dragons all around' [353] when they hurry out of the castle.[32]

The heroine of *The Eve of St Mark*, written a week or so after the completion of *The Eve of St Agnes*, in some ways resembles Madeline. Among the 'thousand things' perplexing Bertha in the volume she pores over are 'stars of Heaven, and angels' wings, / Martyrs in a fiery blaze, / Azure saints in silver rays' [29–32]. Enwrapped in the legend of St Mark, 'dazed with saintly imag'ries' [56], she ignores the life in the village around her, and cuts herself off from reality – a 'poor cheated soul' [69], 'lost in dizzy maze'[33] and mocked by her own shadow.

The wretched knight-at-arms in *La Belle Dame sans Merci* is similarly a hoodwinked dreamer. La Belle Dame is 'a faery's child'; she sings 'A faery's song', speaks 'in language strange', and takes him to an 'elfin grot'. When he awakens from his vision he finds himself 'On the cold hill's side'. But he is still the dupe of his dream, still hoodwinked, because he continues, in a barren landscape, 'Alone and palely loitering', hoping for a second meeting with La Belle Dame. And he denies himself participation in the actual world, which, in contrast to his bleak surroundings, is represented as a more fruitful scene, where 'The squirrel's granary is full, / And the harvest's done'.

In *Lamia*, the hoodwinked dreamer is of course Lycius, who falls in love with the serpent-woman Lamia, in whose veins runs 'elfin blood', who lingers by the wayside 'fairily', with whom he lives in 'sweet sin' in a magical palace with a 'faery-roof' [I 147, 200; II 31, 123]. 'She seem'd, at once, some penanced lady elf, / Some demon's mistress, or the demon's self' [I 55–6]. What she promises to do for Lycius is what, according to the *Ode on Melancholy*, cannot be done for mortal men: 'To unperplex bliss from its neighbour pain; / Define their pettish limits, and estrange / Their points of contact, and swift counterchange.' The inseparability of pleasure and pain is for her a 'specious chaos'; she will separate them 'with sure art' [I 192–6] – or so the blinded Lycius thinks. But *'Spells are but made to break'*, wrote Keats, in a passage subsequently omitted from the text.[34] 'A thrill / Of trumpets' reminds Lycius of the claims of the 'noisy world almost forsworn' [II 27–33], and he holds a wedding feast, at which 'cold philosophy', in the form of his old tutor Apollonius, attends to put 'all charms' to flight. The 'foul dream' Lamia vanishes under the tutor's piercing eye, and Lycius, too engrossed in his dream to survive, falls dead.

From *Lamia*, we may merely dip into *The Fall of Hyperion* to recall Keats's condemnation of dreamers.[35] They are 'vision'ries', 'dreamers weak', who seek out wonders, but ignore what is most important, the human face [I 161–3]. 'Only the dreamer venoms all his days' [I 175], the speaker learns on the steps of Moneta's temple. 'The poet and the dreamer are distinct, / Diverse, sheer opposite, antipodes. / The one pours out a balm upon the world, / The other vexes it [I 199–202].

Keats's mature view of dreamers illuminates perhaps most importantly the two best odes, *On a Grecian Urn* and *To a Nightingale*. In each poem the speaker begins as dreamer, hoodwinked with the idea that he can unperplex bliss from its neighbor pain, that he can find an anodyne to the ills of the flesh by joining the timeless life pictured on an urn, or by fading away into the forest with a bird. In each case the result is an awareness that spells are but made to break: the speaker recognises the falseness of the dream, the shortcomings of the ideal he has created, and he returns to the mortal world. Life on the urn is at first attractive: unheard melodies are sweeter; the lovers will remain young and fair; the trees will never lose their leaves. Yet it is a static situation. Love must be enjoyed, not be stopped forever at a point when enjoyment is just out of reach. The final judgement is that the urn is a 'Cold Pastoral', a 'friend to man' that, as a work of art, teases him out of thought but offers no possible substitute for life in the actual world.

In the *Ode to a Nightingale*, the speaker would fade away with the bird, and forget 'The weariness, the fever, and the fret' of the mortal world, 'Where Beauty cannot keep her lustrous eyes, / Or new Love pine at them beyond to-morrow'. But when he imaginatively joins the bird in the forest, he immediately longs for the world he has just rejected: 'Here there is no light. . . . I cannot see what flowers are at my feet.' 'In embalmed darkness' he is forced to 'guess each sweet' of the transient natural world. As he continues musing, the bird takes on for him the fairy-tale associations that we saw earlier connected with Madeline's dream, La Belle Dame, and Lamia: its immortal voice has charmed 'magic casements . . . in faery lands forlorn'. The realisation that the faery lands are forlorn of human life tolls the dreamer back to his sole self, and he wakes up. The nightingale, symbol of dreams and the visionary imagination, has turned out to be a 'deceiving elf'. The fancy 'cannot cheat so well'.

The metaphysical critics are right in asserting Keats's early trust in the imagination. What they sometimes fail to recognise, themselves eager for glimpses of heaven's bourne, and to an extent hoodwinked with their own rather than Keats's metaphysics, is that before Keats wrote more than a handful of poems we would not willingly let die, he in large part changed his mind.[36] Late in January 1818, on sitting down to read *King Lear* once again, he wrote a sonnet bidding goodbye to romance: 'Let me not wander in a barren dream.' A few days later he called it 'A terrible division' when the soul is flown upward and the body 'earthward press'd'. In March he wrote, 'It is a flaw / In happiness to see beyond our bourn', and about the same time he recognised that 'Four Seasons' – not just eternal spring, as the visionary might conjure up – 'Four Seasons fill the Measure of the year'. Similarly 'Four Seasons are there in the mind of Man', who 'hath his Winter too of pale Misfeature, / Or else he would forget his mortal nature'.[37] In July, on his walking trip to Scotland, he wrote:

Scanty the hour and few the steps beyond the bourn of care,
Beyond the sweet and bitter world, – beyond it unaware!
Scanty the hour and few the steps, because a longer stay

Would bar return, and make a man forget his mortal way:
O horrible! . . .

. . .

No, no, that horror cannot be, for at the cable's length
Man feels the gentle anchor pull and gladdens in its strength.

['Lines Written in the Highlands', 29–40]

It is the gentle anchor of mortality that ties us to the world; man gladdens in its strength. 'Fancy', said Keats to Reynolds, 'is indeed less than a present palpable reality'.[38] It would be a distortion of fact to maintain that he always held this later view, but it is worth noting that even when he and his fancy could not agree, he declared himself 'more at home amongst Men and women', happier reading Chaucer than Ariosto.[39]

The dreamer in Keats is ultimately one who turns his back, not merely on the pains of life, but on life altogether; and in the poems of 1819, beginning with *The Eve of St Agnes*, his dreaming is condemned. If the major concern in these poems is the conflict between actuality and the ideal, the result is not rejection of the actual, but rather a facing-up to it that amounts, in the total view, to affirmation. It is a notable part of Keats's wisdom that he never lost touch with reality, that he reproved his hoodwinked dreamers who would shut out the world, that he recognised life as a complexity of pleasure and pain, and laid down a rule for action: achievement of the ripest, fullest experience that one is capable of. These qualities make him a saner if in some ways less romantic poet than his contemporaries, and they should qualify him as the Romantic poet most likely to survive in the modern world.

SOURCE: article in *Studies in Philology*, 58 (1961), pp. 533–55; reproduced as a chapter in *The Hoodwinking of Madeline and Other Essays on Keats's Poem* (Urbana, Ill. and London, 1971), pp. 67–93.

NOTES

[Reorganised and renumbered from the original – Ed.]

1. Douglas Bush, *John Keats: Selected Poems and Letters* (Boston, Mass., 1959), pp. *xvi*, 333. See also Bush's 'Keats and His Ideas', in *The Major English Romantic Poets: A Symposium in Reappraisal*, ed. Clarence D. Thorpe et al. (Carbondale, Ill., 1957), pp. 239–40. This view is sanctioned by Keats himself, who thought the poem was in some ways like *Isabella* – 'too smokeable', with 'too much inexperience of . . . [life], and simplicity of knowledge in it'; 'A weak-sided Poem'. When he later planned a new attempt in poetry, it was 'the colouring of St Agnes eve' that he would 'diffuse . . . throughout a Poem in which Characters and Sentiment would be the figures to such drapery' (*The Letters of John Keats*, ed. Hyder E. Rollins [Cambridge, Mass. and Cambridge, 1958], II, pp. 174, 234).

2. R. H. Fogle, 'A Reading of Keats's *Eve of St Agnes*', *College English*, VI (1945), pp. 328, 325.

3. For example, Earl R. Wasserman, *The Finer Tone: Keats's Major Poems* (Baltimore, Md., 1953), pp. 97–137 [excerpted above – Ed.]; R. A. Foakes, *The Romantic Assertion* (London, 1958), pp. 85–94; and, at some points, Bernard Blackstone, *The Consecrated Urn* (London, 1959), pp. 275–88. While Foakes discusses among Keats's poems only *The Eve of St Agnes*, the metaphysical critics as a group represent not so much an interpretation of the poem as a view of all Keats's poetry. As will presently appear, I think *The Eve of St Agnes* illuminates a quite different view of his concerns and achievement.

4. *Letters*, ed. Rollins (op. cit., note 1), I, pp. 184–5.

5. *I stood tip-toe*, 190; *Endymion*, I 294–5.

6. The simile occurs in a letter to J. H. Reynolds, 3 May 1818 (*Letters*, I, pp. 280–1). Porphyro's eagerness to get to Madeline hardly accords with Keats's idea that 'we care not to hasten' to 'the second Chamber'; the identification of Madeline's bedroom with 'the Chamber of Maiden-Thought' seems similarly unbefitting, since one of the effects of arriving in the latter is 'that tremendous one of sharpening one's vision into the heart and nature of Man–of convincing ones nerves that the World is full of Misery and Heartbreak, Pain, Sickness and oppression'. Wasserman develops the comparison (op. cit., pp. 116–25), only to withdraw the letter from consideration (because 'the reading of the romance in the light of the prose statement suggests an allegorical interpretation', pp. 131–2); but he subsequently (pp. 159, 164) returns to 'the chambers of life'.

7. So the critics sometimes write; for example, Wasserman (op. cit., p. 114): 'Porphyro has recognised that the dream-vision for which Madeline is preparing is an ascent to the "chief intensity", to the spiritual repetition of what we call happiness on earth; and therefore the feast and the music represent the sensuous and imaginative entrances into the essence before the spiritual entrance through love. Consequently, when Porphyro passes into Madeline's chamber, he first prepares the remarkably rich foods. . . .'

8. *Romeo and Juliet*, I v 96–7, 105; II ii 26, 55, 61; III iii 29–30, 18; II ii 28; III iii 37; II ii 114; III ii 82.

9. *Isabella*, 2, 64 and the rejected stanza following line 56: *The Poetical Works of John Keats*, ed. H. W. Garrod, 2nd edn (Oxford, 1958), p. 217.

10. See, among others, H. Buxton Forman (ed.), *The Poetical Works and Other Writings of John Keats* (London, 1889), II, p. 84 n.; and Roy P. Basler, *Explicator*, III (1944), item 1.

11. *Poetical Works*, ed. Garrod, p. 244.

12. For the variants, see ibid., pp. 245, 253.

13. *Leigh Hunt's London Journal*, II (1835), p. 18.

14. Sir Sidney Colvin, *John Keats: His Life and Poetry* (London, 1917; new edn New York, 1925), p. 87 n.; F. E. L. Priestley, 'Keats and Chaucer', *MLQ*, V (1944), p. 444.

15. *The Poetical Works and Other Writings of John Keats*, ed. H. B. and M. B. Forman (New York, 1938–39), V, p. 310. (This edition is hereafter cited as 'Hampstead Keats'.)

16. See Thomas B. Stroup, '*Cymbeline*, II ii and *The Eve of St Agnes*', *English Studies*, XVII (1935), pp. 144–5; Claude L. Finney, *The Evolution of Keats's Poetry* (Cambridge, Mass., 1936), II, pp. 557–8; and *Times Literary Supplement* (6 April, 4 May, 1 June 1946), pp. 163, 211, 159.

17. Samuel Richardson, *Clarissa Harlowe* (1747–48; Shakespeare Head edn (Oxford, 1930)), V, pp. 339–40.

18. Hampstead Keats (op. cit., note 15), V, p. 318.

19. Foakes (op. cit., note 3), p. 91 n., relates the feast to 'Paynims' in line 241, but says that 'such suggestions are discontinued as Porphyro is transformed' by kneeling by the bed [297, 305–6] and by being 'saved' through the completion of a spiritual journey [337–9].

20. I quote the revised stanza from the second Woodhouse transcript (*W²* in Garrod's *Poetical Works*). After hearing the new version, Woodhouse wrote to the publisher John Taylor (19 Sept. 1819): 'I do apprehend it will render the poem unfit for ladies, & indeed scarcely to be mentioned to them among the "things that are"'. Taylor replied six days later that, if Keats 'will not so far concede to my Wishes as to leave the passage as it originally stood, I must be content to admire his Poems with some other Imprint' (*Letters*, II, pp. 163, 183). According to Woodhouse's note heading one of the transcripts of the poem, Keats 'left it to his Publishers to adopt which [alterations] they pleased, & and to revise the Whole' (*W²*). [Ed.: In an appendix to his book, Wasserman puts forward an argument for establishing a new text of the poem, 'embodying revisions found in the late fair copy (Garrod's *E*) and those noticed as alterations (*w*) in the second Woodhouse transcript (*W²*)'.]

21. *Paradise Lost*, IV 800.

22. Ibid., IX 782–4.

23. *Letters*, II, p. 163.

24. Ibid., II, p. 174.

25. Ibid., I, p. 34.

26. Hampstead Keats, V, p. 309.

27. For example, the lame and anti-climactic justification, 'in sooth such things have been', as Porphyro's imagination expands from 'sight of Madeline, / But for one moment', to the progression 'speak, kneel, touch, kiss' [78–81]; the picture of Porphyro gazing on Angela 'Like puzzled urchin' [129]; and some of Porphyro's reactions, relayed with tongue in cheek by the narrator: 'The lover's endless minutes slowly pass'd' [182], 'lo! – how fast she slept' [252], 'It seem'd he never, never could redeem / From such a stedfast spell his lady's eyes' [286–7].

28. *Letters*, II, p. 80.

29. This is the version recorded in the W^2 transcript. In Ben Jonson's quatrain, quoted by Hunt from Brand's *Popular Antiquities* and often cited in notes to Keats's poem, the assurance that the ritual produces 'an *empty dream*' is worth recalling: see *Leigh Hunt's London Journal*, II (1835), p. 17.

30. *Hamlet*, IV vii 176–9. The point is made by Stuart M. Sperry Jnr, 'Madeline and Ophelia', *Notes and Queries*, new series, IV (1957), pp. 29–30.

31. Keats's conclusion seems a matter for unending debate. The metaphysical critics, remarking that the storm is 'an elfin-storm from faery land' and that the lovers 'glide, like phantoms' out of the castle, uniformly agree that Madeline and Porphyro transcend mortality, entering an otherworld of eternal felicity, while Angela, the Beadsman and the warriors remain to die or writhe benightmared. But the 'elfin-storm' is Porphyro's explanation; the narrator calls it 'a tempest fell' of 'frost-wind' and 'sharp sleet', and other critics – e.g., Amy Lowell, *John Keats* (Boston, Mass., 1925), II, p. 175; Herbert G. Wright, 'Has Keats's *Eve of St Agnes* a Tragic Ending?', *MLR*, XL (1945), pp. 90–4; Bernice Slote, *Keats and the Dramatic Principle* (Lincoln, Neb., 1958), pp. 35–6 – have suggested that the lovers face reality, perhaps even perish, in the storm. Still another view – Wright, op. cit., p. 92 – is that the lovers face penance in 'that second circle of sad hell', the circle of carnal sinners in the fifth canto of Dante's *Inferno*, in which (as Keats described in his sonnet 'On a Dream') lovers are buffeted about in a storm very much like the one in *The Eve of St Agnes*. It is possible that Porphyro is evil only to the extent that Madeline is a hoodwinked dreamer: that when she awakens from her dream the evil represented by him is correspondingly reduced, and a happy human conclusion is justified. But it seems doubtful, and one may at this point have to fall back on the remark of the publisher J. A. Hessey: '[Keats] is such a man of fits and starts he is not much to be depended on' – Edmund Blunden, *Keats's Publisher* (London, 1936), p. 56; or that of Haydon: 'never for two days did he know his own intentions' – *The Diary of Benjamin Robert Haydon*, ed. Willard B. Pope (Cambridge, Mass., 1960), II, p. 317. Whatever the fate of the lovers, Woodhouse noted that Keats 'altered the last 3 lines to leave on the reader a sense of pettish disgust. . . . He says he likes that the poem should leave off with this Change of Sentiment' (*Letters*, II, pp. 162–3).

32. When I read an earlier version of this paper before the English

Faculty of the University of Illinois, it was suggested that if Porphyro awakens Madeline to reality, he should be considered an agent of good in Keats's terms. It may be observed, however: 1. that Madeline dreams through the consummation; and 2. that Porphyro does not necessarily represent all aspects of reality, or even one aspect consistently throughout the poem. Contradiction arises mainly from the assumption of allegory.

33. A variant following line 68 (*Poetical Works*, ed. Garrod, p. 451).

34. Ibid., p. 205.

35. I use the term 'dip' advisedly. Moneta is speaking more narrowly of *poet*-dreamers, and part of the condemnation occurs in a passage that Woodhouse thought Keats 'intended to erase'.

36. Glen O. Allen, 'The Fall of Endymion: A Study in Keats's Intellectual Growth', *Keats-Shelley Journal*, VI (1957), pp. 35–57; he argues authoritatively that the change occurred during the winter of 1817–18, while Keats was completing and revising *Endymion*. David Perkins, *The Quest for Permanence* (Cambridge, Mass., 1959), p. 220, feels that 'the over-all course of [Keats's] development might be partly described as a periodic, though gradually cumulative, loss of confidence in the merely visionary imagination'.

37. *Letters*, I, pp. 215, 221, 262, 243.

38. Ibid., I, p. 325.

39. Ibid., II, p. 234.

Walter E. Houghton   The Meaning of
The Eve of St Mark   (1946)

Most criticism of *The Eve of St Mark* has been sterile because it has been out of touch with the poem, busy with popular superstitions about St Mark's Eve; with speculation about how the narrative was to develop, or how the hypothetical story was to express Keats's personal relations with Fanny Brawne; or with the later use of similar names and images in 'The Cap and Bells'. Such matters, of course, can be of real critical value, but only in so far as they are brought to bear upon the actual text, and their relevance is determined by the fresh insight, if any, that they yield. Yet these controlling principles have been largely ignored, with the result that scholarship has either distracted attention from the poem or distorted its meaning.

Where, on the other hand, the focus has been on the text, the results have been better, but still not adequate, because criticism has not gone beyond or below the 'pictorial beauties'. No one has asked if and how the various pictures are inter-related, or what kind and quality of mood they induce, or whether under the surface details there is not a unifying concept.

By its form as well as by its pictorial character, *The Eve of St Mark* has been peculiarly exposed to both these critical hazards. In form, it is a fragment, and apparently the introduction to a romance. On 14 February 1819, Keats wrote to his brother and sister:

In my next packet, . . . I shall send you my Pot of Basil, St Agnes' eve, and if I should have finished it a little thing called the 'eve of St Mark'[. Y]ou see what fine Mother Radcliffe names I have–it is not my fault–I do not search for them.[1]

Eight months later he again took up the poem and copied it out, in a letter to the same correspondents, '[as] far as I have gone'. He did not know, he said, whether he should ever finish it.[2]

Given the fragmentary form, plus a title at once suggesting analogy with the legend already used for *The Eve of St Agnes*, and the direction of most criticism is predetermined. It first appears in a letter from Dante Gabriel Rossetti to H. B. Forman, published by the latter in 1883:

I copy an extract which I have no doubt embodies the superstition in accordance with which Keats meant to develope his poem. It is much akin to the belief connected with the Eve of St Agnes.

'It was believed that if a person, on St Mark's Eve, placed himself near the church-porch when twilight was thickening, he would behold the apparition of those persons in the parish who were to be seized with any severe disease that year, go into the church. If they remained there it signified their death; if they came out again it portended their recovery.'[3]

This note was followed by another after Rossetti, sometime later, had pounced on a passage in Keats's letters to Fanny Brawne. Keats had said, 'I could write a Poem which I have in my head, which would be a consolation for people in such a situation as mine. I would show some one in Love as I am, with a person living in such Liberty as you do.'[4] To Rossetti the poem referred to – though there is no evidence – was almost certainly 'none other than the fragmentary *Eve of St Mark*'.[5] And so at once he coupled this letter with the superstition – and got the story:

> By the light of the extract . . . I judge that the heroine – remorseful after trifling with a sick and now absent lover – might make her way to the minster-porch to learn his fate by the spell, and perhaps see his figure enter but not return.[6]

In Claude Finney's opinion this is the key to the complete poem as planned, and he thinks Rossetti's conjecture confirmed by all that we now know of Keats's state of mind and body in February 1819, as well as in August 1820, when the letter was apparently written – very jealous, confined to his room with a sore throat, with Fanny going to a round of balls.[7]

All this speculation would be harmless enough except for the fact that once we read these notes, then we start reading the actual poem, almost in spite of ourselves, in the light of an unwritten and quite hypothetical story. After all, in the poem Bertha is not in love and not remorseful, and not remotely interested in who is or is not entering the cathedral. She is fascinated by a legend, but it is not the legend of St Mark's Eve; it is the legend 'Of Saintè Markis life and dethe'. But ever since 1883 thousands of readers, faced with these notes, especially that on the superstition, in almost every edition, scholarly or textbook, have been persuaded to look hard for something which is not there, with the result that very few, I suspect, have been able to see what is there. What happened to a professional like Sidney Colvin must surely have happened to many an amateur: his knowledge of the superstition caused him unconsciously to apply to the fragment what is true, if at all, only of the poem as it might have been completed: 'Nearly allied with *The Eve of St Agnes*', he wrote in the popular English Men of Letters series, 'is *the fragment* in the four-foot ballad metre, *which Keats composed on the parallel popular belief* connected with the eve of St Mark'.[8]

It is true that Keats had this belief in his mind; that he wrote sixteen lines describing it in his own Middle English; and even that those sixteen lines have been placed between lines 98 and 99 by at least four distinguished scholars. But what are the facts? In 1906 Forman examined a holograph leaf from a scrapbook of Keats's (the so-called Sabin Scrapbook) which contained on one side lines 99–114 of the poem, and on the other side sixteen lines, also in 'Middle English', which had not been known before, and which gave a simplified account of the superstition.[9] This passage was on the righthand leaf, and thus made possible the assumption that it preceded the similar 'Middle English' passage on the reverse side, which begins at line 99 of the poem. Furthermore, there was a rejected reading of the last couplet which, had it been retained, would have made an easy transition to line 99:

> And everichon shall by the[e] go
> Truly mine auctour says it so.

After which supposedly, the poem continued, 'Als writith he of swevenis, . . .'

In 1913 there turned up a second MS. of *The Eve of St Mark* containing the extra lines, the second volume of the Woodhouse transcripts. Woodhouse had copied them from the Sabin leaf,[10] but he had not drawn any such conclusions as those suggested above. Instead, he had put them at the end after a blank space, separating them from the poem as it stands 'as if they were new verses which Keats had not interwoven into the text'.[11] And that is everything we know about the lines. They do not appear in either of the autograph MSS. of the poem; nor in any other transcript; nor in the first printed version by Lord Houghton in 1848.[12]

On the basis of these facts, what seems a sound conclusion? That the passage *belongs* after line 98 and should be printed there? By no means. That the passage *probably* belongs after line 98 and consequently may be printed there? Hardly. All that the evidence warrants, I think, is that Keats knew the legend and probably intended to work it into the poem; and – though this is more doubtful – that at one time he considered inserting the sixteen lines describing it after line 98, to be followed by lines 99–114, but thought better of it (for a reason suggested below), cancelled the final couplet that made the transition easy, and reversed the lines for possible insertion later on. Something like that seems a reasonable deduction. And Middleton Murry has come to much the same conclusion. After quoting the lines in a note to the poem, he said: 'This passage . . . appears to have formed no part of the original version. Possibly it marks an abandoned attempt to continue the poem in the autumn of 1819. Its chief value is that it confirms the established opinion as to the legend which Keats had in mind.'[13] Precisely: had in mind, but not in the original version.

Yet, strange as it seems, Forman and de Selincourt, Colvin and Garrod have all accepted the lines as part of the original poem. And still stranger, Forman and Colvin, for all their positive conclusions, have expressed the gravest doubts! Though Forman introduced the passage by saying, 'Here are the sixteen lines, which immediately precede line 99', only a moment before he was remarking that it was 'not of equal quality with what we had already', and that it 'may have been specially rejected, not merely dropped with the whole scheme of the unfinished poem'.[14] Colvin printed the passage after line 98 without any note of caution, when in point of fact he believed, as we learn from the general preface, that in the light of the Woodhouse transcript 'there is no certainty about this' – no certainty, that is, that it belonged in the text at all.[15] But unhappily there has been only certainty for hundreds of trusting readers of the poem who did not happen to read Colvin's preface. And now within the past few years both Garrod and Forman have even inserted the lines into the poem, Garrod at least numbering them with letters,[16] but Forman not giving the slightest indication of their very questionable status.[17] Since these scholars and their editions carry the greatest prestige, there is real danger that on far too shaky evidence the passage may become a permanent part of *The Eve of St Mark*, and thus make it still more difficult for the future readers to grasp the real meaning of the poem as it stands.

Other critics who have avoided the distractions mentioned above and looked directly at the text have adopted the aesthetic approach, accepting 'pictorial beauties' as the end and aim of the poem. 'What', asks George Ford in his [*Keats and the Victorians*], 'What is the fragmentary *Eve of St Mark* if not pure word-painting?', and he need not stay for an answer.[18] It was the Pre-Raphaelites and the critics trained in their school, notably Colvin and Amy Lowell, who have made that a commonplace of criticism.[19] We must 'not merely read', said Amy Lowell, 'but *see*, first the Minster square, then the panelled room . . .', on to the aesthetic conclusion that 'nothing matters here but the extraordinary beauty of the poem itself.'[20] In one respect, however, Amy Lowell went further. If she would not define the mood created by the pictures, nor yet look below the surface to the unifying idea, she saw that *The Eve of St Mark*, fragment though it is, was none the less a completed work of art. '*St Mark* ranks so high among Keats's works as to be the equal of any. . . . It is as nearly perfect of its kind as a poem can be. . . . There is not a redundant word, and not a word too few.' This is an exaggeration but at least it is the exaggeration of a truth. It points toward the poem and not away from it.[21] If we now turn to the text with the intention of analysing its 'wholeness', we may come closer to its meaning.

The Eve of St Mark is built on the principle of contrast. We are aware at once of two pictures, complementing each other. Outside is the cathedral town, the city streets washed by April rain, the tolling Sabbath bell, the people moving quietly to evensong, and the surrounding hills and valleys, green and chilly in early spring. Inside is a girl, sitting in a panelled room overlooking the minster-square, reading her book. Both pictures are not only sharply etched, they are also skilfully interwoven. After the shift to the inside [23–38], we glance back to the cathedral street through Bertha's window [39–47]; then return to her reading [at 48], until, as night comes down, we hear 'the still foot-fall of one returning homewards late', and notice that the clamorous daws are now asleep [57–66], before we turn back again to the room and the reading [67–119]. The important thing to notice, however, is that this contrast, when looked at organically, really disappears, because in the major and basic contrast which is at the core of the poem both outside and inside unite to support the same pole. And, indeed, Keats finally brought them together in lines 67–8:

All was silent, all was gloom,
Abroad and in the homely room:[22]

That suggests at once the opposite elements in the poem which are far from gloomy and homely, and so points to the real antithesis that underlies its meaning.

This is the juxtaposition, so dear to the romantics, of the near and familiar, the conventional and commonplace, with the strange, curious, and far-off, the visionary and the exotic. In the poem this contrast is given both pictorial and conceptual expression. Pictorially the initial setting – town and room and a heroine with the quite ordinary name of Bertha, staidly dressed in black and white – is mundane and contemporary. 'The dull and quiet Sunday evening represented', wrote William Bell Scott in 1885, 'is of our time in any cathedral town in England, not the Sunday evening of old when morning Mass was the religious observance, and the evening was spent in longbow and popinjay games and practice. . . . Every item of the description is modern.'[23] Every item, that is, except the 'curious volume' and the oriental screen. The volume is brilliant with medieval illumination of 'a thousand things' far-away and mysterious – saints and martyrs, the breastplate of Moses, a winged lion, and so on. This effect is reinforced by the later passage in 'Middle English' – by its very language, of course, as well as by what it says. And the closing reference to Venice, it should be noted, is to medieval Venice, when the body of St Mark was supposedly brought home from Alexandria by Venetian sailors. In creating the broad antithesis of past and present, Keats has used an effective distinction in color. The 'golden broideries' and 'golden mice', the 'fiery blaze' of martyrs, the 'azure saints in silver rays', the 'golden star, or dagger bright', with 'the tapers' shine at Venice', all have a brilliance and warmth, and a touch of unreal exaggeration, in comparison with which the quieter, cooler hues of green valleys and chilly faint sunset outside, and within, the gloomy chamber, presently streaked with shadows from 'the dismal coal', and Bertha's black dress, suggest the known and familiar life of a nineteenth-century town.

The romantic theme is then given fresh development, as in music, with the introduction into this 'homely room' of an oriental screen, as exotic as the manuscript. And the second image is not only linked to the first by the reference to 'Lima mice' (cf. the 'golden mice' of 38), but contrasted, like the first, with the near and commonplace when a macaw (who, by the way, is brilliantly colored, in addition to living far from England) is contrasted with Bertha's home-bred variety of parrot.

Finally, the theme undergoes a subtle modulation as the strange in the sense of the exotic passes into the strange in the sense of the fantastic, given a touch of the preternatural. After Bertha lights the fire,

> Her shadow, in uneasy guise,
> Hover'd about, a giant size,
> On ceiling-beam and old oak chair,
> The parrot's cage, and panel square; . . .
> . . .
> Glower'd about, as it would fill
> The room with wildest forms and shades,
> As though some ghostly queen of spades
> Had come to mock behind her back,
> And dance, and ruffle her garments black.   [73–6, 84–8]

The juxtaposition of fantasy and reality – related, as we shall see, to the conceptual meaning – rests not only on the contrast of the 'ghostly queen' with the 'maiden fair' [39], but also on that of the 'wildest forms and shades' with 'patient folk and slow' [20], with

> staid and pious companies,
> Warm from their fire-side orat'ries;
> And moving, with demurest air,
> To even-song, and vesper prayer.   [15–18]

In passing, we see again how the antiphonal notes of 'inside' and 'outside' become one note, like a base and treble C, in the larger and fundamental antithesis of the poem.

Beneath its pictorial embodiment, this antithesis is also expressed dramatically, and in terms which can be translated into an 'idea'. To see this we have to concentrate on Bertha, on the direction of her thinking and the circumstances of her life. 'All day long, from earliest morn', the volume has 'taken captive her two eyes', but by no means merely for its pictures or its romantic 'color'. She is reading the text (note 48, 83, 89), and the text is a medieval *Legenda Sanctorum*, that is, 'Readings in the Lives of the Saints'.[24] Bertha's mind is on 'saintly imageries' [56], on

> Martyrs in a fiery blaze,
> Azure saints in silver rays,   [31–2]

and above all on the Evangelist Mark, who was both saint and martyr. For this being his eve, her turning at last to St Mark is altogether natural; and the function of the eve in the poem as we have it is to suggest the legend, not the superstition. St Mark's lion is first mentioned [35], then his legend [52], which Bertha is reading as the daylight fails. Whereupon, too excited to stop, she strikes 'a lamp from the dismal coal' and continues:

> Untir'd she read the legend page,
> Of holy Mark, from youth to age,
> On land, on sea, in pagan chains,
> Rejoicing for his many pains.   [89–92]

Then follows the quotation from the MS., and as we *now* read it, we see that its rôle is by no means simply to reinforce the medieval atmosphere but rather to reiterate the theme of sainthood and martyrdom, and again to focus specifically on St Mark.

—'Als writith he of . . .
. . .
. . . how a litling child mote be
A saint er its nativitie,
Gif that the modre (God her blesse!)
Kepen in solitarinesse,
And kissen devoute the holy croce.
Of Goddes love, and Sathan's force, –
He writith; and thinges many mo:
Of swiche thinges I may not show.
Bot I must tellen verilie
Somdel of Saintè Cicilie,
And chieflie what he auctorethe
Of Saintè Markis life and dethe' :   [99, 103–14]*

St Cecilia, of course, is the Roman virgin who suffered martyrdom at the hands of Almachius, provost of Rome, in the third century. For St Mark's death I quote a passage from Caxton's version of *The Golden Legend*, which in future editions of Keats ought to displace, I think, the old quotation from Brand's *Antiquities* about St Mark's Eve:

Now it happened on Easter day, when S. Mark sang mass, they assembled all and put a cord about his neck, and after, drew him throughout the city, and said: Let us draw the bubale [the ox] to the place of bucale [the abattoir]. And the blood ran upon the stones, and his flesh was torn piecemeal that it lay upon the pavement all bebled. After this they put him in prison, where an angel came and comforted him, and after came our Lord for to visit and comfort him, saying: Pax tibi Marce evangelista meus. Peace be to thee Mark, mine Evangelist! be not in doubt, for I am with thee and shall deliver thee. And on the morn they put the cord about his neck and drew him like as

* [Ed.] In some editions, with the text of this part of the poem variant from that used by Houghton, the relevant line-references are 117, 121–32. (See Houghton's discussion, earlier in this article, of the MS. researches of 1906 and 1913.)

they had done tofore, and cried: Draw the bubale, and when they had drawn he thanked God and said: Into thy hands Lord, I commend my spirit, and he thus saying died. Then the paynims would have burnt his body, but the air began suddenly to change and to hail, lighten and thunder, in such wise that every man enforced him to flee, and left there the holy body alone. Then came the christian men and bare it away, and buried it in the church, with great joy, honour, and reverence. This was in the year of our Lord fifty-seven, in the time that Nero was emperor.

And it happed in the year of grace four hundred and sixty-six in the time of Leo the emperor, that the Venetians translated the body of S. Mark from Alexandria to Venice.[25]

That, or some similar passage, was exactly what Bertha's eyes finally fell upon:

> At length her constant eyelids come
> Upon the fervent martyrdom;
> Then lastly to his holy shrine,
> Exalt amid the tapers' shine
> At Venice, –   [115–19]*

The important thing to grasp is not merely that the theme of sainthood and martyrdom runs right through the poem, reaching its high point in the final lines, but also that Bertha's reaction is almost ecstatic. The book holds her captive, all day long and on into the night [26–7]; she is too excited to be tired [83, 89] and too enthralled to take her eyes off the page [115]; she rejoices for his many pains [92], that is, rejoices at the divine faith and the divine support which sustained St Mark in the midst of suffering; she pauses a moment, and looks up

> With aching neck and swimming eyes,
> And daz'd with saintly imageries.   [55–6]

There, so to speak, is the dream, the longing. And the reality? The humdrum life of a provincial town in nineteenth-century England, 'fill'd with patient folk and slow', shuffling by, to the

---

* [Ed.] Or lines 133–7.

church and home again, tomorrow and tomorrow and tomorrow; and Bertha looking out on the same minster which was once the animating center of what a different world. Could it be that the basic contrast of the poem is a tragic contrast, and that the ideal, the vision of saintly glory, is brought into pitiful contrast with the actual? Is there a tragic suggestion of frustration at the bottom of the poem? There are the lines (with my italics):

> All was silent, all was gloom,
> Abroad and in the homely room:
> Down she sat, *poor cheated soul!*
> And struck a lamp from the dismal coal;[26]   [67–70]

One thinks at once of the Prelude to *Middlemarch*, which I shall quote at some length, since it seems to me a most illuminating commentary on the poem:

> Who that cares much to know the history of man, . . . has not dwelt, at least briefly, on the life of Saint Theresa, has not smiled with some gentleness at the thought of the little girl walking forth one morning hand-in-hand with her still smaller brother, to go and seek martyrdom in the country of the Moors? Out they toddled from rugged Avila, wide-eyed and helpless-looking as two fawns, but with human hearts, already beating to a national idea; until domestic reality met them in the shape of uncles, and turned them back from their great resolve. That child-pilgrimage was a fit beginning. Theresa's passionate, ideal nature demanded an epic life; . . . fed from within, [she] soared after some illimitable satisfaction . . .
>
> That Spanish woman who lived three hundred years ago, was certainly not the last of her kind. Many Theresas have been born who found for themselves no epic life wherein there was a constant unfolding of far-resonant action; perhaps only a life of mistakes, the offspring of a certain spiritual grandeur ill-matched with the meanness of opportunity; perhaps a tragic failure which found no sacred poet and sank unwept into oblivion . . .
>
> Here and there is born a Saint Theresa, foundress of nothing, whose loving heartbeats and sobs after an unattained goodness tremble off and are dispersed among hindrances, instead of centring in some long-recognizable deed.

This is not to claim that Keats sat down with any such definite idea in his mind. Had he done so, the tragic note would have been more explicit and pointed, and not, as it is, implicit, felt more than recognised. What happened, I suspect, is pretty much what Eliot once described as a common occurrence. 'What is the experience', he asked, 'that the poet is so bursting to communicate?' And answered, 'By the time it has settled down into a poem it may be so different from the original experience as to be hardly recognisable. The ''experience'' in question may be the result of a fusion of feelings so numerous, and ultimately so obscure in their origins, that even if there be communication of them, the poet may hardly be aware of what he is communicating; and what is there to be communicated was not in existence before the poem was completed.'[27] Keats sat down, let us say, to write another romance on another superstition, this time St Mark's Eve. He began perhaps with nothing more specific in mind than to introduce the heroine, living near a cathedral. As he started writing, a number of 'feelings', to use Eliot's term, caught his imagination. He focused, as we know, on 'the sensation of walking about an old country Town in a coolish evening'.[28] Shifting inside, the same pictorial vision was turned on the room, and especially on the screen and the shadows. Then, as he sketched the heroine reading, the theme of martyrdom, suggested by St Mark, was introduced and gradually developed until it dominated the poem, not unconnected, in those obscure origins which Eliot speaks of, with his own death-wish on the one hand, and on the other, his sense of frustration. By the time he reached line 119 [sc. 137 – Ed.], Keats must have known that his 'introduction' had gone off on another tangent, unfitted now for the story he had planned. The legend of St Mark, and not of his Eve, had run away with him. If the sixteen lines written about the latter had ever actually gotten into the poem, after line 98, he now cut them out (they were clearly irrelevant), and left the fragment as it stood, a poem in its own right.[29]

I attach no value to this hypothetical reconstruction in itself. Its value is purely critical. It helps us to understand how the poem could have been written. It isolates and accounts for its limitations: the excessive attention given the screen, for though the screen harmonises with the exotic strain in the poem, it is not integral to the main theme of martyrdom; the amount of detail devoted to the shadows, for though, here again, to the extent that the shadows set up a contrast with Bertha and the townsfolk, they harmonise with the deeper suggestion of vision and reality, nevertheless they may be said to combine rather than to fuse with that suggestion; and finally the failure, partly for the reason just given, partly from its placing in the poem, to make the tragic implication sufficiently sharp. Are not these exactly the sort of deficiencies we might have predicted in a poem whose meaning evolved, in some way as I have conjectured, during the course of writing? Had Keats intended from the start to write the poem he did, he might have avoided them, or been more willing to rectify them. As it was he let them stand – with an apology: 'I hope you will like this', he said, 'for all its Carelessness',[30] a remark which, since it can hardly refer to the careful choice of diction and imagery, must refer to the form.

But the carelessness is not great. Though tempted toward a series of loosely connected pictures, Keats managed to fasten his imagination on a unifying principle, the romantic contrast of the familiar and the strange. He gave it embodiment in the figure of a modern girl in an English town reading medieval legends and dreaming of martyrdom. And he cut under the surface to suggest the human tragedy implicit in the situation.

SOURCE: article in *ELH: A Journal of English Literary History*, 13 (1946), pp. 64–78.

NOTES

[Numbering as in the original but with some abbreviations and revisions – Ed.]

1. *The Letters of John Keats*, ed. M. B. Forman (Oxford, 1931), II, p. 322.
2. Ibid., II, p. 453, under the date 20 Sept. 1819.
3. *The Poetical Works and Other Writings of John Keats*, ed. H. B. Forman (London, 1883), II, p. 320–1, in a note to the text.
4. *Letters*, II, p. 548, dated '[August 1820?]' by M. B. Forman.
5. *Poetical Works* (1883), II, p. 321.
6. Ibid. It is fair to note that Rossetti added a qualification (on p. 322): that the poem might not have been commenced with Fanny Brawne in

mind, but that, after beginning it, Keats probably saw how well the story would fit his own situation.

7. Claude L. Finney, *The Evolution of Keats's Poetry* (Boston, Mass., 1936), II, pp. 566–7.

8. Colvin, 'English Men of Letters' series (London, 1887), p. 164. The italics are mine.

9. The announcement was made by Forman in *The Bookman* of London, XXXI (Oct. 1906), pp. 16–17.

10. According to H. W. Garrod in his edition of *The Poetical Works of John Keats* (Oxford, 1939), p. 452 n., this is shown by Woodhouse's notes.

11. Finney, op. cit., II, p. 565; and cf. p. 708.

12. See the Garrod edition, p. 452 n. and p. 449 for a list of all the MSS.

13. J. Middleton Murry, *The Poems and Verses of John Keats* (London, 1930), II, p. 584.

14. See *The Poetical Works of John Keats*, ed. H. B. Forman (Oxford, 1906), and later editions, (p. 1); and under the reproduction of the holograph (1906 edn, facing p. 342), Forman wrote: 'A hitherto lost passage belonging between lines 98 and 99.'

15. Sidney Colvin, *The Poems of John Keats* (New York, 1915), II, p. 81, for the text; I, p. *xiv*, for the confession in the preface.

16. Garrod edition, op. cit., pp. 452–3.

17. *The Poetical Works and Other Writings of John Keats*, ed. H. B. and M. B. Forman (New York, 1938–39), IV, pp. 175–6.

18. George Ford, *Keats and the Victorians* (New Haven, Conn., 1944), p. 36.

19. Cf. Colvin, *Keats* (1887), op. cit., p. 165, where he finds the chief interest of the poem to lie in 'its pictorial brilliance and charm of workmanship', and goes on to draw the obvious connections with Rossetti and Morris, both of whom admired it greatly.

20. Amy Lowell, *John Keats* (Boston, Mass. and New York, 1925), II, pp. 327, 329. The quotation that follows is on p. 326.

21. This may also be said of Arlo Bates's remark, in *Poems by John Keats* (Boston, Mass. and London, 1896), p. 297: 'The completeness and harmony of the impression in this fragment are by no means the least of the wonders of Keats's poetry.'

22. Cf. Finney's interpretation, op. cit., II, p. 569, which, based on a slightly different reading, also records an impression of harmony rather than contrast: 'Here, as in *The Eve of St Agnes*, there is a series of enveloping settings; but here they create an effect of harmony instead of contrast. The bluish hills and "green vallies cold" enfold the silent streets of the cathedral town, filled with "patient folk and slow"; . . . and the silent streets . . . crowded with "staid and pious companies", enfold the silent room overlooking the minster-square.'

23. In a letter to Sidney Colvin, quoted in the latter's *John Keats: His Life and Poetry, His friends, Critics and After-Fame* (London, 1918), p. 440.

24. The most famous example of the type is the *Legenda Aurea*, compiled

by Jacobus de Voragine in the 13th century, subsequently translated and printed by Caxton in 1483, and by G. Ryan and H. Ripperger in 1941, as *The Golden Legend*. It contains 'Saintè Markis life and dethe' as well as an account of St Cecilia, mentioned by Keats in line 112 [sc. 130 – Ed.]. It is worth noticing that when Keats speaks of 'the *legend* of St Mark' [52] or 'the *legend* page of holy Mark' [89–90], he is using the word quite properly in the medieval sense to mean, not myth or fable (and therefore *not* the 'legend' or superstition of St Mark's Eve), but the actual story of St Mark.

25. *The Golden Legend, or Lives of the Saints, as Englished by William Caxton* (London, 1900), III, pp. 136–7.

26. Cf. what Yeats said of Synge's tragic heroes and heroines in his 'Preface to Synge's Poems and Translations', *Essays* (London and New York, 1924), p. 383: 'Person after person in these laughing, sorrowful, hcroic plays is, "the like of the little children do be listening to the stories of an old woman, and do be dreaming after in the dark night it's in grand houses of gold they are, with speckled horses to ride, and do be waking again in a short while and they destroyed with the cold, and the thatch dripping, maybe, and the starved ass braying in the yard".'

27. T. S. Eliot, *The Use of Poetry and the Use of Criticism* (London and Cambridge, Mass., 1933), p. 131.

28. *Letters*, II, p. 453 (20 Sept. 1819): journal letter to George and Georgiana Keats.

29. If at some future date a new letter or a new MS. should prove, despite all the present evidence to the contrary, that Keats's final intention was to use these lines after line 98, that would not change the meaning of the poem as it stands. It would only lessen its artistic value by lessening its coherence, and I should then add the passage to the list of limitations which I mention in the next paragraph.

30. *Letters*, II, p. 456 (20 Sept. 1819).

David Perkins 'Ambiguity of Theme and Symbol in *La Belle Dame sans Merci* and *Lamia*' (1959)

. . . One can discuss *La Belle Dame sans Merci* in connection with *Lamia* and so highlight parallels in theme and symbol. The union of the knight with La Belle Dame is one of Keats's many mortal-immortal pairings, and, as in *Lamia*, questions about the visionary imagination are posed in the equivocal character of the lady. The usual interpretation has been that La Belle Dame is Circe, cruelly leading men to their destruction. Lately, however, it has been argued that, since there is no indication that she wilfully banished the knight from her 'elfin grot', the union of the lovers is broken by the knight's own inability to retain the vision.[1] But the fact is that either interpretation may be maintained, or rather that the poem brings together both points of view as it mirrors a conflict in Keats's own mind.

The first three stanzas serve as an introduction, defining the tone of the poem and establishing the situation. It is a ballad with medieval trappings, but unlike the ballads of Scott, for example, it is an openly visionary poem. One feels that the action takes place not so much in some historical period as in a timeless realm of imagination. The speaker meets a knight-at-arms who is 'haggard', 'woe-begone', and even seems to be dying:

> I see a lily on thy brow,
>   With anguish moist and fever dew;
> And on thy cheeks a fading rose
>   Fast withereth too.

He asks 'what can ail' the knight, and the question expresses the naïve character of the speaker, puzzled at the deathly appearance of the knight and assuming that in the approach of winter he ought not to be 'palely loitering'. And, of course, the naïveté helps to create the overtly simple, fairy-tale atmosphere of the ballad. The questions also serve as a description, and the time of year has a loose metaphor significance. Not only summer but autumn, the fulfillment of the summer, is now over. Only winter and death remain. The poem then goes on to resolve those questions. The pallor of the knight turns out to be that of the 'pale kings', the 'pale warriors, death-pale' he sees in his dream, and he is loitering on 'the cold hill's side' in a vain wish to meet again the lady and re-enter her elfin grot.

After this introduction, the knight begins his tale. He 'met a lady in the meads'. She was an immortal, a 'faery's child'. He wooed her with flowers, and she him with song. She had all his attention so that he 'nothing else saw all day long', thus indicating his entire and whole-souled commitment to a life of vision. And the lady, in turn, 'look'd' at the knight 'as she did love,/ And made sweet moan' – 'as', of course, meaning 'as if', implying the impossibility of being sure of anything about this strange being from other world. Again, no more than the knight can the reader feel secure in interpreting the sweet moan which the lady made. It may be similar to the 'delicious moan' of the 'virgin-choir' in the *Ode to Psyche*, a song merely expressing her love, or it may also be a moan of sadness, implying, as the phrase 'sighed deep' two stanzas later may imply, the lady's own recognition that their union must be short-lived. The lady, says the knight,

> found me roots of relish sweet,
> And honey wild, and manna dew,
> And sure in language strange she said –
> 'I love thee true'.

The food here recalls the 'manna and dates' which Porphyro offers to Madeline in *The Eve of St Agnes*, but without going into nuances of symbolic implication suggested by this association, one need only point out that roots, honey and manna might be appropriate for a 'faery's child', but they would not provide much nourishment to a knight-at-arms. The lady's intentions may be loving, but the food she offers makes clear a radical difference in the character of the two lovers. The poem then suggests the consummation of their union in the elfin grot. The slumber of the mortal-immortal lovers at this point – 'and there I shut her wild wild eyes/ With kisses four'; 'And there she lulled me asleep' – represents the security and the paradoxical repose amid intensity Keats envisioned as an ideal.

To this point in the poem, everything has implied that the love affair cannot go on for very long, but there has been little reason to question that the lady's love is genuine. Even after having awakened upon 'the cold hill's side', the knight does not deny that she loved him. He remarks that 'she said – / "I love thee true"'', and seems to believe it. But she said it in 'language strange', so neither the reader nor the knight can really be sure about anything but the strangeness of the language. That is indeed the point. The lady is a 'faery's child'. One simply cannot be positive about her nature, for humanity cannot establish any certain contact with her. Yet even with this reservation in mind, the knight's account of the dream he had after being lulled asleep still remains puzzling.

> I saw pale kings, and princes too,
> Pale warriors, death-pale were they all;
> They cried – 'La belle Dame sans Merci
> Thee hath in thrall!'

> I saw their starved lips in the gloam,
> With horrid warning gaped wide,
> And I awoke and found me here,
> On the cold hill's side.

Whatever one makes of this dream, two things, at least, are reasonably certain. It breaks up the union of the lovers and the knight regrets it – 'Ah woe betide!' Secondly, it has its pernicious effect by picturing the desolation which will come with the knight's return to actuality. Indeed, the warning might be no more than that man cannot hold visionary experience for very long, and that when he awakens he becomes starved for lack of it. What is puzzling, however, is that the warning seems to be about the character of the lady, that she is sinister, cruel, without pity or mercy, and the poem has scarcely prepared the reader for this interpretation. These 'pale warriors' are exact equivalents of the pale 'knight-at-arms'. The phrase 'starved lips' certainly suggests that they too have been with the lady in her elfin grot, and are in that 'second circle of sad Hell' of the 'pale' lovers described in Keats's sonnet 'On a Dream', written the same month as *La Belle Dame*. The very fact that there are many with starved lips suggests the victims of a Circe. We may also remember that, in *Endymion*, Glaucus is caught by the 'cruel enchantress', Circe, in 'a net' of 'thraldom' [III 427]. The attitude toward

La Belle Dame then, seems to shift during the course of the poem, so that at the end one is tempted to infer that the knight has been deliberately seduced and then banished to the cold hillside to die. But the inference does not necessarily follow; and the poem is not only uncertain but a poem about uncertainty.

In *Lamia* an analogous story also resulted in ambiguity. Lycius, of course, resembles the knight as he is briefly drawn into an affair with a 'lady elf' or demon, and if Keats describes his plight with sympathy, he can also make use of Apollonius to voice a withering contempt. As in *La Belle Dame sans Merci*, the attitude to Lamia seems to shift through the course of the poem, revealing an irresolution in Keats himself. But as compared with the odes, at least, both *La Belle Dame* and *Lamia* embody a more settled state of mind. The doubt concerns only what attitude to take in exposing the visionary imagination. The escape it offers may be sweet but impossible to possess for very long. Or, as in *Lamia*, the condemnation may be sterner in character, emphasising that the vision deceives. The lover of vision may be only the innocent victim of his own quest for happiness, or he may be a fool as well. In any case, he is certain to become a 'wretched wight'. We may remember what Endymion comes to acknowledge:

> There never liv'd a mortal man, who bent
> His appetite beyond his natural sphere,
> But starv'd and died.   [IV 646–8]

The very opening of *Lamia* is in marked contrast with the *Ode on a Grecian Urn* and the *Ode to a Nightingale*. In these two odes, as in so much of Keats's earlier poetry, the desire or interest had been to bring together human life and the Greek pastoral or visionary world. Now, however, in the opening of *Lamia* the over-all effect is to distinguish sharply between them. For the poem begins with a pretty love affair between the god Hermes and a nymph. There are elements, in this little prefatory idyll, that suggest the sort of ideal union represented or symbolised by the recurrent pairs of lovers in Keats's earlier poems. The difference is that now the whole affair is relegated to a non-human realm. With it, to some extent, is also relegated the issue that was a central concern in so much of Keats's earlier poetry: the hope of waking from a dream to find it actual. There is almost the suggestion that this awaking to find it truth, this authenticating of the visionary imagination, takes place only in the realm of myth, where dream and actuality are interchangeable. So Hermes, desiring to find the nymph, at last sees her –

> It was no dream; or say a dream it was,
> Real are the dreams of Gods, and smoothly pass
> Their pleasures in a long immortal dream.   [I 126–8]

Indeed, the significance of this episode, as Mr Wasserman has said, is that the human world does not in any way participate in it.[2] By implication, the affair between Hermes and the nymph suggests the impossibility of any such fulfillment in the human world of process and mortality. This prefatory episode can have little purpose otherwise. It has no necessary, organic connection with the story that follows. In a rather artificial way, it is used to introduce the main story. But it is then dismissed.

We can only assume that this half-playful, slightly mocking idyll is to highlight, by contrast, the principal narrative. And the narrative that follows, whatever else can be said of it, is an exploration of the nature of illusion, and of the effect of disillusion on the human imagination. Significantly, none of the principal characters is a thoroughly desirable type. Lamia, the immortal serpent-woman, is no stable embodiment of the ideal: she is a shifting, evanescent thing, liable to vanish before the cold light of reason. Lycius, her mortal lover, is far from Shakespearean, to say the least; he has little to characterise him except an extraordinary capacity for wish-fulfillment, a desire to retreat with his vision, and a lack of flexibility. And the third principal character, Lycius's old tutor, Apollonius, whose sharp-eyed gaze penetrates to

Lamia's true identity, makes her vanish by doing so, and thus indirectly kills his equally humorless pupil, has, aside from a certain dignity, only negative virtues to recommend him. He is free from illusions – at least of the visionary sort. But there is nothing positive; and he is almost as far as Lycius from approaching the ideal of the 'mighty and miserable Poet of the Human Heart', of which Keats spoke shortly before beginning *Lamia*. There is, however, this difference. Whatever Apollonius represents cannot be disregarded. It must in some way be faced and subsumed.

Lamia is not quite of the same order as the god Hermes. But she is able to take on some of the same properties; and similarities are suggested. The god is described in terms of astronomical or heavenly images – 'star of Lethe' or 'bright planet' – and possesses a 'serpent rod'. Lamia is equally associated with astronomical images – for example, her 'silver moons', 'mooned body's grace', 'stars', and 'starry crown'. The fact that Hermes and Lamia can each grant the love aspirations of the other suggests another similarity. But Lamia desires a mortal. She thus becomes a revised model of a familiar symbol – the immortal lady whose sexual union with a mortal symbolises the human yearning to retain forever the apex of passionate intensity. She is La Belle Dame sans Merci, the 'faery's child', and so is described as a 'lady elf', as having 'elfin blood', and as lingering 'faerily' by the roadside. The moon imagery links her with Cynthia. But she is also a serpent, which is to say that Cynthia has now become a serpent. In view of the many Miltonic echoes scattered through the poem, we may feel that, as a serpent, Lamia even suggests Satan.[3] At least, the Lamia theme may have attracted Keats because the serpent would be associated, however unconsciously, with temptation. Also Lamia is a 'cruel lady' (though kind to the woodland nymph) with a 'Circean head', and the reference to Circe suggests that she lures and seduces men to their own destruction.

But at least in the first part of the poem, she is described in a tone tinged with mockery. Hermes, for example, addresses her as a 'beauteous wreath' and the periphrasis certainly shades into satire. The poet describes her as a grotesquerie:

Striped like a Zebra, freckled like a pard,
Eyed like a peacock, and all crimson barr'd.   [I 49–50]

The quick, college-cheer movement of the verse, the incongruity of the menagerie, and the kaleidoscope of color all define an attitude toward her. Moreover, her array of patterns and colors, 'golden, green, and blue', shifts, flickers and dazzles as she breathes, and together with her over-lavish collection of other ornament her 'silver moons' and her 'crest . . . Sprinkled with stars', it does not seem to be a highly tasteful display. She reminds one of a burlesque dancer. These wonders are topped by the bizarre absurdity of the mingling of woman and serpent.

Her head was serpent, but ah, bitter-sweet!
She had a woman's mouth with all its pearls complete.   [I 59–60]

This is not far from caricature if one tries to visualise it; and the mocking humor is delicately enforced by calling attention to the 'complete' set of 'pearls' or teeth in her mouth. On the whole, this tone is maintained throughout the first half of the poem. Significantly, Keats, in opposition to his earlier antipathy to the style of Dryden and Pope, is now taking Dryden as a model. The gusto of Dryden, and his gift for ridicule, are caught up here, and they accentuate the ironic detachment. At the outset, then, the poet pictures Lamia as altogether mixed with contrarieties, and her ultimate attractions as highly ambiguous.

In her 'serpent prison-house' Lamia was able to dream 'of all she list', and 'once, while among mortals dreaming thus,/ She saw the young Corinthian Lycius'. She 'fell into a swooning love of him', and wants to make her dream a reality. Having adopted a woman's form, she is now 'a maid/ More beautiful' than any human maiden. She is paradoxically

A virgin purest lipp'd, yet in the lore
Of love deep learned to the red heart's core:

Not one hour old, yet of sciential brain
To unperplex bliss from its neighbour pain.   [I 189–92]

She seems to offer, that is, an escape from process to a pure bliss, unmingled with sorrow. Having stationed herself by the road side, she calls to Lycius as he walks by, and he turns to her, at once seized with wonder and passion:

For so delicious were the words she sung,
It seem'd he had lov'd them a whole summer long:
And soon his eyes had drunk her beauty up,
Leaving no drop in the bewildering cup.   [I 249–52]

Here are the familiar symbols, song, summer and wine, so frequently associated, as in the *Ode to a Nightingale*, with the movement into the world of vision. In this case, of course, the 'bewildering cup' of Lamia's beauty merely suggests the wine symbolism. Lycius recognises her as a 'goddess' or immortal. The situation now begins to repeat the established pattern. Lycius fears that instead of his becoming united with the vision it will fade from his human eyes, and begs Lamia to stay:

For pity do not this sad heart belie –
Even as thou vanishest so shall I die.   [I 259–60]

But Lamia, 'growing coy', reminds him that immortals cannot live in the human world 'where no joy is, – Empty of immortality and bliss'. And when she pretends to say farewell, Lycius, like the 'pale warriors' of *La Belle Dame sans Merci*, turns pale and swoons away. This fit of oblivion, of course, represents the death Lycius prophesied if Lamia should vanish. So far the encounter has pursued the course of *La Belle Dame sans Merci*.

The difference is that Lamia has been 'coy'. The 'cruel lady' now

Put her new lips to his, and gave afresh
The life she had so tangled in her mesh.   [I 294–5]

Lycius thus revived, Lamia 'threw the goddess off', and declared herself to be a mortal lady dwelling in Corinth. It might seem that at this point Lycius has died out of process into an immortal bliss. Similarly, the goddess has put off immortality to become a woman. But one recalls the serpentine nature of Lamia and the delicate mockery with which she is described. Moreover, Lycius is not an immortal about to fade into the 'green-recessed woods'. Instead, he has only swooned; and he will shortly return to Corinth. Similarly, Lamia has put on only the shape and appearance of a woman, but her nature remains untransmuted. She retains her magical powers, and by a spell reduces the distance to Corinth to a few paces.

In other words, the union of Lamia and Lycius is not an actual experience of what is desired. Only in the subjective imagination of Lycius does the situation seem to enact the ideal permanence, just as the love of Hermes and the nymph exists only in the pastoral world, the age-old repository of human wish-fulfillment. When Lycius and Lamia come to Corinth, they take for their dwelling a house where 'none but feet divine / Could e'er have touched'. Like the 'unheard' melodies of the *Ode on a Grecian Urn*, this house represents a withdrawal into purely imaginative activity; for it is known only by Lycius. Other human beings cannot see it, and when subsequently the wedding guests arrive, they

> enter'd marveling: for they knew the street,
> Remember'd it from childhood all complete
> Without a gap, yet ne'er before had seen
> That royal porch, that high-built fair demense.   [II 152–5]

As a mortal, Lycius must live in Corinth. He cannot escape to the Cretan Elysium where Hermes found his nymph. But he can live in Corinth wholly engaged with his own fantasies and without sharing the life around him, and that is what he does. In short, Lycius is a 'dreamer', to borrow the vocabulary of *The Fall of Hyperion*, seeking to become thoughtless or unaware in the fond haven of an unreal paradise, and the poem explores the consequences of such a life. Now as long as the dream is at least partially recognised as only a dream, and in the privacy of the imagination cherished and protected from the intrusion of fact or truth, it can be maintained and enjoyed. As soon as actual human life is vividly represented, it exposes the falsehood of the dream and destroys it. At first, Lycius seems to half-realise that he is indulging a dream. As he enters Corinth with Lamia he endeavors not to be seen – 'Muffling his face, of greeting friends in fear'. In particular, he fears the sharp eyes of Apollonius. Even to look at Apollonius as he comes near makes Lycius uneasy; for 'he seems / The ghost of folly haunting my sweet dreams'.

The character of Apollonius, the philosopher, has probably provoked most of the critical disagreement about the poem. A traditional view was that he represents science or 'consequitive reasoning' dispelling imagination, and the passage beginning 'Do not all charms fly / At the mere touch of cold philosophy?' can be cited:

> Philosophy will clip an Angel's wings,
> Conquer all mysteries by rule and line,
> Empty the haunted air, and gnomed mine –
> Unweave a rainbow, as it erewhile made
> The tender-person'd Lamia melt into a shade.   [I 234–8]

But to interpret the poem in these terms is to make the unwarranted assumption that, if a poem contains a passage of abstract statement, this passage necessarily summarises the poem. The same notion has vitiated much criticism of the *Ode on a Grecian Urn*, in which the poem has been tortured to make it reveal how or in what sense the urn demonstrates that 'Beauty is truth'. More recently, critics have pointed out that, however harsh and crabbed Apollonius may be, he is not for that reason the villain of the poem, for Lycius himself is illuded and a dreamer. Both these interpretations are helpful but incomplete. The important point is that within the poem Apollonius is penetrating and Lycius deceived. Lamia is, after all, a serpent, and however loving she may be, she still preys on him, as Apollonius says, by absorbing him to the point that he is incapable of any wider concern. Hers is a frightened, selfish love that would keep its object from growing up in order to continue to possess it. And one might add that from the start Lycius has no chance against this 'Virgin . . . in the lore / Of love deep learned to the red heart's core'. We know from the letters that Keats was increasingly tending to equate philosophy with truth at the expense of poetry:

Though a quarrel in the Streets is a thing to be hated, the energies displayed in it are fine . . . This is the very thing in which consists poetry; and if so it is not so fine a thing as philosophy—For the same reason that an eagle is not so fine a thing as a truth.[4]

Again, at the very time he was writing *Lamia*, he said in another letter: 'I am convinced more and more every day that (excepting the human friend Philosopher) a fine writer is the most genuine Being in the World.'[5] But *Lamia* does not contrast the philosopher with the poet; it contrasts him only with the visionary poet or dreamer.

Apollonius, then, represents a clear though perhaps a single-eyed view of reality. In fact, symbolism of eyes is important in the poem. The vision of Lycius is filled and intoxicated by Lamia:

> his eyes had drunk her beauty up,
> Leaving no drop in the bewildering cup,
> And still the cup was full.   [I 251–3]

Lycius is 'blinded' [I 347], or looks solely into Lamia's 'open eyes, / Where he was mirror'd small in paradise' [II 46–7]. 'Ah, Goddess, see / Whether my eyes can ever turn from thee', he says [I 257–8]. Her existence increasingly depends on the complete subjective commitment of his eyes to her, which also permits him to see himself mirrored. Only when at the feast he takes his eyes from Lamia to look at Apollonius does Lamia begin to vanish; for at this point, as we shall see, only Apollonius, of all the people at the feast, remains fixed in the realities of mortal existence, refusing to enter or share the dream:

By her glad Lycius sitting, in chief place,
Scarce saw in all the room another face,
Till, checking his love trance, a cup he took
Full brimm'd, and opposite sent forth a look   [II 239–42]

to his old teacher. In contrast to Lycius, Apollonius has 'sharp
eyes', or 'quick eyes' or 'eyes severe' [I 364, 374; II 157]. To
the dreamer they are 'juggling eyes', or 'demon eyes' to be
threatened with 'blindness', for they banish the dream with
their unilluded gaze:

the sophist's eye,
Like a sharp spear, went through her utterly,
Keen, cruel, perceant, stinging.   [II 299–301]

It is true that Apollonius appears as a character of sour
disposition. Of course, one could argue that, if he is now harsh
to the dreamer, he had previously been a 'trusty guide / And
good instructor' to Lycius. Moreover, he is seen, to some
extent, through the dreamer's eye. But if he is crabbed, that is
also partly the attitude of the poem to what he represents. The
dreams are sweet, but they are still folly, and however
unpleasant, Apollonius's is the completely unilluded
perception. To quote from *Hyperion*, he to some extent
represents 'the pain of truth, to whom 'tis pain'. Keats is
posing an unhappy dilemma, but it is not the core of the poem.
Instead, the poem is largely about the consequences of being a
dreamer.

The second part of the poem begins with a 'doubtful'
conundrum. In keeping with the attitude to reality reflected in
the poem, the actual passion of mortals is 'love in a hut, with
water and a crust'. The love of 'faery land' is 'love in a
palace'. Neither is satisfactory, but 'perhaps at last' the love of
faery land is 'More grievous torment than a hermit's fast'[II 1–
5]. The poem then presents Lamia and Lycius enjoying their
bliss. The time is summer and they lie upon a couch, reposing

Where use had made it sweet, with eyelids closed,
Saving a tythe which love still open kept,
That they might see each other while they almost slept.   [II 23–5]

This, of course, is the familiar slumberous repose of Keats's mortal-immortal lovers. But Lycius hears the sound of trumpets, which carries his thoughts out of this 'purple lined palace' and 'into the noisy world almost forsworn'. Lamia, 'ever watchful',

> Saw this with pain, so arguing a want
> Of something more, more than her empery
> Of joys.   [II 35–7]

Having recollected the varied life of the human world, Lycius begins to find the dream insufficiently satisfying by itself. Inevitably, he wishes to convert the dream to an actuality in his human life, where Apollonius walks. To translate this into the symbolism of the poem, he and Lamia have been living in 'sweet sin', but he now wants to marry her and to have her take a place beside him in his mortal life, together with other companions and interests. As this desire reveals, he has begun to confuse the dream with reality. Up to now, he has not asked Lamia her name, 'ever thinking thee', as he says, 'Not mortal, but of heavenly progeny,/ As still I do'. But he now treats her as a mortal woman, brow-beating her, and asking whether she has 'any mortal name' or any 'kinfolk'. The questions are similar to the questions addressed to the Grecian urn – 'What men or gods are these' – and bespeak the same state of mind; for, as I mentioned, the poet, as the *Ode on a Grecian Urn* begins, has confused 'marble men and maidens' with 'deities or mortals', and the initial confusion of imaginative vision with earthly reality tends, at the end, to make for a sharper distinction between them. In *Lamia*, however, Keats reaches further. By confusing dream and reality, the dreamer, who is to have an unhappy end, brings them together. Confronted with actuality, the dream is inevitably dispelled. By contrast with the heart's illusion, reality appears meager and crabbed. Meanwhile, the dreamer, having lived so long with his illusion, has become incapable of dwelling in the actual human world. He cannot bear mortal life as it really is, and crumples at the impact.

It is unnecessary to trace the further development of the poem in detail. Lycius decides on a wedding feast to which he will invite his fellow Corinthians. At the feast, things seem at first to go well. With the 'wine at flow', the garlands and the music of powerful instruments – all habitually associated with the paradise that is now viewed as an illusion – the guests seem to enter or share Lycius's state of mind. 'Every soul' is 'from human trammels freed', and Lamia appears 'no more so strange'. Only Apollonius remains surely fixed in human realities; but he is enough. When Lycius looks at him, as we have seen, the illusion begins to dissolve under the steady, withering eye of the philosopher. Finally it is destroyed, and Lycius dies.

Of course, Keats's early poetry had often depicted a similar situation. After his first dream-union with Cynthia, Endymion awakens into the life of process and is sore dissatisfied with it:

> all the pleasant hues
> Of heaven and earth had faded: deepest shades
> Were deepest dungeons; heaths and sunny glades
> Were full of pestilent light.   [*E.* I 691–4]

Also, shortly after Endymion decides that he has been deluded, has 'lov'd a nothing, nothing seen / Or felt but a great dream' [*E.* IV 637–8], he senses that he is going to die:

> Why, I have been a butterfly, a lord
> Of flowers, garlands, love-knots, silly posies,
> Groves, meadows, melodies, and arbour roses;
> My kingdom's at its death, and just it is
> That I should die with it.   [*E.* IV 937–41]

Numerous similar instances might be cited. For example, in the early epistle *To My Brother George*, Keats had written:

> Yet further off, are dimly seen their bowers,
> Of which, no mortal eye can reach the flowers;
> And 'tis right just, for well Apollo knows
> 'Twould make the Poet quarrel with the rose.   [43–6]

But if the conclusion of *Lamia* recalls these earlier passages, it does so in a sterner mood. The poet is no longer willing to 'quarrel with the rose' for the sake of visionary bowers. We may also recollect that in *The Fall of Hyperion*, where Keats projects himself directly as the protagonist, he almost dies on the steps because he has been a dreamer. In a sense, *Lamia* may be regarded as Keats's version of Wordsworth's

> farewell the heart that lives alone,
> Housed in a dream, at distance from the kind!
> Such happiness, whatever it be known,
> Is to be pitied, for 'tis surely blind.[6]

SOURCE: excerpted from *The Quest for Permanence: The Symbolism of Wordsworth, Shelley and Keats* (Cambridge, Mass., 1959; repr. 1965), pp. 260–76.

NOTES

[Slightly revised from the original – Ed.]

1. Earl R. Wasserman, *The Finer Tone: Keats's Major Poems* (Baltimore, Md., 1953; repr. 1967), pp. 74–7. Despite the disagreement here with the general tendency of his interpretation, I am indebted for numerous suggestions to Mr Wasserman's searching discussion of the poem.
2. Ibid., pp. 159–62.
3. Cf. the phrase 'serpent prison-house' [203] with Keats's marginalia in *Paradise Lost* [IX 179–91]: 'Satan having enter'd the Serpent, and inform'd his brutal sense – might seem sufficient – but Milton goes on . . . whose head is not dizzy at the possible speculation of Satan in the serpent prison?'
4. *Letters of John Keats*, ed. Hyder E. Rollins, 2 vols (Cambridge, Mass. and Cambridge, 1958), II, pp. 80–1.
5. Ibid., II, p. 139.
6. Wordsworth, 'Elegiac Stanzas, suggested by a Picture of Peele Castle', lines 53–6.

Mario L. D'Avanzo   'A Poem about Poetry and Imagination: *La Belle Dame sans Merci*'   (1967)

La Belle Dame sans Merci describes perfectly the poet's semicircular arc of imaginative ascent, fulfilment and decline into the world of reality. Within the poem we find almost all of Keats's recurrent metaphors describing the poetic process: metaphors used so economically because of the strict limitations of the ballad form, and so subtly that the meaning of the poem is not readily apparent. More than in any other single poem, [we] need the whole corpus of Keats's figures . . . to understand *La Belle Dame sans Merci* as a poem about poetry and imagination; for without that background, . . . the reader would most likely regard the poem as a mere excursion into balladry on Keats's part, rather than as a symbolic narrative about poetic experience. One of the most private of all of his poems, *La Belle Dame sans Merci* could only have been written at a point in his poetic career when all of the figures he had been habitually using recur as 'almost a Remembrance', albeit woven into new combinations.

The poet begins and ends with a stark picture of a dying season. The sedge, a common grass of marshes and swamps, has withered; no birds sing. We are thrust at once into the mutable world which the poet must recurrently endure after falling out of his imaginative trance. The wretched knight is presently experiencing the same pain felt by Endymion after his 'mad pursuing of the fog-born elf'. Both are lured into the desolate, thorny mire of reality: a purgatory whose landscape mirrors the desolation within Keats's disillusioned poets. Like the sedge, the knight is withered; like the speaker in the *Ode to a Nightingale*, forlorn; and like Lycius, anguished and deathly pale. If these other victimised mortals represent the poet, agonised by the world of reality, we may identify the knight-at-arms as a poet also.

And now the question: why a knight-at-arms? We should remember that all Keats's heroes in search of poetic insight are characterised as royal Apollonian in feature and manner, visionary wanderers, and lovers. Endymion, for example, is not only a shepherd and pastoral poet, but also a 'prince' [*E*. II 227]. Lycius, too, springs from royal lineage. Both he and Endymion, are charioteers and, therefore, identified as Apollo figures. As lovers, both dedicate themselves to poetry, represented as a woman. The knight-at-arms is like Endymion and Lycius. We may regard him as a latter-day Calidore in Keats's poetry: a youthful wayfarer on a quest; an altruist who hopes to serve humanity but, unhappily, seems to have forsworn his duty as he falls under the strange power of the beautiful lady without pity; a courtier who in the courtly fashion of his age dedicates his love to this lady without the slightest hope that she will requite it. We should also bear in mind that, as a rule, the medieval knight in France played the important role of the troubadour. As artist he achieved excellence in his poetry through the inspiration of love. Thus his lady's beauty finds its mirror in the troubadour's poem.

Further, we must pay special attention to the pastoral setting of the poem for it contributes significantly to our identification of the knight as a poet and to our reading of the poem as a symbolic statement of the knight's initiation into poetic experience. The youthful, questing poet-knight meets his beautiful lady in the isolation of the meads. If we may assume that Keats's choice of character has a wider significance than has been recognised, we may say the same for his choice of setting. Traditionally, the first poetry written by novice troubadours are pastorals set in meadows and fields. These poets often sing plaintively of their ill-fortuned love of an indifferent mistress. We may with some justification, therefore, identify the knight as a pastoral poet, an Endymion figure, who ascends to the heights of imaginative vision under the inspiration of La Belle Dame sans Merci. Keats's subtle characterisation of the knight as the poet demonstrates once more the ingenuity with which his poetry ' "load[s] every rift" of [its] subject with ore'. Critics have failed to see the weighty implications in Keats's choice of a knight-at-arms as a character. Earl R. Wasserman, for example, provides a much too simple explanation of Keats's choice of a knight as his hero. He claims correctly that 'all mortals who engaged in "Imagination's struggles" are knights-at-arms', but fails to see the several other reasons, noted herein, for the appropriateness of a knight as the character of the poet.

In stanza four, the knight-at-arms begins his narrative account of how he has arrived at the mental and physical state described in the first three stanzas. Quite by chance he has met a lady whose beauty and singing enthral him almost immediately. Like Lamia, she is born 'a faery's child' and sings 'A faery's song'. We associate her with the light and winged elfin, poetic imagination. In calling attention to her 'wild eyes' and long hair, Keats refers to two particular physical characteristics of his other women-muses which repeatedly fascinate and charm the admiring poet. For example, the beauty of Cynthia's abundant 'golden tresses' inspires him to the poetic frenzy and leads him to enthralment:

                                    she had,
    Indeed, locks bright enough to make me mad;
    And they were simply gordian'd up and braided.   [*E.* 1 612–14]

A part of the loveliness of Keats's poetic vision in *Sleep and Poetry* involves the muses, 'Parting luxuriant curls' [334], 'Dancing their sleek hair into tangled curls' [150], and 'sing[ing] out and sooth[ing] their wavy hair' [180]. Indeed, sleep itself is described as the 'Silent entangler of a beauty's tresses' [15]. These examples demonstrate that a woman's tresses are recurrently associated with imaginative inspiration and imaginative vision. La Belle Dame's long hair very subtly identifies her as a companion to Cynthia and the muses.

But this subtle linkage of image (wavy hair) and idea (poetic experience) does not end here. The connection is rooted in Keats's Apollo-worship. On many occasions he tends to identify himself as that ideal poet he was striving to become, as for example, in the writing of the two Hyperion fragments and in *Sleep and Poetry*, where he might die and follow the 'great

Apollo / Like a fresh sacrifice' [59–60]. One of the most prominent features of the god's beauty, as Lemprière points out, lies in his 'long hair', a detail which seems to have continually fascinated Keats. *Hyperion*, for example, mentions Apollo's 'golden tresses famed / Kept undulation round his eager neck' [*H*. III 131–2]. By a process of association in Keats's mind, this particular feature of the god finds its way into other poems describing poetry and imagination. Apollo's wavy hair and chariot figure prominently in the short poem, 'On Leaving Some Friends at an Early Hour', which recounts Keats's initial imaginative visions dancing before his eyes as he begins to write. The images of 'wavy hair' and 'pearly car', which allude to Apollo and his chariot, are clearly linked with inspiration. Passing across Keats's inward eye, they excite him to 'write down a line of glorious tone'. Apollo's curly hair, associated with the controlling idea of poetry and imagination, and carrying secondary connotations of beauty, fertility, youth and vigor, is transferred to La Belle Dame. She becomes in this poem the female presider of poetry.

The beautiful lady's 'wild' eyes also prove to be a significant detail. They suggest not only the Maenad-like frenzy of the Apollonian priestesses, but also the untamed energy of imagination which the knight is attempting to subdue. Her wildness seems closely associated with the frantic and violent nature of Lamia in the process of metamorphosing from serpent to woman:

> her elfin blood in madness ran,
> . . .
> Her eyes in torture fix'd, and anguish drear,
> Hot, glaz'd, and wide, with lid-lashes all sear,
> Flash'd phosphor and sharp sparks, without one cooling tear.
>
> [*L*. I 147, 150–2]

Such virulence and yet beauty in the same woman suggest the ambiguous nature of the imagination as it inspires and at the same time destroys the poet. Like Lycius, the knight attempts to tame this wildness in his beautiful lady, with the direst results.

If stanza four describes the initial confrontation of knight and lady and suggests her bewitching physical appearance, stanza five pictures the knight being progressively drawn to her by her beauty and singing. Significantly, the lady begins to sing her 'faery's song' only after the knight places her on his 'pacing steed'. With the perfect fixity of the poet in trance, his eyes are trained on the regularly moving, singing lady 'all day long'. This first of two deeds which the knight performs for the lady, placing her on his steed, appears to lead directly to his trance and to her singing. One notes the use of the conjunction 'for', suggesting this cause and effect relationship. Stanza four, in effect, speaks metaphorically of the poet's curbing his wild imagination by metre. Keats here revives one of his recurrent metaphors for poetry, the steed, whose regular pace in other poems served as a figure for metrical regularity. Note that the lady is 'set', not 'put' or 'placed', on the steed. Keats's diction is extremely precise here, for the word used denotes that which is regulated or put in order. Having been 'set' or regularised temporally by the poet, the imagination, in consequence, sings. And while she sings, the poet becomes charmed by what he has put in order and set into motion.

The poet-knight takes an active part in the process that is enthralling him. He weaves a garland in honor of her, just as Endymion weaves his flowers 'dyingly' to Cynthia. We may interpret the garland as either the woven poem or the poetic coronal. In either reading, his act seems to parallel Endymion's worshipful indulgence to his imagination. The poet states to Cynthia:

No one but thee hath heard me blithely sing
And mesh my dewy flowers all the night.
No melody was like a passing spright
If it went not to solemnize thy reign. . . .   [*E.* III 156–9]

With equal devotion, the transfixed knight-at-arms offers to his lady 'bracelets' and 'fragrant zone', as well as his woven garland. One may question the appropriateness of the first two of these gifts to the overall theme of the poem. They subtly suggest that the knight would bind and hold forever his evanescent imagination; for, like Lycius and Endymion, he hopes for a permanent intensity of poetic passion in the arms of La Belle Dame. Sadly, the knight's attempt fails, as the first three stanzas indicate. His suffering and haggardness may be attributed to the loss of his passion as his beautiful lady fades and disappears.

La Belle Dame takes his gifts and returns the knight's fixed glance 'as she did love', while at the same time making 'sweet moan'. Her plaintive yet paradoxically beautiful utterances suggest that in the very temple of the poet-knight's imaginative delights, melancholy has her sovereign shrine; for the beautiful lady of imagination provides not only the transcendent pleasures of poetic experience but also its inevitable pains, both suggested in the word 'moan'. Before she vanishes, the knight knows an ever-ascending series of delights in love, that is, imaginative feeling. Its inevitable decline, thrusting the knight back into the world of reality, seems anticipated in La Belle Dame's making 'sweet moan'. We should recall a like utterance from Lamia, who fills her palace of poetry with moans 'as fearful the whole charm might fade' [*L.* II 124]. And yet the grammatical structure of stanza five suggests that the beautiful lady, like Circe, is wilfully deceiving the knight. The line, 'She look'd at me as she did love' expresses the conditional and should read, 'She look'd at me as *if* she did love'; she seems to be practising a feminine wile that leads to his enthralment.

The exchange of gifts in stanzas five and seven further suggests the perfect interaction of poet and imagination. The beautiful lady gives her knight the manna-dew of inspiration, thereby preparing him for the greater sensory pleasures soon to come in her 'elfin grot'. In addition to the honey of imagination, the lady finds him 'roots of relish sweet'. On the literal level of meaning, this act seems just another of the delights provided by the beautiful lady. But on a metaphorical level of meaning, her gift, like her bestowal of manna-dew of inspiration, seems to plant within the poet roots of music. Keats's use of the words 'roots' and 'relish'[1] refers not only to gustatory pleasure in some fairy-like, unnamed tuber, but also to the fundamental chords (i.e., 'roots') being struck within the fertile depths of the poet-knight's own soul of imagination.[2] For in making 'sweet moan', in speaking 'language strange', and in singing 'a faery's song', La Belle Dame is nurturing the musical and verbal roots of the imagination, which in the organicism of creation will grow and develop into poetry. Thus, Keats seems to be saying, 'she provided me with the basic and most pleasurable roots of melody and words', roots granted in a similar manner by Cynthia, who strings and plucks the 'lyre of [Endymion's] soul' until it is 'Aeolian tun'd' [*E*. II 866]. The knight's deeply seated, divinely activated musical power seems to be what Keats calls the 'relish', or the extreme pleasure of quickening imaginative feeling in a life of sensations.

Intoxicated by manna-dew, honey and her fairy song, the knight hears the first protestations of La Belle Dame's love for him 'in language strange'. Her language is 'strange' because any supreme visitation of the poetic imagination, in Keats's estimation, proves extraordinary, unfamiliar and inexplicable. The entranced poet cannot account for the mysterious music playing on his inner ear, nor for the wild visions dancing before his eyes. Imaginative frenzy opens up an unfathomable world of new sensory experience in the poet. We recall, in this regard, Endymion's perception of 'strange minstrelsy' while he is locked in 'magic sleep' [*E*. I 457, 453], of Cynthia's 'strange voice' singing to him in a sexual-imaginative embrace [*E*. II 849], of the unannounced and inexplicable 'strange influence' of bowers, nymphs and intoxicating bays, all of which induce the frenzied creation of verse within the poet. To Keats, the gratuitous visitation of intense poetic feeling seems so strange and mysterious

That we must ever wonder how, and whence
It came. . . .   [*Sleep & Poetry*, 70–1]

Raised to the heights of passionate and therefore imaginative intensity by the beautiful lady's confession of love ('I love thee true'), the knight gains entrance to her 'elfin grot', which we have already identified as a recurrent metaphor for the sanctuary of poetry and imagination, a place alive with the spontaneous music of animistic nature, as we have seen elsewhere. In the haunts of her labyrinthine 'gnomed mine', he finds complete imaginative fulfilment in sexual union with her. And yet in the very act of lovemaking, she sighs 'full sore', knowing well that all fertile, impassioned acts of imagination must perforce come to an end. Their perfect seizure subsequently leads to visionary dreaming as a poet and imagination slumber, much like the lovers entwined in each other's arms in *Ode to Psyche*.

If stanza seven sets the knight's dream in the 'elfin grot', stanza eight abruptly places him 'on the cold hill side'. We must consider this swift transition as characteristic of the ballad form; we must also presume that some time has lapsed between the initial stages of the knight's warm and impassioned love-dream in the grot and its final stages on the cold hill side, where he had a vision of his complete enthralment. We are told only of the knight's 'latest dream', that is, his most recent vision, which presumably follows all the others in the elfin grot. That final, waking dream of troubled visions on the cold hill side announces the death of imagination and the ensuing pains of the poet's return to the numbing world of reality.

He hears 'pale kings and princes', the former victims of the beautiful lady's charms, crying that the knight, like themselves, has been enthralled by a beautiful but deceiving fancy. Whereas she once nourished the poet with manna-dew of inspiration and fulfilled his hunger for poetic vision by offering him a long love-dream, she pitilessly withdraws her favors, starving, enfeebling and destroying all those who dedicate themselves to the strenuous pursuit of poetry and imagination.

We may identify these starving, enslaved kings and princes as poets who, like the knight-at-arms, have journeyed the path of poetry and have destroyed themselves in searching for its visions. In *Sleep and Poetry* Keats remarks:

And they shall be accounted poet kings
Who simply tell the most heart-easing things. . . .   [267–8]

In this poem, however, his poet-kings painfully tell the most
heart-breaking things. In identifying kings and princes as the
most fanciful of mortals, Keats is not being arbitrary or even
private in his association, but rather is relying on classical
myth for the source of his analogy. From Ovid [in Sandys's
translation] he learned that Morpheus's son, Phantasus,
provides the power of fancy solely to kings and princes:

Phantasus

Of different facultie, indues a tree,
Earth, water, stone the severall shapes of things
That life enjoy not. These appeare to Kings
And Princes in deepe night: The rest among
The vulgar stray.[3]

The knight as well as the kings and princes has been unable to
realise the risks and dangers involved in attempting to capture
and bind the wily imagination, which thrives and breeds only
for the moment and then, with elfin fickleness, vanishes. The
poet's quest involves the greatest hazards even to poet-kings;
for as Keats warns in *Endymion*,

There never liv'd a mortal man, who bent
His appetite beyond his natural sphere,
But starv'd and died.   [*E.* IV 646–8]

Awakening from his 'latest dream', the knight appears to
possess all the symptoms of pain found in other poet-heroes
who have fallen out of poetic frenzy. The inevitable waning of
imaginative ecstasy leaves him sapped of strength and vitality.
We may regard the knight's 'anguish moist and fever dew' as
the painful, consumptive effects of a short, but intense, life of
imaginative sensation. Indeed, does not the knight's
experience describe the inevitable fever that Keats himself
suffers after a day of writing poetry? He remarks that the

'artificial excitement' induced by his imagination 'goes off more severely from the fever I am left in'. We have already commented on his own awareness of the pernicious effect of poetry on his mind and body; and yet that enthralling love affair with poetry seems never to have estranged itself. For Keats knew that with the passage of time his painful fever would vanish, and hopefully, would be followed by another visitation of the poetic imagination. Although the knight-at-arms suffers, he 'sojourns' on the cold hill side, 'alone and palely loitering', without muse or music and significantly too, without his steed. Horseless at this point in his career, the knight remains immobile, directionless, and wholly out of the world symbolised in his most cherished personal possession, the elemental gift of rhythm and music. His loitering denotes aimless and idle stops and pauses that stand in direct contrast to the regularity of movement and the intensity of purpose of La Belle Dame as she sits and sings on his pacing steed. His sojourning and loitering are with hopes that he may again fall upon his beautiful lady of poetry and have another exalted, though temporary, love-dream. What is more likely, he will die in enthralment, as rapidly as the color of the fading rose. For in describing the end of a season, the withering of organic life, and the end of a dream, Keats suggests that the imagination, too, has its inevitable and natural decline, forcing the poet back to the fever, the palsy, and the fret of the real world. That inevitable process returns him not to the warm and blossoming meads of springtide, but to the flowerless, songless, cold and profitless world of late autumn. . . .

SOURCE: excerpted from ch. 8 of *Keats's Metaphors for the Poetic Imagination* (Durham, N.C., 1967), pp. 192–202.

NOTES

[Reorganised and renumbered from the original – Ed.]

1. We should also note that the word 'relish', in an archaic sense, denotes 'a grace or embellishment in old music', according to Webster's Dictionary.

2. Perkins's reading of stanza seven seems inadequate for its assumption that La Belle Dame provides literal nourishment to the knight. He remarks: 'One need only point out that roots, honey and manna might be appropriate for a "faery's child", but they would not provide much nourishment to a knight-at-arms.' (*The Quest for Permanence*, p. 262 [see preceding excerpt in this selection – Ed.].) Metaphorically, the knight acquires poetic inspiration by these agents, Perkins's remark is representative of the critical tack taken by many scholars.

3. George Sandys, *Ovid's Metamorphoses Englished* (London, 1626), p. 232. Colvin's comment, 'that Keats, more than from any other source, made himself familiar with the details of classic fable' – *John Keats: His Life and Poetry, His Friends etc.* (London, 1917), p. 171 [see excerpt in Part Three, above – Ed.] – seems helpful in further establishing the source of Keats's analogue of the poet as king.

Kenneth Muir   The Meaning of *Hyperion*   (1952)

The facts about the composition of *Hyperion* are now fairly well established. Keats began thinking of the subject soon after the publication of *Endymion*. He prepared himself for his task by the study of *Paradise Lost* and of Cary's translation of Dante, which he took with him on his walking-tour in Scotland. He returned from that tour, with an ominous sore throat, to watch by the bedside of his dying brother, Tom; and though he had intended to study for a longer time before beginning his poem, he found himself obliged to 'write and plunge into abstract images to ease' himself of Tom's 'countenance, his voice and feebleness'. He had told Woodhouse that he would write no more; but this was a momentary mood, for he was 'that very instant . . . cogitating on the characters of Saturn and Ops'. By the time Tom died, on 1 December 1818, Keats had finished the first two books of the poem. Freed from his responsibility to Tom, he became attracted by Fanny Brawne; but it was under the influence of Mrs Isabella Jones that he wrote *The Eve of St Agnes*. Just before, or just after, writing this poem, he abandoned *Hyperion* in the middle of Book III.[1] After a period of indolence, a fallow period, Keats spent the spring and early summer of 1819 in writing five of his odes. Then, during the composition of *Otho the Great* and *Lamia*, he took up *Hyperion* again, recasting it as *The Fall of Hyperion*. This he abandoned on 21 September; and during the autumn he seems to have been preparing the original *Hyperion* for the press, revising it with the help of *The Fall of Hyperion*. Brown's statement that Keats devoted his autumn evenings to the writing of *Hyperion* has been taken to mean that he had gone back on his resolution to abandon *The Fall of Hyperion*. But this can hardly be, since the lines quoted in the letter of 21 September are near the end of the poem; and what followed, even if it had not then been written, was an adaptation with the minimum of alteration of the corresponding lines of the first *Hyperion*. The composition to which Brown refers must have been confined to a few verbal changes, in either of the two versions. Indeed, from a comparison of the manuscript with the 1820 text, it can be seen that some readings of *The Fall of Hyperion* were incorporated in the earlier poem.

This account of the composition of the two versions would now be accepted, without much modification, by all critics; but on the interpretation of the poem, on the reasons why Keats finally abandoned it, and on the relative merits of the two versions something may still be said.

I

To understand the full meaning of the first *Hyperion* it is expedient to read the second. In the summer of 1819 Keats was able to interpret the earlier poem with the help of what he had learned in the interval; and the second poem, precisely because it embodied this new knowledge, is both different from the first, and indispensable to its interpretation. Even during the actual composition of *Hyperion* Keats was developing rapidly, and the original conception was altered and deepened as he wrote. It is probable that the poem was conceived, at least vaguely, before the completion of *Endymion*, and that Keats's original intention was merely to fill out the old myth with poetical ornament: he trusted that the theme would acquire significance as he wrote, as had happened with *Endymion* itself. But in the year that elapsed before he began the poem he had learnt to tell a story more effectively by writing *Isabella*; he had studied and thought deeply; he had been reading Milton and Wordsworth, and from them and from Dante he had derived some valuable lessons. He had decided that ideas could be better expressed in poetry by embodying them in narrative form, than by using the more direct method of *The Excursion* – a poem he had regarded not long before as the poetic masterpiece of his time. He was determined to attempt the epic form, and for that purpose blank verse was the obvious choice of a medium. He knew that he could write better blank verse than Cary; and he hoped to excel that of *The Excursion*, with *Paradise Lost* as his nearest model.

As he brooded on his subject it began to acquire a contemporary significance. At the time when he began to write the first *Hyperion*, and again when he abandoned the second, Keats's mind turned to the subject of politics. 'As for Politics', he wrote in October 1818,

They are in my opinion only sleepy because they will soon be too wide awake–Perhaps not–for the long and continued Peace of England itself has given us notions of personal safety which are likely to prevent the re-establishment of our national Honesty—There is of a truth nothing manly or sterling in any part of the Government. There are many Madmen in the Country, I have no doubt, who would like to be beheaded on Tower Hill merely for the sake of eclat, there are many Men like Hunt who from a principle of taste would like to see things go better . . . but there are none prepared to suffer in obscurity for their Country. . . . We have no Milton, no Algernon Sidney. . . . Notwithstanding the part which the Liberals take in the Cause of Napoleon I cannot but think he has done more harm to the life of Liberty than any one else could have done.

It is clear from this that Keats disliked the reactionary government of his day; that he realised that 'a principle of taste' was not a satisfactory foundation for political action – a lesson some have still to learn; and that he disagreed with English Bonapartists such as Hazlitt.

Eleven months later, in the very letter which announced the

abandonment of *Hyperion*, Keats returned to the subject of politics:

> In every age there has been in England for some two or three centuries subjects of great popular interest on the carpet: so that however great the uproar one can scarcely prophesy any material change in the government, for as loud disturbances have agitated this country many times. All civilized countries become gradually more enlighten'd and there should be a continual change for the better.

He goes on to describe how the tyranny of the nobles was gradually destroyed, and how in every country the kings attempted to destroy all popular privileges:

> The examples of England, and the liberal writers of France and England sowed the seeds of opposition to this Tyranny—and it was swelling in the ground till it burst out in the French Revolution. That has had an unlucky termination. It put a stop to the rapid progress of free sentiments in England; and gave our Court hopes of turning back to the despotism of the 16th century. They have made a handle of this event in every way to undermine our freedom. They spread a horrid superstition against all innovation and improvement. The present struggle in England of the people is to destroy this superstition. What has rous'd them to do it is their distresses—Perhaps on this account the present distresses of this nation are a fortunate thing—tho so horrid in their experience. You will see I mean that the French Revolution put a temporary stop to this third change, the change for the better. Now it is in progress again and I think it an effectual one. This is no contest between whig and tory—but between right and wrong.

That is why Keats hoped before he died 'to put a Mite of help to the Liberal side of the Question'.

I am not suggesting that Keats's political views found direct expression in *Hyperion*, and still less that it is an allegory of the French Revolution. But it is not fanciful to suggest that the revolutionary climate of the time contributed to, if it did not suggest, the subject of the poem. It is, on one level, a poem on Progress. Keats's desire for an England in which the progress interrupted by the Tory reaction after the revolution in France would be resumed and accelerated is reflected in the poem. The

great speech of Oceanus expresses Keats's belief in progress.
The Titans

<blockquote>
cower beneath what, in comparison,
Is untremendous might,   [II 154–5]
</blockquote>

even as the tyrants of the world would cower before those who
strove for freedom; and Saturn himself cries to Thea –

<blockquote>
Tell me, if thou seest
A certain shape, or shadow, making way
With wings or chariot fierce to repossess
A heaven he lost erewhile; it must, it must
Be of ripe progress.   [I 121–5]
</blockquote>

But to discover the deeper meaning of the poem it is necessary
to consider Keats's idea of progress, and the difference
between the new gods and the old. It is here that Keats most
obviously developed during the composition of the poem.
Until he reached the end of the second book, he had intended
to make Apollo merely more beautiful than Saturn and
Hyperion. The speeches of Clymene and Oceanus make it
clear that the law of progress envisaged by Keats was a
development towards a greater perfection of beauty, in
accordance with the eternal law –

<blockquote>
That first in beauty should be first in might;   [II 229]
</blockquote>

but when he wrote the third book his conception of beauty had
deepened. Already, in the first two books, Keats was groping
towards the conception of Apollo expressed in Book III. In
Thea's face sorrow had made

<blockquote>
Sorrow more beautiful than Beauty's self;   [I 36]
</blockquote>

and the 'living death' in Apollo's music had made Clymene

sick 'Of joy and grief at once'. We can trace the germs of this conception to passages in *Endymion*, and to letters written after the completion of that poem. Keats had declared that 'what the imagination seizes as Beauty must be truth', and that 'Sorrow is Wisdom'; and he had spoken of his 'mighty abstract Idea . . . of Beauty in all things' – in sorrow, as well as in joy. Beauty, wisdom, and sorrow he had accepted as correlatives.

Before he began the composition of *Hyperion*, Keats had been considering what he called 'Men of Achievement' and 'Men of Power'. Men of genius, he wrote,

> are great as certain ethereal Chemicals operating on the Mass of neutral intellect—but they have not any individuality, any determined Character—I would call the top and head of those who have a proper self Men of Power.

A few weeks later, he declared that the quality which 'went to form a Man of Achievement, especially in Literature', was Negative Capability. He returned to the subject in October 1818, when he told Woodhouse that the poetical character

> is not itself—it has no self—it is everything and nothing—It has no character—it enjoys light and shade; it lives in gusto, be it foul or fair, high or low, rich or poor, mean or elevated—It has as much delight in conceiving an Iago as an Imogen. What shocks the virtuous philosopher, delights the camelion Poet.

This idea of the poetical character was partly derived from some of Hazlitt's essays in *The Round Table*; and from Hazlitt, too, Keats took the term *identity*:

> A poet is the most unpoetical of any thing in existence; because he has no identity—he is continually informing and filling some other Body—The Sun, the Moon, the Sea and Men and Women who are creatures of impulse are poetical and have about them an unchangeable attribute—the poet has none; no identity—he is certainly the most unpoetical of all God's creatures.

Keats was aware of the defects and dangers inherent in

negative capability. He felt that the poet's personality was liable to be 'incoherent' and disintegrated:

It is a wretched thing to confess; but it is a very fact that not one word I ever utter can be taken for granted as an opinion out of my identical nature—how can it, when I have no nature?

Tom's identity pressed upon him so much that sometimes he was obliged to go out. He became the person contemplated, and suffered with him – just as he was able to identify himself with a sparrow pecking about the gravel, or even a billiard ball:

The identity of every one in the room begins to press upon me that I am in a very little time annihilated—Not only among Men; it would be the same in a Nursery of children.

In view of these quotations, it is noteworthy that Saturn and the other Gods of the old dispensation possess identities. Saturn speaks of his 'strong identity', his 'real self'; but Apollo has no identity. He possesses to a supreme degree the negative capability that Keats had laid down as the prime essential of a poet. In other words, the old gods are men of power, the new gods are men of achievement. The poem describes the victory of the men of achievement. That is its primary meaning; linked with it, and almost equally important, is the account of the price that must be paid for being a man of achievement.

It is sometimes said that Keats could not finish the poem because he had expended all his powers in describing the nobility and beauty of the old gods, so that he was unable, as the poem demanded, to make the new gods superior to them. The criticism is not valid because, unless Saturn had been made noble, Oceanus genuinely wise, and Hyperion beautiful, the poem would have lost half its tragic beauty. The old order is great and beautiful – otherwise its downfall would have lacked significance. The best of the past must be conquered by the new gods. In a similar way, Blake in his poem on the

French Revolution did more than justice to his representatives
of the *ancien régime.*

In the first two books of *Hyperion* we are given to understand
that Apollo is superior in beauty and wisdom to the old gods,
but on his first appearance in Book III we find him overcome
with sorrow. Oceanus had declared that the 'top of
sovereignty' was

> To bear all naked truths,
> And to envisage circumstance, all calm.   [II 203–4]

But such a stoical submission to nature's law was not enough.
Keats wished to show that sorrow could be creative; and it has
even been said that his whole poetic output can be regarded as
an attempt to find a justification for suffering.[2] Apollo, with no
personal reasons for grief, takes upon himself the sorrows of
mankind, and by so doing he is deified. He is superior to
Oceanus in much the same way as Jesus, in Keats's opinion,
was superior to Socrates; and he is superior to Hyperion in the
same way that the poet is superior to the great heroes of which
he writes. Although Keats may not at the time have been fully
conscious of the identification, there is no doubt that his
account of the deification of Apollo by disinterested suffering is
a symbolic presentation of the 'dreamer' becoming a great
poet. But the reference is wider. Keats, in his famous parable,
wrote of the world, not as a vale of tears, but as a vale of soul-
making; so that the deification of Apollo is symbolic of the
birth of a soul in all who are thus reborn. The vale of god-
making in *Hyperion* is the same as the vale of soul-making; and
since, as Blake put it, 'The Poetic Genius is the true man',
Keats, in describing his own conversion from dreamer to poet,
was writing of the birth of the soul in all men. Apollo, though
ostensibly a god, has to be deified because he represents both
the poet and man:

> Knowledge enormous makes a God of me,
> Names, deeds, grey legends, dire events, rebellions,
> Majesties, sovran voices, agonies,

Creations and destroyings, all at once
Pour into the wide hollows of my brain
And deify me, as if some blythe wine
Or bright elixir peerless I had drunk
And so become immortal.   [III 113–20]

This new knowledge Apollo learns from the silent face of Mnemosyne, who is the personification of the vision and understanding of human history, and a mirror of the inescapable suffering inherent in historical change and in the human condition itself.

This description of 'dying into life' is the conclusion of the poem. When Keats had written so far he handed the manuscript to Woodhouse, realising that he had reached the limit of his experience. He may have intended, as de Selincourt thought, to write another book and a half, in order to describe the submission of the old gods to the new; but any such ending would have been merely formal, since the old and new had already been contrasted.

Even *Endymion* had been something more than a mythological narrative: Keats had used it to express a personal dilemma. *Hyperion*, in which he had once again 'touched the beautiful mythology of Greece', is only superficially about the ancient gods: its real subject, as we have seen, is human progress; and the new race of men imagined by the poet were not stronger or cleverer than their predecessors, but more sensitive and vulnerable – not characters, but personalities.[3]

The weaknesses of the poem, apart from its too Miltonic style, are that Keats's narrative power is only intermittently displayed; the rhythmical impetus frequently exhausts itself at the end of a paragraph; and the fable itself is not perfectly adapted to the meaning Keats tried to impose on it. It was in an attempt to remedy these faults that he began to recast the poem in the summer of 1819.

II

Between the two versions of *Hyperion* several months elapsed; and we can trace Keats's development during this time, not merely in the narrative poems, sonnets and odes, but also in his letters, particularly in the long journal-letter to George and Georgiana, begun in February and finished in May. He is led from the news of the approaching death of Haslam's father to a consideration of disinterestedness. He points out that 'very few men have ever arrived at a complete disinterestedness of Mind'; but that though we are involved, with the animals, in a struggle for survival, 'we have all one human heart', and can rise to deeds of heroism and self-sacrifice. A few weeks later, Keats, who had been reading Robertson's *America* and Voltaire's *Siècle de Louis XIV*, discusses the lamentable plight of the common people in a civilised as well as in an uncivilised society:

Man is originally a 'poor forked creature' subject to the same mischances as the beasts of the forest, destined to hardships and disquietude of some kind or other. If he improves by degrees his bodily accommodations and comforts—at each stage, at each ascent there are waiting for him a fresh set of annoyances—he is mortal and there is still a heaven with its stars above his head.

Even if Godwinian perfectibility were possible – and Keats regards it as a Utopian illusion – man would still die; and the more unalloyed his worldly happiness, the bitterer death would be. This leads Keats to his parable of the world as a vale of soul-making, which is in a sense an interpretation, or a forerunner, of the third book of *Hyperion*. A world of pains and troubles is necessary 'to school an intelligence and make it a Soul'. Here Keats was trying to find a purpose in human suffering, and setting up as an ideal the disinterested and sympathetic sharing of the sorrows of others. The climax of his poem, he realised, was not merely the deification of Apollo, but, compressed into a single experience, his own acceptance of human suffering. One other passage in the same letter is significant for our present purpose:

Though a quarrel in the Streets is a thing to be hated, the energies displayed in it are fine. . . . By a superior being our reasonings may take the same tone—though erroneous they may be fine—This is the very thing in which consists poetry; and if so it is not so fine a thing as philosophy.

On the surface Keats is saying that philosophy is finer than poetry; but he probably meant merely that poetry, to be great, must be an image of truth. It is a reaffirmation at a deeper level of his former intuition that what the imagination seizes for beauty must be truth; and it looks forward to the *Ode on a Grecian Urn*.

The significance of these passages in the journal-letter is that Keats, by accepting suffering, had transcended it. The 'dark passages' of which he had written in May 1818 he had now been exploring. He was able to face the 'eternal fierce destruction' from which he had recoiled in March 1818. Now in the odes he wrote before turning again to *Hyperion* after contrasting the immortality and joy of poetry with the miseries of this mortal life (in the *Ode to a Nightingale*), he accepted the inseparability of joy and sorrow (in the *Ode on Melancholy*), and concluded, not by escaping from life into art, but by contemplating life as though it were a work of art (in the *Ode on a Grecian Urn*), and finding that there too the disagreeables evaporate. . . .

III

The Fall of Hyperion is cast in the form of a dream or vision, and J. L. Lowes has demonstrated the pervasive influence of Dante's *Purgatorio*.[4] It is very much a purgatorial poem, and the steps symbolise, as they do in Dante, the striving of the Dreamer towards the truth. We may agree, too, with Bridges who remarked that Keats had now 'added to his style a mastery of Dante's especial grace'.

The first 280 lines of the poem are new; the remainder is a

recast of the earlier version. In the 'induction' Keats distinguishes between the fanatics, who 'weave a paradise for a sect', and the poets who alone are able to tell their dreams by means of 'the fine spell of words'. There is an implied contrast between the true poet, who reveals the meaning of life, and those who propagate a false view of life, just as in Coleridge's 'Allegoric Vision', to which Keats was also indebted,[5] superstition is contrasted with religion.

The landscape described in the next section of the poem [12–60] corresponds closely both to Keats's first period of poetry that culminated in *Sleep and Poetry*, and also to the Chamber of Maiden Thought. The draught with which the Dreamer pledges the living and the renowned dead symbolised poetry – the poetry Keats has used in order to escape from 'the weariness, the fever, and the fret' and from the consciousness that 'the world is full of misery and heartbreak, pain, sickness and oppression'. The wine is both the 'dull opiate' and the 'draught of vintage' of the *Ode to a Nightingale*; and the Dreamer 'started up As if with wings' just as Keats in the ode had been borne on the 'viewless wings of poesy'. The Dreamer finds himself in an old sanctuary, the Temple of Saturn, which has been interpreted as 'the temple of knowledge' and as 'the temple of life becomes conscious of itself in man'. Whatever it represents, there is a certain ambiguity in Moneta's position, for she had been the priestess of Saturn and also the foster-parent of Apollo. Apparently Keats intended her to be the priestess of Truth, who had outlived the various manifestations of truth in different ages of the world. She tells the Dreamer that he has felt 'what 'tis to die and live again before' his fated hour; and she explains that he has been 'favoured for unworthiness' because he is one of

> those to whom the miseries of the world
> Are misery, and will not let them rest.   [148–9]*

---

* [Ed.] Line-references for *The Fall of Hyperion* in this study relate to the first canto.

She tells him, nevertheless, that he is less worthy than those

> Who love their fellows even to the death,
> Who feel the giant agony of the world,
> And more, like slaves to poor humanity,
> Labour for mortal good.   [156–9]

Keats is careful not to claim for himself, what could only be known after his death, that he is a poet rather than a dreamer. The lines that follow [187–210] were apparently meant to be deleted, and in the Houghton transcript they are omitted. De Selincourt, however, claims that they are necessary to complete the argument about the difference between the poet and the dreamer: without these lines Moneta would appear to condemn all poets. Keats wrote the passage in order to make the distinction; but he may have felt it was untrue to his real conviction to class himself categorically with the dreamers, and also that the attack on Byron was irrelevant and uncontrolled. He therefore repeated the words 'Majestic shadow, tell me', rewrote the lines describing how Moneta's breath moved the linen folds about a golden censer, and continued with the poem – meaning, perhaps, to rewrite the dialogue on the poet and the dreamer, or else to salvage some of its lines for a later part of the poem. Middleton Murry argues forcibly that the lines should be deleted; and in view of the repetitions they should at least be relegated to a footnote.

The unveiling of Moneta is a repetition of the scene in the first *Hyperion* in which Apollo gazes into the eyes of Mnemosyne; and this fact is the strongest argument for the identification of Keats and Apollo, and for Murry's assumption that the deification of Apollo represents the transformation of a romantic dreamer into a great poet:

> Then saw I a wan face,
> Not pin'd by human sorrows, but bright blanch'd
> By an immortal sickness which kills not;
> It works a constant change, which happy death
> Can put no end to; deathwards progressing
> To no death was that visage; it had pass'd

The lilly and the snow; and beyond these
I must not think now, though I saw that face –
But for her eyes I should have fled away.
They held me back, with a benignant light,
Soft mitigated by divinest lids
Half closed, and visionless entire they seem'd
Of all external things – they saw me not,
But in blank splendor beam'd, like the mild moon,
Who comforts those she sees not, who knows not
What eyes are upward cast.   [*F.H.* 256–71]

There is nothing Miltonic about these lines. In them, and in many others in the first canto of *The Fall of Hyperion* Keats is writing in a style peculiarly his own. This blank verse – and the maturity it expresses – was perhaps Keats's greatest achievement as a poet.

H. W. Garrod has argued that allegory is the natural refuge 'of timid minds brought up against facts, and too conscientious to ignore them altogether';[6] and that Keats printed the first *Hyperion* rather than the second, to 'save his work of allegory'. But it should be sufficiently clear that it was from no 'shyness of the actual' that Keats wrote in an allegorical form. The second *Hyperion* is more allegorical than the first, and yet it is obviously more courageous and more direct in the way it faces life. What Keats had to say could not have been more directly expressed than in the vision of Moneta. It is even arguable that the expression is too direct for the highest poetry. Spenser constructed a complicated system of belief, which he converted into allegory; Keats, on the other hand, expressed his own experience as directly as possible. *The Fall of Hyperion* is an attempt to express an intuition about the ultimate nature of reality in the only way possible, the parabolic.

The contrast between the poet and the dreamer, which is the real theme of the poem, is a final expression of a conflict which had agitated Keats as early as *Sleep and Poetry*. 'The strife and agonies of human hearts,' of which he speaks in that poem, may indeed refer to his ambition to write tragedies; but this ambition was closely connected with his desire to write poetry which would not be merely the opium of the middle classes or the expression of personal emotions. In *Endymion* the same conflict is symbolised by the hero's love for Diana and the Indian Maiden: and it is there resolved by the conviction that a poet will best help humanity by his poetry. But from his letters in the autumn of 1818 and the spring of 1819, we know how cruelly the miseries of humanity pressed in upon Keats. By the time he conceived Moneta he had come to think not only that the very condition of writing great poetry is that the poet should feel the miseries of the world as his own, but that ordinary good men and women are more valuable than 'romantic' poets.

We need not agree with Keats's condemnation of his own earlier poetry, though his judgement should warn us against the temptation to read too much into it. Yet it may be admitted that if the odes remain great in spite of Keats's criticism, they are, compared with what he was ambitious to write, comparatively minor poetry.

IV

The second half of the poem is adapted from the first *Hyperion*: and in the opinion of most critics, Murry and Ridley being honourable exceptions, Keats has done little but maim the original. To discover whether in fact his powers were already beginning to show a decline, it will be necessary to examine several passages in some detail. In *Hyperion*, Thea is thus described:

> She was a Goddess of the infant world;
> By her in stature the tall Amazon
> Had stood a Pigmy's height: she would have ta'en
> Achilles by the hair and bent his neck,
> Or with a finger eas'd Ixion's toil.
> Her face was large as that of Memphian Sphinx
> Pedestal'd haply in a Palace court
> When Sages look'd to Egypt for their lore.
> But oh! how unlike Marble was that face:
> How beautiful, if sorrow had not made
> Sorrow more beautiful than beauty's self.   [I 26–36]

In *The Fall of Hyperion* the corresponding lines are:

'That divinity
Whom thou saw'st step from yon forlornest wood,
And with slow pace approach our fallen King,
Is Thea, softest-natur'd of our Brood.'
I mark'd the goddess in fair statuary
Surpassing wan Moneta by the head,
And in her sorrow nearer woman's tears.*

The Amazon, the pigmy, Achilles and Ixion, even the
Memphian Sphinx and the last two lovely lines, all are gone.
The reasons are apparent. The Amazon-pigmy comparison
was a deliberate echo of Milton, and the whole passage has too
obviously a Miltonic ring. The passage disturbs the balance of
the poem, for the reader's interest should here be concentrated
on Saturn. The essence of the last two lines had already been
used to describe Moneta, and it was impossible to leave them
in without repetition.

The next passage is an interesting example of the way Keats
endeavoured to eliminate his exclamations. In *Hyperion* it
reads:

O aching time! O Moments big as years,
Each as ye pass swell out the monstrous truth
And press it so upon our weary griefs
That unbelief has not a space to breathe.
Saturn sleep on: O thoughtless, why did I   [I 64–8]
. . .

The rhythm of these lines is slightly monotonous, and Keats
was right to condense them into the three lines of the later
version:

With such remorseless speed still come new woes
That unbelief has not a space to breathe.
Saturn, sleep on:—Me thoughtless, why should I . . .
. . .

---

* [Ed.] Verse-excerpts for which no line-references are given in this
reproduction of Muir's essay are of Keats's revision which, in the outcome,
were not established in the first printed text.

The new line, with its Shakespearian echo, effectively conveys the essence of the previous passage, though, as Bridges observed, 'Me thoughtless' is more Miltonic than the expression it replaces.

The famous simile of the trees, as Ridley has shown, is improved rather than weakened in the later version:

As when upon a tranced summer night
Those green rob'd Senators of mighty woods
Tall Oaks, branch-charmed by the earnest Stars,
Dream and so dream all night without a stir
Save from one sudden solitary gust
Which comes upon the silence and dies off
As if the ebbing Air had but one wave:
So came these words and went;   [II 72–9]

The second of these lines, beautiful as it is, has to go, because it distracts attention from the purpose of the simile, which is to describe the *sound* of Thea's words. The oaks are changed to forests, so that we hear them, rather than see them. *Stir* is likewise changed to *noise*, a word which reproduces the sound of the wind and concentrates our attention on that, rather than on the movement of the trees. The regular rhythm of the sixth of these lines is changed into one which suggests what it describes –

Swelling upon the silence; dying off.

The changes in this passage alone would serve to show that Keats's power as a poet had suffered no decline, or at least that he was still able to improve on his earlier work.

The lines describing Saturn and Thea –

And still these two were postur'd Motionless
Like natural Sculpture in cathedral cavern   [I 85–6]

– were altered to what Ridley calls 'a rather awkward conceit':

> Long, long, those two were postured motionless,
> Like sculpture builded up upon the grave
> Of their own power.

Exception has been taken to 'up upon';[7] but in other respects the new version is an improvement. It is superior to the first from the point of view of euphony; and the image is more relevant than that of the cathedral cavern to the theme of the poem. It springs from and illuminates the subject – it is not a decorative addition. To find a parallel to it one would have to go to one of Shakespeare's best images:

> Yet thou doest looke
> Like patience, gazing on Kings graues, and smiling
> Extremitie out of act.[8]

As a last comparison, we may take the two versions of Saturn's speech:

> O tender spouse of gold Hyperion
> Thea I feel thee ere I see thy face—
> Look up and let me see our doom in it.
> Look up and tell me if this feeble shape
> Is Saturn's, tell me if thou hear'st the voice
> Of Saturn, tell me if this wrinkling brow
> Naked and bare of its great Diadem,
> Peers like the front of Saturn! What dost think?
> Am I that same—O chaos who had power
> To make me desolate? Whence came the Strength
> How was it nurtur'd to such bursting forth
> While fate seem'd strangled in my nervous grasp?
> But it is so; and I am smothered up
> And buried from all godlike exercise
> Of influence benign on Planets pale,
> Of admonitions to the Winds and Seas,
> Of peaceful sway above Man's harvesting,
> And all those arts[9] which Deity supreme
> Doth ease its heart of Love in—I am gone
> Away from my own Bosom—I have left
> My strong Identity—my real self
> Somewhere between the Throne, and where I sit

Here on this bit of earth—Search Thea search!
Open thine eyes eterne, and sphere them round
Upon all space: space starr'd and lorn of light,
Space region'd with life air; and barren void—
Spaces of fire, and all the yawn of Hell—
Search Thea search! and tell me if thou seest
A certain Shape or Shadow making way
With wings or chariot fierce to repossess
A heaven he lost erewhile—it must, it must
Be of ripe progress—Saturn must be King—
Yes, there must be a golden Victory;
There must be gods thrown down, and trumpets blown
Of Triumph calm; and hymns of festival
Upon the gold clouds metropolitan—
Voices of soft proclaim and silver stir
Of strings in hollow shells; and there shall be
Beautiful things made new, for the surprise
Of the Sky-children—I will give command—
Thea! Thea! Thea! where is Saturn?   [I 95–134]

———

'Moan, brethren, moan; for we are swallow'd up
And buried from all godlike exercise
Of influence benign on planets pale,
And peaceful sway above man's harvesting,
And all those acts which Deity supreme
Doth ease its heart of love in. Moan and wail.
Moan, brethren, moan; for lo! the rebel spheres
Spin round, the stars their antient courses keep,
Clouds still with shadowy moisture haunt the earth,
Still suck their fill of light from Sun & Moon,
Still buds the tree, and still the sea-shores murmur.
There is no death in all the universe
No smell of Death—there shall be death—Moan, Moan;
Moan, Cybele, moan, for thy pernicious babes
Have chang'd a God into a shaking Palsy.
Moan, brethren, moan; for I have no strength left,
Weak as the reed—weak—feeble as my voice—
O, O, the pain, the pain of feebleness.
Moan, Moan, for still I thaw—or give me help:
Throw down those Imps and give me victory.
Let me hear other groans, and trumpets blown
Of triumph calm, and hymns of festival
From the gold peaks of Heaven's high piled clouds;
Voices of soft proclaim, and silver stir
Of strings in hollow shells; and let there be

Beautiful things made new for the surprize
Of the sky children'—So he feebly ceas'd,
With such a poor and sickly sounding pause,
Methought I heard some old Man of the earth
Bewailing earthly loss.

The radical changes in Saturn's speech have been variously lamented. The orthodox opinion would seem to be that 'as poetry the second version is hardly comparable with the first'. Yet it is not difficult to see the reason for all the alterations. The speech is no longer addressed to Thea, because all her sympathy can avail him nothing. His power is gone; and most of the changes were made to enable the speech to reflect his fallen state. The oft repeated moans exhibit his impotence. The reference to progress has to be cut since it is the new gods alone who stand for progress. Saturn is no longer obeyed, so the final resolution, 'I will give command', is omitted. Keats in the first version had described Saturn as speaking with a palsied tongue; these words are now inserted in the text of the speech, and its tone is altered to suit the description. Saturn is humanised, because in the plan of the poem his sorrows are a reflection of the sorrows of humanity. He now seems like

> some old Man of the earth,
> Bewailing earthly loss.

The hope that animated the first version is expunged, since those who retain hope have not plumbed the depths of despair. In the first version, both of this speech and of the next, Saturn still hopes to be able to create:

> Cannot I form? Cannot I fashion forth
> Another World, another Universe,
> To overbear and crumble this to naught?   [I 142–3]

In the second version, by a stroke that is both psychologically and poetically truer, Saturn can only think of destruction; since he cannot create, he will destroy:

There is no death in all the universe,
No smell of death—there shall be death.

So the passage relating to the stars is changed from a description of the heavens, where Thea is to watch for the approach of Hyperion, to a dramatic use of the same properties: the fact that the stars no longer obey Saturn leads directly to his desire for destruction. Other changes in the speech are more obviously improvements. Keats wisely eliminated the ugly phrase and jingle –

> Where I sit
> Here on this bit of earth*

and he changed a Miltonic to a Keatsian phrase;

> Upon the gold clouds metropolitan

becoming

> From the gold peaks of Heaven's high piled clouds.

Keats's motives for altering the speech are therefore clear. If the two versions are considered in isolation divorced from their contexts, the first may well seem to be poetically superior; but its Miltonic grandeur is obtained at the expense of characterisation and dramatic appropriateness. The statement that the revision is a product of Keats's failing powers cannot be substantiated.

Nevertheless Keats was right to print the first version. It was more likely to be acceptable to the public taste; it was more complete than the revision; it was more polished; and it was less vulnerable to the sneers of the reviewers, to whom the soul-

---

* [Ed.] Reproduced as 'this spot of earth' in printed versions [I 116].

searching of the second version would have been an easy target.

The decision to abandon the second *Hyperion* was taken on 21 September. The reason given by Keats is that there were too many Miltonic inversions in it:

The Paradise Lost though so fine in itself is a corruption of our Language—it should be kept as it is unique—a curiosity—a beautiful and grand Curiosity. The most remarkable Production of the world. A northern dialect accommodating itself to greek and latin inversions and intonations. . . . I have but lately stood on my guard against Milton. Life to him would be death to me.

On the same day, he was telling Reynolds:

I have given up Hyperion—there are too many Miltonic inversions in it—Miltonic verse cannot be written but in an artful or rather artist's humour. I wish to give myself to other sensations. English ought to be kept up.

He goes on to ask Reynolds to mark in the manuscript lines which illustrate 'the false beauty proceeding from art' and others which display 'the true voice of feeling'. As Reynolds did not have the manuscript of *The Fall of Hyperion*, we must suppose that Keats was referring to a copy of the first version. This would seem to imply that he had abandoned both poems. He had realised that he could never finish *The Fall of Hyperion*, for a reason obvious enough but never mentioned by him: he had already used up the climax of the first poem in the first canto of the second version. Apart from this, he had found that he could not entirely eliminate the Miltonic influence from it. Driven back to the first version, he found that the new verse he had achieved in the other made him profoundly dissatisfied with the artificiality of the verse of the first. Murry, indeed, has argued that the rejection of Miltonic verse symbolised also the rejection of an attitude to life; and it is true that the financial difficulties of his brother had made Keats decide to come to terms with the public. Yet the fact that he had been writing *Otho the Great* during the summer with a reasonable hope of its being performed, means that we should not overemphasise the mood of withdrawal. His primary reason for getting away from London – and from Fanny – was so that he could write without distraction. It is significant that he wrote nothing of importance in the five months that remained to him before his first haemorrhage.

The conflict apparent in *The Fall of Hyperion* was not resolved: but it was allayed by being faced. If Keats had not been compelled to abandon the poem, there would still have been only an arbitrary solution to its central problem. This could be solved only in action, by an integration of theory and practice – in other words, by writing the kind of poetry of which Moneta would have approved. *To Autumn*, written immediately afterwards, shows that Keats had attained, if only for a few days, to a mood of grave serenity. He was at last able to reconcile beauty and truth in a vision in which imaginative understanding reveals reality as a whole of significance and value, satisfying both to the man and to the poet. In the meeting with Moneta imagination and reality have been reconciled; and the way to reconciliation had lain through the vale of soul-making. *To Autumn* represented the first fruits, and the last fruits, of Keats's new understanding.

Some critics have regretted that Keats was not contented to be a 'romantic' poet, the Dreamer of *The Fall of Hyperion*. Garrod's witty but misleading book was written to show that Keats's best work was written only when he escaped from philosophy, politics, action and character, into 'the world of pure imaginative forms'. A more subtle variation of this error is to be found in de Selincourt's view that Keats escaped from life into nature:

. . . The supreme truth to the poet is not to be found in the lessons of nature, but in her mysterious beauty, and in her never failing power, whencesoever it may spring, to respond to every mood of the changing heart of man. . . . Here lies the mystery: here, too, in a world of barren facts, of arid controversies, of idle speculations, the irresistible appeal.[10]

That Keats sometimes sought relief from the fever and fret of existence in the beauty of nature is not to be denied; but in his greatest poetry the moon beams in blank splendour, and he describes autumn objectively. Indeed, only by extreme sensitivity to the external world is it possible to be objective. Whatever our views on the relative merits of the odes and the two *Hyperions*, it is impossible to accept Garrod's theory that Keats was continually being led away from poetry by his thirst for 'reality'; for he could not have written *The Eve of St Agnes* and *To Autumn* if he had not elsewhere attempted to philosophise. The determination to be faithful to his own experience and his sensitive recording of the external world were really inseparable. If he had not sought truth, he could not have written great poetry.

SOURCE: article in *Essays in Criticism*, 2 (1952), pp. 54–75; reproduced in *John Keats: A Reassessment*, ed. Kenneth Muir (Liverpool, 1958; 2nd edn 1969), pp. 103–23.

NOTES

[Reorganised and renumbered from the original – Ed.]

1. It is possible, as Middleton Murry argues, that the Mnemosyne scene was written in March 1819, immediately after the soul-making parable.

2. Stephen Spender, *Forward from Liberalism* (London, 1937), p. 31.

3. Keats seems also to imply by deification through creative suffering that supernatural religion would be superseded by the natural religion of a love of one's fellow-men; but he did not share Leigh Hunt's rather shallow Abou-Ben-Adehmism.

4. J. L. Lowes in *TLS* (11 Jan. 1936) and *PMLA* (1936), pp. 1098 ff.

5. J. L. N. O'Loughlin in *TLS* (6 Dec. 1934).

6. H. W. Garrod, *The Poetical Works of John Keats* (Oxford, 1939), p. 68.

7. If the line is read with a caesura after *up*, the juxtaposition need not offend.

8. Shakespeare, *Pericles, Prince of Tyre*, Act V.

9. Keats probably intended to write *acts*, which is the reading of the 1820 volume.

10. E. de Selincourt, *The Poems of John Keats*, 5th edn (London, 1926), p. *lxvii*.

Paul D. Sheats Stylistic Discipline in
The Fall of Hyperion (1968)

The summer of 1819 abundantly fulfilled Keats's prediction, in June, that his 'discipline was to come, and plenty of it'.[1] In virtual retirement from the world at Shanklin and Winchester, he apprenticed himself to the new styles and forms of *Otho* and *Lamia* in a deliberate attempt to become a 'popular writer' [*Letters*, II, p. 146]. During these months he observed and welcomed the growth in himself of another sort of discipline: a 'healthy deliberation' that could bear the buffets of the world calmly and with dignity. As he put it to Reynolds in July, he was 'moulting: not for fresh feathers & wings: they are gone, and in their stead I hope to have a pair of patient sublunary legs' [II, p. 128]. On the last day of the summer he acknowledged to his brother that a similar change had taken place in his poetry. 'Some think I have lost that poetic ardour and fire 't is said I once had–the fact is perhaps I have: but instead of that I hope I shall substitute a more thoughtful and quiet power' [II, p. 209].

Perhaps the most direct expression of this artistic and personal self-discipline is *The Fall of Hyperion*, which was substantially complete by the summer's end. As several critics have noted, the style of this fragment, as well as its 'purgatorial' theme, reveals a radical change in Keats's practice of poetry.[2] He not only moderated the 'artful' and Miltonic idiom of the first *Hyperion*, as his own comments suggest [II, p. 167], but went on to relax the prosodic discipline that had been one of the great achievements of his stylistic development. As W. J. Bate has observed, the 'entire metrical character' of the *Fall* abandons the ideal of 'intensity' that had guided his artistic self-discipline through 1818 and the spring of 1819.[3] As fundamental a break with the past is revealed by aspects of this style that have received less critical attention than its prosody. The imagery of the *Fall*, in particular, seems the product of a 'more thoughtful and quiet power', and offers additional evidence that in this last attempt on the 'cliff of poesy' Keats deliberately sought an artistic self-discipline that was ethical and philosophic in its authority.

The characteristics of Keats's earlier style are not only famous but distinctive, and detailed description would be superfluous.[4] The odes of April and May 1819 may be viewed as the culmination of his continuing attempt to achieve a complete poetic statement of concrete sensuous richness. A concrete thing typically becomes the object of a contemplation that willingly abandons discursive or 'consequitive' modes of apprehension, and seeks instead an instinctive 'intensity' of sensation that is communicated by patterned vowels and consonants, a weighty and predominantly spondaic rhythm, and densely clustered, often synaesthetic images. Keats's imagery frequently implies a physical approach to the object contemplated, as his imagination 'pounces upon' and 'gorges' its beauty. The empathic identification that often results, as David Perkins has observed, is 'so massive that it obliterates consciousness not only of self but also of anything other than the object focused upon'.[5] Nearly all the odes of the spring, for example, are structured by an approach to and withdrawal from an object that promises (or threatens) 'intensity' of sensation, and several display a concurrent 'rise', 'progress' and 'setting' of imagery. In the third book of *Hyperion* Keats's impulsive apostrophe to the isle of Delos becomes a lingering appreciation of its sensuous richness:

> Rejoice, O Delos, with thine olives green,
> And poplars, and lawn-shading palms, and beech,
> In which the Zephyr breathes the loudest song,
> And hazels thick, dark-stemm'd beneath the shade.   [III 24–7]

When Apollo enters the poem, a few lines later, he seems less of an autonomous character than a vehicle for the poet's further imaginative approach to the 'leafy luxury' of the setting:

> [He] wandered forth
> Beside the osiers of a rivulet,
> Full ankle-deep in lilies of the vale.   [III 33–5]

In the last line Keats characteristically employs a suggestion of tactual intimacy to convey utter abundance of luxurious sensation.

When he revised *Hyperion*, Keats transferred this passage to the prologue of the *Fall* and converted it into an allegorical representation of the first phase in the development of a poet.[7] Although several particulars remain the same ('palm' and 'beech'), the character of the imagery is drastically changed:

> Methought I stood where trees of every clime,
> Palm, myrtle, oak, and sycamore, and beech,
> With Plantane, and spice blossoms, made a screen. [*F.H.* I 19-21]

This rapid roll call of unqualified specific names prevents the "intense' contemplation of concrete particulars, and serves instead to exemplify logically the unnatural variety of this allegorical garden. Fixed at a uniform distance, the setting functions to 'screen' and conceal rather than to surrender itself to the imagination of the beholder.

A similar discipline is imposed on imagery throughout the nearly four hundred lines Keats added to the poem during the summer of 1819.[8] He represses any manifestation of an instinctive 'intensity', and emphasises instead the logical, thematic or moral significance of concrete particulars. Extended passages in the prologue, for example, establish patterns of abstract categories within which images, if they occur at all, function as typifying examples. The 'sort of induction' that opens the *Fall* distinguishes two species of dreamers, the 'fanatic' and the 'savage' [I 1–4], each of whom is associated in the following lines with appropriate images ('vellum' and 'indian leaf' [I 5]). These species are then subsumed within the genus of inarticulate dreamers, and opposed to the poet who can tell his dreams [I 8]. A final evaluation of the fame (and by implication the validity) of the present 'dream' – the *Fall* – is then conceived as a suspended classification within the relevant categories:

> Whether the dream now purposed to rehearse
> Be Poet's or Fanatic's will be known
> When this warm scribe my hand is in the grave. [*F.H.* I 16–18]

In beginning *Endymion*, over two years before, Keats had proceeded from an initial generalisation to restatements that synthesise rather than analyse and categorise concrete particulars. The 'thing of beauty' of the first line becomes all beautiful things, and every image that follows embodies but diverts attention from the initial abstraction. Within a few lines, the poet's spirit openly 'clings and plays about its fancy' [*E.* I 620–1] with more concern for the sensuous richness than the logical significance of, for example, 'clear rills / That for themselves a cooling covert make / 'Gainst the hot season' [*E* I 16–18].

Later in the *Fall* [I 147–202], Moneta divides men into four sharply defined groups: the disinterested and the selfish, the practical and the visionary.[9] If the vigor of her discriminations promises a logical coherence this draft did not attain, the rigorous classification of concrete particulars remains an expression of moral judgement, as it is throughout the *Divine Comedy*. The 'things' that had puzzled the will and tempted the imagination 'out of thought' in the *Epistle to Reynolds* [76–7], fifteen months earlier, Keats here sorts and classifies with something of the authority of a Minos.[10] He passes over whatever 'intensity' they may offer the senses, and seeks to determine instead their 'moral properties and scopes'.

In those passages of the *Fall* that are primarily descriptive, Keats frequently selects imagery that possesses a broadly thematic significance. A number of images refer to sickness and medicine, for example, and repeated images of cold and the color white endow both sensations with obvious moral implications. Purity of character is on occasion summarised by the physical setting, as, for example, when Moneta sits 'on a square-edg'd polish'd stone, / That in its lucid depth reflected pure / Her priestess garments' [*F.H.* II 51–3].[11] Similes refer to theme with a conscious allusiveness new to Keats's poetry: the mention of Eve [I 31] implies the consequences of the Dreamer's 'appetite' [I 38], and Proserpine [I 37], like the Dreamer, knows 'what 'tis to die and live again' [I 42].[12] As Ridley and Muir have shown, Keats revised the first *Hyperion* so as to clarify relevance and coherence of imagery. The excised 'green-rob'd senators of mighty woods' [*H.* I 73] added little to the relevance of the simile it adorned (which was concerned with a sound) and did not point to a theme of the narrative.[13] The artful but thematically irrelevant similes that had emphasised Thea's size [*H.* I 26–33] are replaced in the *Fall* by a brief but more efficient comparison of Saturn to his image in the temple [*F.H.* I 298–300].

Like the painting that in 1817 inspired Keats's formulation of the ideal of 'intensity', the external world depicted by the prologue offers the reader 'nothing to be intense upon' [*Letters*, I, p. 192]. Although the garden and sanctuary contain objects that promise sensuous luxury to and evoke an intense response from the Dreamer, the style itself remains detached, and neither displays nor encourages imaginative entanglements with physical things. Objects that promise intensity of sensation are half-concealed from the reader by a veil of generalised diction, which parts to reveal images that frequently discourage or repel imaginative approach. The Dreamer comes upon

> a feast of summer fruits,
> Which nearer seen, seem'd refuse of a meal
> By Angel tasted, or our Mother Eve;
> For empty shells were scattered on the grass,
> And grape stalks but half bare, and remnants more,
> Sweet smelling, whose pure kinds I could not know.   [*F.H.* I 29–34]

Unlike its predecessor in *The Eve of St Agnes* [264–70], this feast is generalised and visual. On closer approach the mildly pleasant 'summer fruits' are 'seen' as 'refuse' – Keats's sole use of the unlovely noun.[14] This generalisation is then resolved into concrete particulars that discourage the involvement of taste and touch, and emphasise privation rather than abundance: the shells are empty, the stalks half-bare. In the *Nightingale* ode the privation of sense had stimulated a compensatory effort by the imagination to 'guess each sweet' [43], but these 'remnants' evoke no impulse whatever; the Dreamer records his inability to classify them – 'whose pure kinds I could not know' – and passes on. The simile that follows diverts our attention from the 'plenty' it sets out to describe:

More plenty than the fabled horn
Thrice emptied could pour forth, at banqueting
For Proserpine return'd to her own fields,
Where the white heifers low.   [*F.H.* I 35-8]

Keats's imagination passes rapidly over several associations he
had explored in earlier poems, and moves from the concrete
abundance of the feast to the 'fair field / Of Enna' of *Paradise
Lost*,[15] which he touches with a gentler pathos than Milton,
reminding us not of the young girl's violent abduction but of
her return from the dead.[16] The starkly unqualified final image
suggests a beauty that lies beyond the grasp of the gusto and
perseverance Keats had praised in *Paradise Lost*, and conveys a
pathos that, like Dante's, is 'brief'.[17]

Throughout the following descriptions the imagery remains
brief and sensuously neutral. The Dreamer's desires are
detached from the concrete objects that evoke them by solitary
abstractions: 'And appetite / . . . Growing within, I ate
deliciously; / And, after not long, thirsted' [*F.H.* I 38-41]. If the
'full draught' that relieves this thirst performs the functions of
the wine in the *Nightingale* ode, it is purged, as an image, of all
but the most delicate promise of sensuous richness: 'a cool
vessel of transparent juice, / Sipp'd by the wander'd bee' [I 42-
3]. The potency of this drink is not manifested stylistically, by
clustered and synaesthetic imagery, but by a spare statement
of its dramatic effect: 'the cloudy swoon came on, and down I
sunk' [I 55].

The rapid movement of the Dreamer's attention becomes
more striking in the following description of the sanctuary, the
proportions of which are established by broad, sweeping
movements of the eye. The relics littering the pavement are
enumerated rapidly and with deliberate vagueness:

strange vessels, and large draperies,
Which needs had been of dyed asbestos wove,
Or in that place the moth could not corrupt,
So white the linen; so, in some, distinct
Ran imageries from a sombre loom.   [*F.H.* I 73-7]

Unlike those carved on Madeline's casement [*St Agnes*, 208–16], these 'imageries' are not approached or explored, even though they are explicitly 'distinct'.

Keats's revisions of *Hyperion* also suggest his desire to prevent prolonged contemplation of concrete things. He deliberately split the opening scene [*H.* I 1–14] by introducing a long passage that describes the dynamic growth of the Dreamer's powers of vision [*F.H.* I 297–310]. The interpolation tends to prevent absorption in the concrete setting of the shady vale, and to dissipate the mood of intense stasis it had implied. Later in the *Fall* Keats abstracts and names this mood – 'eternal quietude' [I 390]. He clarifies the significance of imagery but moderates its power to evoke intensity of sensation.

The many organic images in the *Fall* act more emphatically to discourage sensuous contemplation. References to the human body are anatomically exact and highly concrete: the carotid arteries become 'those streams that pulse beside the throat' [*F.H.* I 125], and the mouth the 'roofed home' of the tongue [*F.H.* I 229]. Keats disciplines the tactual suggestivity of the adjective 'globed', which he had exploited in the *Ode on Melancholy* [17], by applying it to the 'brain' [*F.H.* I 245]. The focus of tactual imagery in the *Fall* is often anatomical and painful. Cold is mentioned most frequently, and the sensuous appeal of warmth is checked in both of its appearances by immediate shifts to the thought of death [*F.H.* I 18, 98].[18] The imagery of the *Fall* is clearly not selected for its beauty or its promise of sensuous luxury. Like the 'dead stiff & ugly' Angela, whom Keats introduced into the final stanza of the *Eve of St Agnes* in August [*Letters*, II, p. 163], this imagery specifically avoids allowing the sense of beauty to overcome 'every other consideration' [*Letters*, I, p. 194].

A further effect of stylistic discipline in the *Fall* is to discourage empathic identification with natural objects. The Dreamer is consistently stationed at a definite distance from his surroundings, and the senses he most often invokes are those that imply distance, particularly the sense of sight. If tactual or kinesthetic imagery occasionally suggests an intimate apprehension of external objects, such as the blooms that swing 'light' in air [*F.H.* I 27], or the 'soft smoke' that rises from the altar of the sanctuary [*F.H.* I 105], the more frequent focus of tactual imagery on the Dreamer's anatomical self encourages a centripetal movement of attention that is the opposite of empathy. A similar effect results from Keats's frequent references to the process of sensation, a characteristic of this style which may reflect his study of Dante.[19] A 'scent' is known to the 'woodland nostril' [*F.H.* I 406], and the Dreamer's shriek stings his own ears [*F.H.* I 127]. His eyes 'fathom the space' of the lofty sanctuary [*F.H.* I 82], or 'ran on / From stately nave to nave' [*F.H.* I 53-4]. Even at moments of extreme emotion the diction notices the autonomous functioning of the Dreamer's senses:

> I heard, I look'd: two senses both at once
> So fine, so subtle, felt the tyranny
> Of that fierce threat.   [*F.H.* I 118–20]

The pathetic contrast between Saturn's words and his appearance elicits a similar formulation:

> Nor could my eyes
> And ears act with that pleasant unison of sense
> Which marries sweet sound with the grace of form.   [*F.H.* I 441–3][20]

Such rigorous segregation of the different senses is the antithesis of synaesthesia, which Keats had employed in earlier poems to render heights of intense sensation. Of the three examples of this figure in the *Fall*, only one encourages imaginative apprehension of a distant object – the 'soft smoke' noticed above. The synaesthetic images evoked by the fragrance of roses and the sound of fountains act quite differently:

> In neighbourhood of fountains, by the noise
> Soft-showering in mine ears; and, by the touch
> Of scent, not far from roses.   [*F.H.* I 22–4]

Tactual imagery ('touch', 'soft-showering') here suggests neither proximity to nor identity with the things observed, but rather affirms their distance.[21] As generalised sense-impressions ('noise', 'scent') impinge upon the tangible periphery of the Dreamer's mind, sensation becomes a process of conscious inference that is far removed from the instinctive outrush of empathy characteristic of the chameleon poet. Keats's attention here moves from the object beheld to the mind that beholds it, and perception results not in self-forgetfulness but in self-consciousness. Like the speaker in the first and last stanzas of the *Nightingale* ode, the Dreamer is firmly stationed within his 'sole self', and any instinct to 'dissolve' or 'fade away' is vigorously controlled by the style. When the pain of self-conscious thought becomes unbearable, he finds solace not in the absorbing beauty of the physical world, but in a moral reality that transfigures that world:

> Deathwards progressing
> To no death was that visage; it had pass'd
> The lily and the snow; and beyond these
> I must not think now, though I saw that face—
> But for her eyes I should have fled away.
> They held me back, with a benignant light,
> . . .
>
> [*F.H.* I 260–5]

However we describe it, the Dreamer's passionate response to Moneta's eyes is hardly aesthetic. Applied to this wan countenance, the 'artful humour' of Keats's earlier phrase – 'sorrow more beautiful than Beauty's self' [*H.* I 36] – seems slightly irrelevant.

The stylistic discipline of 'intensity' is obviously relevant to the allegorical form and the 'purgatorial' action of the *Fall*. Detachment from the physical world emphasises the supersensory power of a vision that 'can see as God sees, and take the depth / Of things' [*F.H.* I 304–5]. The sharp delineation of the Dreamer's consciousness asserts the integrity of his identity, which it is the task of the prologue to establish, and implies that escape from the pain of his initiation, or from the vision that follows it, is impossible. If the style fails to display empathy, the Dreamer is characterised by a sympathy, for both his fellow men and the fallen and humanised Titans, that brings him pain.[22]

The discipline of 'intensity', however, is not limited to the *Fall* itself. Keats's own sense of estrangement from the physical world is clear in several letters he wrote during the summer. He grew 'accustom'd to the privations of the pleasures of sense' [II, p. 186], and took particular delight in the 'beautiful' blank wall beyond his Winchester window [II, p. 141]. If he displays an undiminished power to relish physical sensation, it is mingled with a detached, and amusing, perspective on himself that on occasion seems almost a parody of 'intensity'. 'Talking of Pleasure', he wrote to Dilke in September, 'this moment I was . . . holding to my mouth a Nectarine–good god how fine–It went down soft pulpy, slushy, oozy–all its delicious embonpoint melted down my throat like a large beautified Strawberry. I shall certainly breed' [II, p. 179]. A more painful focus for Keats's powers of imaginative 'intensity' was provided by Fanny Brawne, whom he struggled to put out of his mind [II, p. 137], or imagined behind a veil of mist [II, pp. 137, 140], like the roses and fountains of the *Fall*. He took on the hardness of sensibility the Dreamer displays: a letter is 'flint-worded' [II, p. 142], his heart 'iron' [II, pp. 141, 146], 'A few more moments thought of you would uncrystallise and dissolve me', he wrote to Fanny. 'I must not give way to it' [II, p. 142].

If 'intensity' became something of a personal threat to Keats during the summer of 1819, he perceived its inadequacies as broadly philosophical and ethical. The antithesis he had drawn the year before between 'luxury' and 'philosophy' [I, p. 271] was sharpened and resolved largely in favor of philosophy. He repeatedly questioned the veracity of the imagination of this time, and on one occasion opposed an erroneous but instinctive sympathy for Fanny to the criticisms of a cold but veridical philosophy [II, p. 127]. Perhaps his most pointed philosophical criticism of 'intensity' occurs in the journal-letter of 19 March 1819, where in a deservedly famous passage he recognises that the poetry of 'intensity' is one expression of an instinctive egoism that impels the life of nature as well as most men [II, pp. 78–81]. The eagle that he chooses as an emblem for poetry suggests the predatory pursuit of beauty, and, as a concrete and enthralling thing, itself teases us out of thought, as does 'intensity'. Above the eagle, poetry and instinctive self-interest – which at one point he calls, suddenly, 'sin' [I, p. 80] – Keats ranks the ideal of philosophical disinterestedness, a 'pure desire of the benefit of others' [II, p. 79] which he was to embody in the impartial benignity of eyes that 'beam'd like the mild moon/Who comforts those she sees not' [*F.H.* I 269–70].

That the disciplined style of the *Fall* expresses its author's concern for disinterestedness is suggested by the 'system of Salvation' the poem offers, which everywhere insists on the primacy of selflessness. Moneta condemns those men in the outer world or in the temple who cannot feel the misery of their fellows. The suffering, compassionate Titaness herself is the moral opposite of the amused and detached 'superior beings' [*Letters*, II, p. 80] of the journal-letter.[23] The 'vision' is granted as compensation for the suffering peculiar to the disinterested poet, who cannot act to relieve the misery he perceives. The Dreamer exhibits an acute sensitivity to excessive desire; he represses the impulse to hasten toward the altar of the sanctuary as 'too unholy there' [*F.H.* I 94], and implicitly judges his craving for vision by comparing it to the 'avarice' of a search for gold [*F.H.* I 271–7].[24] Unlike the paradise of the 'fanatic' or 'savage', the spectacle of the fallen Titans inflicts pain, from which the Dreamer fervently desires to escape: 'Oftentimes I pray'd/Intense, that Death would take me from the vale/ And all its burthens' [*F.H.* I 396–8]. This intense desire for dissolution is not indulged, as it was in the *Nightingale* ode, and it seeks escape not into vision but from it. The 'vision' of the *Fall*, that is, no longer subserves the desires of the poet, but disciplines them, just as the style disciplines our instinctive desire to 'gorge' the beauty of the physical world.

A major effect of the revised form of the *Fall* is to divest the epic narrative of *Hyperion* of a theme that had rendered artistic disinterestedness difficult for Keats – the initiation or birth of a poet. The entrance of this theme in the third book of *Hyperion* had provoked an impulsive departure from the style (and seemingly, the action) of the previous books. By transferring this theme to the Dreamer and working it out in the prologue of the *Fall*, Keats altered the epic narrative itself, as we have seen he altered the imagery of his style, diminishing its 'intensity', asserting its distance and impersonality. We may speculate that such a change would have facilitated the deliberate invention necessary to the poem's completion.[25]

The impersonality of the epic narrative, thus revised, is apparent when it is compared with the sensuous or erotic subjects of earlier visions, such as the *Nightingale* ode or *Lamia*. There is also evident in the *Fall* an abatement of the epistemological criticism to which these earlier visions had been subjected with a severity roughly proportional to their 'intensity' and implicit egoism. The imaginative approach to' the nightingale, proves ultimately self-exhausting and of uncertain validity, and Lamia's illusory beauty is exposed and destroyed by the pitiless 'demon eyes' of the philosopher Apollonius. Despite the Dreamer's self-doubts and uncertainties about the value and truth of poetry, he accepts the vision offered him by Moneta gratefully and without question. This vision is seemingly guaranteed by the 'prodigious' toil and proven disinterestedness of its beholder. In the ode *To Autumn*, which in several respects profited from the more deliberate discipline of the *Fall*, epistemological uncertainties have disappeared completely.[26]

Especially in its attempt to control what Samuel Johnson called the 'hunger of the imagintion', Keats's late style seems anti-romantic in tendency.[27] It recalls the later development of Wordsworth, who came to doubt the adequacy of 'chance-desires', and who sought to anchor his faith in a firmer ground than the 'poet's dream'. If Keats sought to free his style from absorption in the compelling intensity of concrete beauty, he did not, however, dedicate it to the abstract and metaphorical exposition of the 'invisible world'. His moral and artistic vision remains fixed on a reality that is sublunary and a world in which, as a younger and more hopeful Wordsworth had said, 'we find our happiness or not at all'. The style of the *Fall* morally informs and chastens our perception of concrete things, and may be said to purge and redeem the 'poet's dream' instead of denying it.[28] The Dreamer of the *Fall* neither seeks nor receives an 'unfeeling armour', but rather opens the 'horn-Book' of his heart to the pain that thought and experience inflict on Titans and men alike. His vulnerability is his strength. If these contrasts between Keats and Wordsworth measure the resilience of the former's youth, they also suggest the specifically artistic promise inherent in a 'more thoughtful and quiet' poetry that, as W. J. Bate has said, was less an ending than a 'final beginning'.

SOURCE: article in the *Keats-Shelley Journal*, 17 (1968), pp. 75–88.

NOTES

[Reorganised and renumbered from the original – Ed.]

1. *The Letters of John Keats*, ed. Hyder E. Rollins (Cambridge, Mass. and Cambridge, 1958), II, p. 116. Subsequent references to letters in the text are to this edition.

2. Although not all critics have agreed with Middleton Murry that *The Fall* is the 'profoundest and most sublime' of Keats's poems, many have noted its philosophical and emotional maturity. Recent assessments include: Kenneth Muir, 'The Meaning of *Hyperion*' (1952 article, repr. in *John Keats: A Reassessment*, ed. K. Muir (Liverpool, 1958), pp. 103–23 [see preceding study in this selection – Ed.]; W. J. Bate, *John Keats* (Cambridge, Mass. and Oxford, 1963), pp. 585–605; and Stuart M. Sperry Jnr, 'Keats, Milton and *The Fall of Hyperion*', *PMLA*, LXXVII (1962), pp. 77–84.

3. W. J. Bate, *The Stylistic Development of Keats* (New York, 1945), p. 176.

4. Bate's study of the stylistic development is complemented by R. H. Fogle, *The Imagery of Keats and Shelley* (Chapel Hill, N.C., 1949), which describes the synaesthetic and empathic aspects of Keats's imagery in detail (pp. 106–22, 152–77).

5. David Perkins, *The Quest for Permanence: The Symbolism of Wordsworth, Shelley and Keats* (Cambridge, Mass., 1959), p. 210.

6. All references to the poetry are to *The Poetical Works of John Keats*, ed. H. W. Garrod (Oxford, 2nd edn 1958).

7. Keats drew as well on Clymene's description of Delos [*H.* II 262–4], in which the movement of attention is slowed by her childlike and admiring repetition: 'I stood upon a shore, a pleasant shore,/Where a sweet clime was breathed from a land/Of fragrance, quietness, and trees, and flowers.'

8. These lines comprise the prologue (293 lines) and eight major interpolations (105 lines) in the narrative of *Hyperion*.

9. I paraphrase (in part) Moneta's description of these categories. In the

disputed lines [*F.H.* I 187–210] she further subdivides the genus of visionaries (those who enter the temple) into 'dreamers' and 'poets'. For a detailed analysis of her frequently contradictory discriminations, see Brian Wicker, 'The Disputed Lines in *The Fall of Hyperion*', *Essays in Criticism*, VII (1957), pp. 28–41.

10. In July 1818, Keats had associated the judge of Dante's *Inferno* with the vigorous and absolute discrimination between a genuine reality and a morally infirm and subjective imagination: 'For who has mind to relish, Minos-wise,/The real of Beauty, free from that dead hue/Sickly imagination and sick pride/cast wan upon it?' ('On Visiting the Tomb of Burns' [9–12]). The *Inferno*, of course, displays many acts of moral judgement that take the form of classifications within the categories of Hell.

11. As several critics have noted, this passage may echo *Paradiso* [II 32] and *Purgatorio* [IX 85–7].

12. Sperry, op. cit. (note 2, above), p. 78, has noted the relevance of the allusion of Eve, and compares it with *Paradise Lost*.

13. M. R. Ridley, *Keats's Craftsmanship* (New York, 1933), pp. 276–7, and K. Muir, op. cit. (note 2, above), pp. 115–16, discuss this passage. [See preceding study in this selection – Ed.]

14. A substantial number of the words that characterise the diction of *The Fall* occur only there. Several of these suggest the new purposes of Keats's style: 'repress' [I 94] and 'confus'd' [I 78]. Abstract uses of 'form' [I 443] and 'kinds' [I 34] are limited to this poem, as are the memorable Latinate polysyllables that dignify its relaxed syntax: 'superannuations' [I 68], 'faulture' [I 70] and 'adorant' [I 283], among others. 'Ascend' [I 107, 124], which is common in *Paradise Lost* and Cary's Dante, Keats used only in *The Fall*.

15. *Paradise Lost* [IV 269–70].

16. The sacrificial animals of ancient Greece had attracted Keats's attention in *Endymion* [I 214] and the *Epistle to John Reynolds* [21], as well as in the *Grecian Urn* ode [33–4]. In earlier poems he had associated Proserpine with Hades and death – *Melancholy* ode [4], *Endymion* [I 944] – and in *Lamia* [63] had pictured her weeping for her 'Sicilian air', like Ruth among 'the alien corn'. In *The Fall* he touches the myth, more benignly, at a time of fulfilment and restoration, and returns the girl to her 'own fields'.

17. In his comment on *Paradise Lost* [IV 269–70] Keats had compared it specifically with the 'brief pathos' of Dante: *The Poetical Works and Other Writings*, V, p. 302.

18. References to cold occur six times, whereas the more pleasant 'cool' is mentioned only once. Precedents in the imagery of the *Divine Comedy* have been noted by J. L. Lowes, '*Hyperion* and the *Purgatorio*', *TLS* (11 Jan. 1936), p. 35.

19. The action of the eyes, for example, is mentioned 39 times in the verses Keats composed during the summer. In 400 lines of *Hyperion* [I 1 – II 43] I have counted 22. Corresponding figures for other senses: auditory 21 and 7; olfactory 3 and 0; tactual 6 and 3; gustatory 0 and 2. A similar formulation of perception is common in the *Divine Comedy*, where the senses

are frequently personified. Among the passages in the *Inferno* that Keats marked we find, for example (in Cary's translation), 'my ken discerned the form of one' [I 59] and 'his eye/Not far could lead him' [IX 5–6]. For other explicit references to the process of sensation, see *Inferno* [IX 73–4, X 126–7, XI 11, XV 19–25, XXIII 27–9]. For transcriptions of Keats's markings in Dante's work, see Robert Gittings, *The Mask of Keats: A Study of Problems* (Cambridge, Mass. and London, 1956), pp. 144–161.

20. Cf. *Purgatorio*: 'One sense cried "Nay",/Another, "Yes, they sing"' [X 54–5].

21. This description of the perception of roses should be compared with the synaesthesia of *Hyperion*: 'like a rose in vermeil tint and shape,/In fragrance soft, and coolness to the eye' [I 209–10]. Of the five examples of synaesthesia that Keats revised, three are retained in *The Fall* [*H*. I 130, 186, 219; *F.H*. I 435, II 30, 55]. He may have intended to use the others [*H*. I 206, 210] later in the narrative.

22. Several interpolations within the narrative of *Hyperion* emphasise the Dreamer's participation in the pain of the fallen Titans, who – as Muir has pointed out of Saturn (op. cit., note 2, above, p. 119 [see preceding study in this selection – Ed.]) – are consistently humanised by the revision. See particularly [*H*. I 331–2, 390 & 441].

23. The Dreamer refers to his salvation as an 'award' [F.H. I 185] and Moneta grants him the vision out of kindness [I 242]. His own disinterestedness is made explicit in the two lines that were deleted from the Woodhouse transcript: 'Mankind thou lovest; many of thine hours/Have been distempered with their miseries' [I 166/7].

24. Cf. *Purgatorio*: 'his feet desisted (slack'ning pace)/From haste, that mars all decency of act' [III 10–11]. Keats could not fail to find conformation of his concern for disinterestedness in the *Divine Comedy*.

25. There is a substantial critical agreement that, by working out the Apollo theme in the prologue, Keats doomed *The Fall* to incompleteness. At least two questions arise here: whether he was capable of the invention required to complete the poem; and whether his material – the Titanomachia – is relevant to the themes advanced in the prologue. If the answer to the first question cannot be known, we should not underestimate Keats's powers of dramatic invention. . . . The relevance of the Titanomachia to his maturing philosophy may be questioned, but it is not obviously inappropriate to the prologue, which seeks, like Keats's other 'systems of Salvation' [*Letters*, II, p. 103], to justify human suffering and to reconcile it with art. The fall of Titans would provide, one might guess, an opportunity to demonstrate the possibility of disinterestedness under tragic circumstance, and, in its relation to the Dreamer, might embody a vision informed by the same value. One might speculate further (since all discussion of this point is speculation) that the Apollo of *The Fall* would have been clearly differentiated from the mortal Dreamer, and that he would bear little resemblance to the bewildered and 'intense' youth of *Hyperion*.

26. The subject of the *Autumn* ode is similarly impersonal and benign. The speaker's presence is felt primarily by his quickness to comfort and

reassure. If the imagery of *Autumn* is less austere than that of *The Fall*, it is organised in terms of the subject itself rather than by the poet's needs.

27. Several critics have commented on the anti-romantic tendencies of *The Fall*. Edward E. Bostetter – 'The Eagle and the Truth: Keats and the Problem of Belief', *JAAC*, XVI (1937), p 371 – finds that the 'despondency' of *The Fall* arose out of Keats's 'questioning of the fundamental tenets of Romantic Poetry'. According to Robert D. Wagner – 'Keats: *Ode to Psyche* and the Second *Hyperion*', *K-SJ*, XIII (1964), p. 36 – the basic structure of *The Fall* 'suggests nothing less than a *revaluation* of romantic values'.

28. This, perhaps, was the point of T. S. Eliot's statement – 'The Metaphysical Poets', *TLS* (20 Oct. 1921), p. 670 – that *The Fall* exhibits traces of a 'unification of sensibility'.

SELECT BIBLIOGRAPHY

EARLY CRITICAL RECEPTION

G. H. Ford, *Keats and the Victorians: A Study of His Influence and Rise to Fame, 1821–1895* (New Haven, Conn., 1944).

G. M. Matthews (ed.), *Keats: The Critical Heritage* (London, 1971).

ENDYMION: A POETIC ROMANCE

Glen O. Allen, 'The Fall of Endymion: A Study in Keats's Intellectual Growth', *Keats-Shelley Journal*, 6 (1957), pp. 37–57.

Walter Jackson Bate, *John Keats* (Cambridge, Mass., 1964): ch. 8, 'A Trial of Invention: *Endymion*', pp. 149–92.

Albert S. Gérard, 'Keats and the Romantic *Sehnsucht*', *University of Toronto Quarterly*, 28 (1959), pp. 160–75; reprinted in Gérard's *English Romantic Poetry* (Berkeley & Los Angeles, Cal., 1968), pp. 194–214.

Clarice Godfrey, '*Endymion*', in *John Keats: A Reassessment*, ed. Kenneth Muir (Liverpool, 1958; reprinted 1969), pp. 20–39.

Bruce E. Miller, 'On the Meaning of Keats's *Endymion*', *Keats-Shelley Journal*, 14 (1965), pp. 33–54.

John Middleton Murry, *Studies in Keats* (London, 1930); 4th edition, revised and enlarged, entitled *Keats* (London, 1955; reprinted New York, 1962). Ch. 3, 'The Meaning of *Endymion*' in the 1930 edition (pp. 34–61), in the 1955 and subsequent editions becomes ch. 4, retitled 'The Cave of Quietude'.

E. C. Pettet, *On the Poetry of Keats* (Cambridge, 1957): chs 4 and 5 on *Endymion*, pp. 123–45.

Jack Stillinger, *The Hoodwinking of Madeline and Other Essays on Keats's Poems* (Chicago & London, 1971): ch. 2, 'On the Interpretation of *Endymion*: The Comedian as the Letter E', pp. 14–30.

Jacob D. Wigod, 'The Meaning of *Endymion*', *Publications of the Modern Language Association of America* [*PMLA*], 68 (1953), pp. 779–90.

ISABELLA: OR, THE POT OF BASIL

Sidney Colvin, *John Keats: His Life and Poetry, His Friends, Critics and After-Fame* (London, 1917): see especially pp. 389–96.

John Jones, *John Keats's Dream of Truth* (London, 1969): Part I – section 3, 'Feel, Sex and *Isabella*' and section 4, 'Negative Capability and again *Isabella*', pp. 11–31.

Judy Little, *Keats as a Narrative Poet: A Test of Invention* (Lincoln, Neb., 1975): ch. 4, 'Hazlitt and New "Axioms" in *Isabella*', pp. 66–86.

Jack Stillinger, 'Keats and Romance: The "Reality" of *Isabella*', *Studies in English Literature*, 8 (1968), pp. 593–605; reprinted in Stillinger's *The Hoodwinking of Madeline and Other Essays . . .* (Chicago & London, 1971), pp. 31–45.

Herbert G. Wright, *Boccaccio in England from Chaucer to Tennyson* (London, 1957): see especially pp. 399–407.

HYPERION and THE FALL OF HYPERION

Walter Jackson Bate, *John Keats* (Cambridge, Mass., 1964): ch. 16, '*Hyperion* and a New Level of Writing', pp. 388–417, and ch. 21, 'The Close of the Fertile Year', sections 7–13, pp. 585–605.

Harold Bloom, *The Visionary Company: A Reading of English Romantic Poetry* (New York, 1961): see especially pp. 409–18.

Edward E. Bostetter, *The Romantic Ventriloquists: Wordsworth, Coleridge, Keats, Shelley, Byron* (Seattle & London, 1963; revised edition 1975): ch. 4, 'Keats' is largely concerned with the two *Hyperion* poems (pp. 136–80 of the revised edition).

Douglas Bush, *Mythology and the Romantic Tradition in English Poetry* (Cambridge, Mass., 1937; reprinted New York, 1963): see especially pp. 115–28 of the 1963 reprint.

J. R. Caldwell, 'The Meaning of *Hyperion*', *PMLA*, 51 (1936), pp. 1080–97.

Irene H. Chayes, 'Dreamer, Poet and Poem in *The Fall of Hyperion*', *Philological Quarterly*, 46 (1967), pp. 499–515.

Walter H. Evert, *Aesthetic and Myth in the Poetry of Keats* (Princeton, N.J., 1965): ch. 5 on *Hyperion*, pp. 225–43.

Geoffrey H. Hartman, 'Spectral Symbolism and the Authorial Self: An Approach to Keats's *Hyperion*', *Essays in Criticism*, 24 (1974), pp. 1–19.

Graham Hough, *The Romantic Poets* (London, 1953; 3rd edition 1967): ch. 5, section iii, 'The Two Hyperions' pp. 180–94 of the 3rd edition.

D. G. James, *The Romantic Comedy* (London & New York, 1948; reprinted 1949): Part II, 'Purgatory Blind', sections 19–22, pp. 134–51 of the 1949 printing.

John Middleton Murry, *Studies in Keats: New and Old* (London & New York, 1939): ch. 7, 'The Poet and the Dreamer', pp. 98–106.

Stuart M. Sperry Jnr, 'Keats, Milton and *The Fall of Hyperion*', *PMLA*, 77 (1962), pp. 77–84; revised and republished in Sperry's *Keats the Poet* (Princeton, N.J., 1973), pp. 310–35.

Norman Talbot, *The Major Poems of John Keats* (Sydney, 1968): see especially pp. 67–81 on *The Fall of Hyperion*.

Brian Wicker, 'The Disputed Lines in *The Fall of Hyperion*', *Essays in Criticism*, 7 (1957), pp. 28–41.
Brian Wilkie, *Romantic Poets and Epic Tradition* (Madison & Milwaukee, 1965): ch. 5, 'Keats and the Mortal Taste', pp. 145–87.

THE EVE OF ST AGNES

Miriam Allott, '*Isabella, The Eve of St Agnes* and *Lamia*', in *John Keats: A Reassessment*, ed. Kenneth Muir (Liverpool, 1958; reprinted 1969), pp. 39–62.
Walter Jackson Bate, *John Keats* (Cambridge, Mass., 1964): ch. 17, sections 11–13, pp. 438–51.
John Bayley, 'Keats and Reality', *Proceedings of the British Academy*, 48 (1962): see especially pp. 117–25.
C. F. Burgess, '*The Eve of St Agnes*: One Way to the Poem', *English Journal*, 54 (1965), pp. 389–94.
Allan Danzig (ed.), *Twentieth-Century Interpretations of 'The Eve of St Agnes'* (Englewood Cliffs, N.J., 1971).
R. A. Foakes, *The Romantic Assertion: A Study in the Language of Nineteenth-Century Poetry* (London, 1958); ch. 5, 'Keats's *The Eve of St Agnes* and Shelley's *Adonais*, pp. 80–110.
R. H. Fogle, 'A Reading of Keats's *Eve of St Agnes*', *College English*, 6 (1945), pp. 325–8.
Gail M. Gibson, 'Ave Madeline: Ironic Annunciation in *The Eve of St Agnes*', *Keats-Shelley Journal*, 26 (1977), pp. 39–50.
Michael Ragussis, 'Narrative Structure and the Problem of the Divided Reader in *The Eve of St Agnes*', *ELH: A Journal of English Literary History*, 42 (1975), pp. 378–94.
Constance Rooke, 'Romance and Reality in *The Eve of St Agnes*', *English Studies in Canada*, 4 (1978), pp. 25–40.
Roger Sharrock, 'Keats and the Young Lovers', *Review of English Literature*, 2 (1961), pp. 76–86.
Stuart M. Sperry Jnr, 'Romance as Wish-Fulfillment: Keats's *The Eve of St Agnes*', *Studies in Romanticism*, 10 (1971), pp. 27–43; revised and republished in Sperry's *Keats the Poet* (Princeton, N.J., 1973), pp. 198–220.

THE EVE OF ST MARK

Jack Stillinger, 'The Meaning of "Poor Cheated Soul" in *The Eve of St Mark*', *English Language Notes*, 5 (1968), pp. 193–6; reprinted in Stillinger's *The Hoodwinking of Madeline and Other Essays* . . . (Chicago & London, 1971), pp. 94–8.

LA BELLE DAME SANS MERCI

Jane R. Cohen, 'Keats's Humour in *La Belle Dame sans Merci*', *Keats-Shelley Journal*, 17 (1968), pp. 10–13.

Charles I. Patterson Jnr, *The Daemonic in the Poetry of John Keats* (Chicago & London, 1970): ch. 4, '*La Belle Dame sans Merci*: The High Point', pp. 125–50.

E. C. Pettet, *On the Poetry of Keats* (Cambridge, 1957): ch. 6 on *La Belle Dame sans Merci*, pp. 203–50.

Bernice Slote, 'The Climate of Keats's *La Belle Dame sans Merci*', *Modern Language Quarterly*, 21 (1960), pp. 195–207.

Francis Utley, 'The Infernos of Lucretius and of Keats's *La Belle Dame sans Merci*', *ELH: A Journal of English Literary History*, 25 (1958), pp. 105–21.

Earl R. Wasserman, *The Finer Tone: Keats's Major Poems* (Baltimore, Md., 1953; reprinted 1967): ch. 3 on *La Belle Dame sans Merci*, pp. 63–83.

LAMIA

Walter Jackson Bate, *John Keats* (Cambridge, Mass., 1964): ch. 20, sections 7–12, pp. 543–61.

Barry Edward Gross, '*The Eve of St Agnes* and *Lamia*: Paradise Won and Paradise Lost', *Bucknell Review*, 13 (1965), pp. 45–57.

Charles I. Patterson Jnr. *The Daemonic in the Poetry of John Keats* (Chicago & London, 1970): ch. 6, '*Lamia*: The Point of No Return', pp. 185–216.

Bernice Slote, *Keats and the Dramatic Principle* (Lincoln, Neb., 1958); ch. 9, '*Lamia*: A Quarrel in the Streets', pp. 138–63.

Stuart M. Sperry Jnr, *Keats the Poet* (Princeton, N.J., 1973): ch. 11, 'Comic Irony: *Lamia*', pp. 292–309.

William C. Stephenson, 'The Fall from Innocence in Keats's *Lamia*', *Papers on Language and Literature*, 10 (1974), pp. 35–50.

Earl R. Wasserman, *The Finer Tone: Keats's Major Poems* (Baltimore, Md., 1953; reprinted 1967): ch. 5 on *Lamia*, pp. 138–74.

NOTES ON CONTRIBUTORS

PART TWO

MATTHEW ARNOLD (1822–88): poet, critic and educationist, Professor of Poetry at Oxford, 1857–62; an outstanding influence in the development of literary criticism in the English-speaking world.

GEORGE G. N. BYRON, 6th Baron Byron (1788–1824): poet, social extrovert and political liberationist.

JOHN WILSON CROKER (1780–1857): Irish-born literary critic and Tory politician, one of the founders of the *Quarterly Review*.

GEORGE GILFILLAN (1813–78): Scottish Presbyterian minister and close friend of De Quincey and Carlyle. In addition to theological and pastoral writings, he published three groups of literary essays on contemporary poets in the *Dumfries Herald*, each entitled 'A Gallery of Literary Portraits' (1845, 1850, 1854).

WILLIAM HAZLITT (1778–1830): essayist, critic and Liberal publicist; a contributor to the *Morning Chronicle*, the *Examiner* and the *Edinburgh Review*. His writings on Shakespeare had an important influence on critical appreciation.

LEIGH HUNT (1784–1859): poet, critic, essayist and Liberal publicist; editor of the *Examiner*, 1808–21, and of other journals. He is prominent in literary history as the champion of Keats and Shelley, and of the early work of Tennyson and Browning.

FRANCIS JEFFREY (1773–1850): Scottish lawyer and a man of letters; co-founder of the *Edinburgh Review* and a strong supporter of the Whig reform movement.

CHARLES LAMB (1775–1834): essayist, critic and poet; a life-long friend of Coleridge and an associate in Leigh Hunt's journalistic and literary circle.

JOHN GIBSON LOCKHART (1794–1854): Scottish man of letters; editor of the *Quarterly Review* and supporter of Tory politics. Son-in-law of Sir Walter

Scott, his *Life* of the poet and novelist is one of the great biographies in the English language.

DAVID MACBETH MOIR (1798–1851): Scottish physician and man of letters; his writings include, in addition to *Sketches of Poetical Literature* (excerpted in our selection), the humorous *Life of Mansie Wauch*, contributed to *Blackwood's Magazine* (book publication 1828).

COVENTRY PATMORE (1823–96): poet and critic, and for many years employed in the Printed Books department of the British Museum; a friend of Ruskin, Tennyson and the Pre-Raphaelites.

WILLIAM MICHAEL ROSSETTI (1829–1919): critic and man of letters; brother of Dante Gabriel and Christina Rossetti. A member of the Pre-Raphaelite group, in later life he wrote an important memoir about it; and he was active in promoting the appreciation of William Blake's work.

JOHN SCOTT (1783–1821): a schoolboy friend of Byron and contributor to the *Morning Chronicle* and other pro-liberal journals.

PERCY BYSSHE SHELLEY (1792–1822): poet and political reformer, associated with William Godwin, Byron and Leigh Hunt.

ALEXANDER SMITH (1830–67): Scottish poet and essayist; his prose writings include *Dreamthorp* (1863), *A Summer in Skye* (1865) and *Last Leaves* (posthumous). His *City Poems* (1857) were much admired by contemporaries.

ALGERNON CHARLES SWINBURNE (1837–1909): poet and critic, and enthusiast for liberty. His writings in literary criticism include *Essays and Studies* (1875), *Miscellanies* (1886), monographs on Shakespeare and other dramatists, and articles on poets and playwrights in the *Encylopaedia Britannica* (including the article on Keats).

RICHARD WOODHOUSE (1788–1834): a lawyer and admirer of Keats, associated in the poet's dealings with his publishers.

PART THREE

SIR SIDNEY COLVIN (1845–1927): art-historian, literary critic and editor; Slade Professor of Fine Art at Cambridge, 1875–85, and Keeper of the Prints and Drawings at the British Museum, 1884–1912. As well as his *Life and Poetry* of Keats, he published an edition of the poet's letters (1887).

MARIO L. D'AVANZO: Professor of English, Queen's College, Ontario; he has published a wide range of studies in English literature.

NEWELL F. FORD: Emeritus Professor of English at Stanford University; in addition to his critical study on Keats, he is the author of numerous articles on the Romantic poets, and editor of Shelley's poetry.

WALTER E. HOUGHTON: Emeritus Professor of English at Wellesley College, Massachusetts; the author of many critical works, notably on Victorian literature, his best-known study is *The Victorian Frame of Mind* (1957).

KENNETH MUIR: King Alfred Professor of English Literature, University of Liverpool, 1951–74, and editor, 1965–79, of *Shakespeare Survey* and of the Casebook on *The Winter's Tale*; widely known for his studies on Shakespeare, Wyatt, Milton, Keats and other poets.

DAVID PERKINS: Professor of English, Harvard University; his publications include, in addition to his study of the Romantic Poets (excerpted in this selection), *A History of Modern Poetry* (1976).

PAUL D. SHEATS: Professor of English at the University of California, Los Angeles; his publications include editions of the poetry of Keats and Wordsworth and critical studies on the Romantic poets, including *The Making of Wordsworth's Poetry* (1973).

LOUISE Z. SMITH: Assistant Professor of English at the University of Massachusetts, Boston.

STUART M. SPERRY JNR: Professor of English at Indiana University, Bloomington; he has published widely on subjects in Romantic literature, especially Keats.

JACK STILLINGER: Professor of English, University of Illinois, and a principal editor of the *Journal of English and Germanic Philology*; his publications include an edition of Keats's poetry (1978) and the important study *The Texts of Keats's Poems* (1974).

EARL R. WASSERMAN (1913–73): at the time of his death, Caroline Donovan Professor of English at The Johns Hopkins University, and editor of *ELH: A Journal of English Literary History*; among his many publications, perhaps the best known – apart from *The Finer Tone*, excerpted in this selection – are *The Subtler Language* (1959) and *Shelley's 'Prometheus Unbound': A Critical Reading* (1965).

INDEX

Poem titles are listed under Keats, with the use of **bold** type for page-numbers relating to critical discussion, as distinct from simple references.